DATE			
APR 20'81			
MAY 8 '80			
—			
MAY 25'81			
NOV 3 0 2007			

CLASS, SEX, and the WOMAN WORKER

CONTRIBUTORS

Miriam Cohen, a member of the history department of the University of Michigan, has specialized in American social and urban history and has published in the *Journal of Interdisciplinary History.*

Thomas Dublin, assistant professor of history at the University of California, San Diego, is the winner of the Bancroft Prize for his work on women and work in Lowell, Massachusetts.

Nancy Schrom Dye teaches in the history department of the University of Kentucky. Her special interest is in women and trade unionism.

Carol Groneman is an assistant professor of history at the John Jay College of Criminal Justice, City University of New York.

Robin Miller Jacoby, assistant professor of history at the University of Michigan, has specialized in British and American women's history. Her essays have appeared in *Feminist Studies* and *Liberating Women's History.*

Elizabeth Jameson, assistant professor of history at the University of Virginia, has worked primarily in women's history and working-class history.

Alice Kessler-Harris is an associate professor of history at Hofstra University.

Susan J. Kleinberg, assistant professor at the Western College of Miami University, has specialized in women's history and urban history. Her articles have appeared in *Labor History* and the *Historical Methods Newsletter.*

Lise Vogel is a free-lance writer who has written on women and labor in New England.

Caroline F. Ware, now retired, taught at Howard University, Vassar, and Sarah Lawrence. Among her earlier works are *The Early New England Cotton Manufacture, Greenwich Village, 1920-30,* and *The Cultural Approach to History.*

Virginia Yans-McLaughlin is an assistant professor of history at the City College of the City University of New York. Her essays have appeared in such publications as the *Journal of Interdisciplinary History* and the *Journal of Social History.*

CLASS,
SEX,
and the WOMAN
WORKER

edited by MILTON CANTOR and BRUCE LAURIE
introduction by CAROLINE F. WARE

CONTRIBUTIONS IN
LABOR HISTORY, NUMBER 1

GREENWOOD PRESS
WESTPORT, CONNECTICUT • LONDON, ENGLAND

Library of Congress Cataloging in Publication Data
Main entry under title:

Class, sex, and the woman worker.

(Contributions in labor history ; no. 1)
Includes index.
1. Women—Employment—United States—History—Addresses, essays, lectures.
I. Cantor, Milton. II. Laurie, Bruce. III. Series.
HD6095.C54   331.4'0973   76-15304
ISBN 0-8371-9032-0

Library of Congress Catalog Card Number: 76-15304
ISBN: 0-8371-9032-0

First published in 1977

Greenwood Press, Inc.
51 Riverside Avenue, Westport, Connecticut 06880

Printed in the United States of America

10 9 8 7 6 5 4 3 2

*To Lillian, Vera, Leslie, and Margaret —
workingwomen all.*

CONTENTS

PREFATORY STATEMENT

Most of the essays in this book originally took the form of papers, which were delivered at various conferences — the women's history conference at the State University of New York, Binghamton, in the summer of 1974, or the second Berkshire Conference on the History of Women at Radcliffe College, in the fall of 1974. Although some of these articles have since been published elsewhere, only Miriam Cohen's essay, Thomas Dublin's article, which first appeared in *Labor History* (Summer 1974), and Caroline Ware's Introduction were not originally written for one of these conferences. Obviously, all these essays reflect the mounting interest in women's history and are products of the women's movement.

Milton Cantor
Bruce Laurie

CLASS,
SEX,
and the WOMAN WORKER

INTRODUCTION

It is a truism that each period rewrites history in the light of its own perspective and in the effort to find meaning in its past. Thus it is not surprising that the new feminism should bring a new concern with the history of women, that the awakened interest in labor history, focused on the rank and file, should direct attention to the woman worker, that ethnic awareness should stimulate interest in cultural influences, and that the new emphasis on people, social processes, and institutions should bring to the fore the role of class in the lives of workers.

The present volume constitutes an effort to apply these current perspectives to the experience of women workers in the United States from the early nineteenth into the twentieth century. The essays are diverse, each focusing on a specific time, place, category of worker, or institution and each using its own conceptual tools and sources of information. Yet they touch on crucial aspects of American industrial development and, in combination, provide significant insights into it.

The Lowell mill workers of the early nineteenth century, studied in the second and third essays, were the instruments of a conscious attempt to create an industrial system which would not rest on a class base and would not produce the conditions which characterized the early industrial system in Great Britain.

The founders of the Lowell textile mills had a vision of industry as an integral part of society along with the yeoman agriculture and commerce with which they were familiar. They had visited England, seen mill conditions there, and observed the depressed population from which industrial workers were drawn (including the large number of child laborers). As a result, they undertook to develop a different system which would not destroy the kind of society which they thought was being built in the United States. Whereas the small southern New England mills which first introduced the factory system had depended very largely on child labor, the major textile corporations in Lowell and nearby cities rejected child labor, introduced the boardinghouse system for young women workers, and became the model for a new industrial experiment. They were the principal factories of any kind employing women in that period.

The design was for a work force only temporarily in the mills. Nobody expected the mill girls to stay on permanently as factory workers, neither the employers who set up the boardinghouses nor the girls who entered the mills. From the employers' point of view, the problem was to make mill work sufficiently attractive to draw young women from an ever-widening rural area. For the women, so long as they could maintain their roots on the land or could look forward to joining the westward migration, the years which they spent in the mills were an episode in their lives, not a commitment to a way of life or status. For neither employer nor worker was the situation defined in class terms. The uniqueness of the Lowell experiment can be appreciated by contrasting it with the earlier Rhode Island mills or with the later industrialization of the Appalachian south, which was based on a poor, dependent, and despised population.

But the noble experiment of an industrial development which would avoid exploitation ultimately failed, although for some forty years it produced a prosperous industry and a distinctive labor experience. At least three fundamental factors contributed to the failure to achieve the vision: the basic terms of employment, the institutional structure and, finally, a new source of immigrant labor.

From the start, factory employment rested on the buying of labor, not the engagement of persons. The basic concept of labor as a commodity to be bought like raw materials, rather than as persons sharing in the process of production, has run through the theory and practice of American industry and has been reflected in economic textbooks, court decisions, hiring and firing practices at the factory gate, and employer attitudes toward industrial safety and labor turnover.

Some of the early labor conflicts focused more on the treatment of workers as people than on the rate of pay for their work. For example, in 1853 woolen workers in Salisbury and Amesbury, Massachusetts, were locked out when they insisted on their right to their traditional morning "grog" break; the women workers walked out to protest "the injustice heaped upon them by a heartless monetary power," and their fellow citizens, in town meetings, appealed to the companies not to set themselves "against the interests of our village." But in this case, and in similar conflicts, the principle prevailed that the mills were simply buying labor and using it efficiently. Neither the vision nor the paternalism of the Lowell mill owners led them to deny this principle.

The issue of labor-as-commodity versus labor's right to elementary human consideration has remained basic and unresolved throughout the history of American industry. Some eighty-five years after the Salisbury episode, a striking union in South Bend, Indiana, counted among the terms of its victory the concession that no worker would be laid off with less than twenty-four-hours' notice. Industries have persistently disclaimed responsibility for the safety and health of workers and have made it difficult to enact and enforce protective legislation against hazardous machinery, fire, black lung, and other threats to health, including chemical and radiation poisoning. The issue was symbolized by the striking garbage workers whom Martin Luther King went to Memphis to support on that fatal day in 1968; they carried placards which stated: "I Am a Man."

A second factor militating against the achievement of a nonexploitative industrial system was the development of the corporation as the major instrument for the management of American industry. In the 1830s, when the Waltham and Lowell mills were established, the corporation's features of limited liability, anonymity, legal personality, and continuity were considered privileges, to be granted sparingly by the state because of the potential power and avoidance of personal responsibility which they offered. The founders of the Waltham and Lowell companies were the first group of industrial entrepreneurs to use the corporate form routinely in industrial organization. As such, they helped to establish an institutional structure whose impersonality and potential for the exercise of power contradicted their social objectives.

The Lowell mill girls were the first to confront the "heartless corporation" which became so familiar an adversary to later generations of workers. And once the corporate form was entrenched, the consequent tendencies toward economic concentration and unlimited growth of giant corporate entities have remained unchecked by efforts at regulation and dominate the American economy even more powerfully today.

The third factor, a change in the character of the labor force, was the most visible. The beginnings of mass Irish immigration after the famine of 1847 were registered almost immediately in the mills, where a pool of immigrants wholly dependent on the mills now became available. The Lowell mill girls looked down on these newcomers as low-class, the type who could be patronized as Yankee girls could not. The immigrant women, in their turn, were entering the mills for long-term employment and did not need to live in boardinghouses. They occupied their own homes and had no prospects for work beyond industrial labor or such alternatives as domestic service.

The change in the character of the mill population meant that the mill experience was discontinuous. The sense of identity developed by the girls and their shared aspirations and grievances, revealed in these essays, were not handed on to the newcomers through institutions or traditions. Rather, the impact of their experience must have been felt in the communities to which they returned or new communities in the West where they spent the rest of their lives.

The next group of essays (four, five, six, and seven), deals with women workers drawn from the masses of new immigrants who came in successive waves from the second half of the nineteenth century up to World War I. These studies examine patterns of employment as they were affected both by the cultural traditions and outlook which these immigrant groups brought with them and by the character of the local job market, which defined the demand for and options of women in the labor force. They deal with three ethnic groups: Irish residents of a mid-Manhattan ward in the mid-nineteenth century; Italian residents of Buffalo, New York, in the early twentieth century and of New York City between 1900 and 1950; and Jewish labor organizers in the garment trades from before World War I up to World War II.

Dependence on the labor of immigrants was a central feature of American industry in the period of its explosive growth. The resulting change in the status of workers bears on the basic issues raised in the book. While many differences existed in relationships among and within nationality groups and in the situations which characterized specific communities, the predominant effect of the entrance of large numbers of immigrants into the labor pool was to widen the gap between those who controlled industry, mainly native Americans, and those who provided the labor. Ethnicity thus had the effect of either reinforcing any class gap which existed or providing a classlike gap of its own.

Once the industrial labor force came to be composed predominantly of aliens, speaking their own languages and living in their own social worlds, it could be — and was — subesteemed by virtue of its "otherness." In all manner of ways, the line was drawn against "hyphenated Americans," who heard themselves denounced as ignorant, unwashed, and addicted to the attributes of poverty as a way of life. The gap was somewhat less great for the Irish, who had no language barrier but, as the first to arrive in large numbers, were stamped with the stereotypes which were then reapplied to each succeeding group of immigrants.

Ethnicity thus provided a ready-made class society, even though many factors stood in the way of class solidarity among ethnic groups and American society was relatively open compared to those most immigrants had known elsewhere. Ethnic hierarchies developed among groups; occupational hierarchies often existed within groups; sometimes there was intragroup exploitation (such as the *padrone* system for recruiting and handling gangs of Italian workers); and sometimes employers deliberately played one group off against others. Nationalities made their way up by occupational ladders that were often related to their initial employment, such as the Irish ascent from pick-and-shovel jobs to straw boss to subcontractor or building materials dealer to builder to developer and contractor, with detours through or links to the political hierarchy, or that followed by some Jews through needle trades to entrepreneurship in the garment industry and the retail and wholesale clothing business, or the familiar Italian route from produce vendor to grocery, florist shop, or restaurant ownership.

Still, ethnic discrimination remained entrenched. Although the melting-pot assumption that newcomers would slough off their foreignness when they touched American soil was as much a fantasy as the immigrant's dream of gold in the streets, it provided a yardstick by which to measure and downgrade all those with visible, audible, and attitudinal differences. Even today, the legal and emotional force of the civil-rights movement and the reassertion of ethnic self-respect have hardly destroyed prejudice in the United States.

Moreover, the arrival of successive waves from different countries, each entering at the bottom of the job pyramid, constantly renewed the downward drag on the status of labor, both by counteracting pressures for wage increases as newcomers eagerly accepted wages which their predecessors had come to reject, and by perpetuating attitudes which downgraded workers as a class.

Immigrant women were generally even more cut off by the barrier of ethnicity than the men. While their children were learning English in school and their men on the job, women who remained at home did not have the same exposure. There were Italian women in New York in the 1930s who had lived there for decades but who literally had never left their blocks, some even their buildings, except perhaps to be taken to church by their children. They had never overcome their fear and sense of helplessness in the face of the alien city. On the other hand, it was sometimes women from immigrant families working at clerical or other white-collar jobs who marked the family's first penetration into higher occupational levels.

The small samples of Irish, Italian, and Jewish women studied in these essays do not pretend to provide a comprehensive or even a representative picture. But they do throw light on some specific patterns of work and raise relevant questions concerning the factors affecting such patterns.

The fourth essay, which looks at Irish women in New York in the mid-nineteenth century, samples the work of women who were members of the first major body of peasant immigrants and examines their adaptation to urban life. It is based mainly on an analysis of the manuscript census returns for a mid-city, lower-income ward. As such, it deals principally with women living in family groups and tends not to include single women in domestic service, whom the census taker would have found living on their employers' premises in the city's more affluent sections. From the records, it appears that Irish women often contributed to family income by taking in lodgers or boarders and by running boardinghouses. They thus performed a very necessary function in an immigrant community which included large numbers of single men. The study does not attempt to establish how far, if at all, the pursuit of this occupation instead of work outside the home was dictated by cultural attitudes toward women's place and women's work. The demand for the service was there, and work within the home permitted immigrant women, transplanted out of their familiar milieu, to carry domestic responsibilities which they could no longer share with an extended family. That there was relatively little cultural resistance to other types of work by women of this ethnic group is suggested not only by the influx of Irish women into the Lowell mills but by their prevalence in domestic service and by such familiar stereotypes as the Irish washerwoman and scrubwoman.

The two essays (five and six) on Italians in Buffalo and New York City, bring somewhat different emphases to the study of the Italian women's perception of work and their place in the economy of the family and the community. The study of Buffalo in the early twentieth century, when Italian immigration was at its height, found Italian women taking in lodgers and boarders, like the Irish before them, and thus meeting the needs of a community where there were 144 Italian men for every 100 women. This study examines the evidence as to how far such a practice was dictated by a strong cultural attitude which predisposed Italian families to keep their women working within the home or under the direct supervision of their own menfolk in such family enterprises as tailor shops or grocery stores. The presumption that such cultural attitudes were a significant factor in the Italian women's avoidance of factory work and domestic service is supported by the contrasting work patterns of Buffalo's other major immigrant group, the Poles, whose women entered factory and domestic employment in large numbers.

The study of Italians in New York City notes the same tendency toward home employment — not only the taking in of lodgers but especially in the form of industrial homework which was wide-spread, particularly among Italians. Nevertheless, there was also a large number and proportion of Italian women in garment facto-ries, seemingly in contradiction to the tendency in Buffalo. An ap-parent change had occurred in traditional attitudes toward women's education in response to the expansion of white-collar employment.

The fifth and sixth studies, then, raise some fundamental ques-tions about the relationship between cultural and economic factors in determining the course of women's work under the particular oc-cupational structure and ethnic composition of each specific community. They raise, too, the issue of whether labor in the home and associated with homemaking is recognized as work. Certainly, it is not only among the Italians that "work" is defined as paid labor outside the home. The same attitude appears among native residents of the Cripple Creek mining community described in the seventh essay. It is, in fact, deeply engrained in the institutions of American society. Only in very recent years have efforts begun to be made to measure the economic value of the homemaker's contri-bution to national production, to estimate the investment represented by her labor in adjudicating property settlements in case of divorce, and to consider the possibility of social security coverage for the homemaker as a worker rather than simply as a dependent. Almost the only formal recognition that home labor has value and constitutes a part of family income has been the awarding by courts of damages to a husband when an accident has resulted in the disability or death of his wife.

The seventh essay, which focuses on three Jewish women who worked as labor organizers, does not attempt the same kind of quantitative analysis of patterns of employment as do the Irish and Italian studies, but rather tries to get at the outlook of immigrant Jewish workers and their views of themselves in the struggle to im-prove the lot of women workers. Organizers for the International Ladies Garment Workers Union (ILGWU) in the early decades of the twentieth century were keenly conscious of sweat-shop con-ditions, and they believed that the class consciousness which they brought as East European Jews was a necessary ingredient which non-Jewish women workers were slow to appreciate. They were particularly aware of the different attitudes of the Italian garment workers and the "Americans," both of whom lacked this class sense.

The seventh and eighth studies look at women in relation to the trade-union movement during its struggle for acceptance at the turn of the century and in the following years. The two situations described could hardly have been more different — the New York garment industry where large numbers of women worked and where the ILGWU came to be one of the best-established unions in the country, and the Cripple Creek mining district of Colorado where the radical Western Federation of Miners was brutally shattered by organized mine owners, aided by state militia, after a strike in 1903. But both yield insights into the experience of women workers in the labor movement and into union treatment of the aspirations of working women.

Viewed from the perspective of the women who worked as ILGWU organizers, the main body of the union and its leadership were largely indifferent to the women workers, who virtually had to organize on their own and then seek admission into the union. At the same time, it was the initiative of the women members that gave the ILGWU its distinctive character and status within the labor movement as the pioneer in the development of union services for members, and that offered a concept of unionism which encompassed the needs of workers as people. It was the women's locals which initiated, against the doubts of their union brothers, the workers' education, health, and recreation programs for which the ILGWU became famous. Nevertheless, the union has remained to this day completely under male leadership, with never more than token participation by women in the upper echelons of the union hierarchy.

In the Cripple Creek district, trade unionism dominated the total scene far more than it did in the metropolis of New York. Mine employees of all types belonged to the Western Federation of Miners, while every other trade in the area had its union. Unions provided many community services, from funerals to libraries, and what claimed to be "the only daily newspaper owned by organized workingmen [the Cripple Creek *Daily Press*]" was published in the area. In this setting, women workers joined the unions of their trades, miners' wives looked to the union for social solidarity and support, and the Western Federation of Miners prided itself on its progressive stand in favor of women's suffrage.

At the same time, the unions helped to reinforce, and to institutionalize within the labor movement, basic community attitudes toward women which assigned them a dependent role rather than an equal and independent place in the work force. They accepted women unionists and respected them as sisters, but they looked on women in general as weak, easily confused, and unable to cope or command. In sum, they shared the perceptions of manhood and womanhood which had become popular during the nineteenth century when industrialization had destroyed the household as a productive unit based on shared activity and substituted the dichotomized, world of work, which was the domain of men, and the home, now defined as women's "natural" sphere. True manhood required being a good provider; true womanhood called for domestic virtues.

The basic demand of the unions, led by the Western Federation of Miners, was for a living wage which would enable a man to support his family in comfort and decency. Couching union wage goals in these terms committed union policy to the principle of women's dependent status. What was considered at the time to be an advanced position, and has survived at the heart of trade-union demands, has in fact been an obstacle to the cause of working women. Other factors have affected the attitudes of trade unionists toward women labor, especially dislike of competition for jobs, but perhaps none is more deeply rooted in the definition of union objectives and in the historic sense of manhood that gives it so strong an emotional hold.

The Cripple Creek study thus throws light on why organized labor has been conservative and often reactionary on issues of women's rights, slow to champion equal pay, reluctant to modify discriminatory seniority systems, and persistent in holding women to the lower ranks of the union structure. It is not surprising that in 1974 women from the major trade unions felt the need to form the Coalition of Labor Union Women (CLUW) because they could not count on their unions to promote women's interests in job opportunities, employee rights, and a fuller status within the union establishment.

The ninth and tenth essays deal with the Women's Trade Union League (WTUL), an organization which brought middle-class and working-class women together in an effort to improve the conditions, raise the status, and promote the unionization of women workers. They examine ways in which the interaction between bonds of sex and barriers of class affected the operation of the organization and achievement of its goals.

The WTUL was a product of the reform movement of the early twentieth century which recognized that industrial development had created intolerable conditions which were incompatible with national democratic assumptions. A mounting concern with conditions of life and labor was expressed in a variety of forms: the settlement-house movement, which brought middle-class people to live in the slums, to experience "how the other half lives" and to become champions of improved housing, municipal services, and humane conditions of work; the formation of the National Consumers League, which mobilized the conscience and buying power of consumers to attack the conditions under which the goods that they bought were made and which, through white lists and support for minimum wage, health, and safety regulations and mothers' pensions, led the fight to eliminate sweatshops, child labor, and the evils of industrial homework; the YWCA's adaptation of parts of its program to the needs of working women; the establishment of the Urban League and the NAACP, both dedicated to the good of the black minority; and the founding of the American Civil Liberties Union (ACLU), which concerns itself with the basic rights of all.

Among these organizations, the WTUL was distinctive in its preoccupation with women workers, its direct involvement in leadership roles, and its initial belief that the trade union would be the main instrument of their advance. In the course of time, however, it devoted itself increasingly to the promotion of social legislation to achieve its goals. The WTUL shared the basic democratic outlook of the reform movement, and although from the start it identified two type of members, workers and "allies," and it numbered class-conscious socialists among its most active elements, it remained a part of the main reform stream. As such, it constitutes a suitable laboratory for analyzing some effects of class and sex.

Although reform movements of the period were by no means limited to women, educated women tended to be more involved than men and they often furnished leadership. Perhaps limitations on other outlets for their talents and energies led them to devote themselves to social concerns. Certainly, they were less likely than men to have personal interests that would have been adversely affected by reform.

There were compelling reasons, too, for focusing reform efforts on the problems of women workers. Not only was it easier for organizations led by women to reach out to female than to male workers, but there was much greater public acceptance of the idea of social responsibility for their welfare. Moreover, as long as courts maintained that the regulation of hours, wages, and conditions of work was an unconstitutional interference with the individual worker's right to contract for his services, the only leverage available (it, too, judicially limited) was on behalf of working women and children. Even for these groups, however, public support for regulation was not easily aroused. As late as the 1920s, a proposed child-labor amendment was turned down by the states after the Supreme Court had twice held such regulation to be beyond the reach of Congress. Protective legislation for women was a major achievement in those years. It was not until the mid-1930s, with new court decisions and the passage of the Fair Labor Standards Act, that legally established labor standards for all workers became possible.

More fundamentally, the WTUL was part of the growing struggle to humanize industry and to consider workers as people rather than as units of labor. In the early 1920s its leaders, and others like them, initiated the workers' education movement for women workers at a time when few trade unionists saw the value of educational programs. The college women responsible for summer schools for women workers, first on the Bryn Mawr College campus near Philadelphia and thereafter at centers in the State of New York, the Midwest, and the South, showed respect for the workers' experience and confidence in their potential by using their experience as teaching material and by sharing the governance of the schools on an equal basis with the worker-students. They offered a curriculum designed to help workers understand the industrial system within which they worked, to give them tools of analysis and communication to cope with it, and to open new dimensions of life through poetry, music, sports, and even astronomy so that they might grow as human beings.

Within this general milieu, the WTUL touched many issues of continuing importance to women workers — the role of legislation, the expanding meaning of "worker" as white-collar occupations assumed increasing importance, the self-image of women as workers, strategies of cooperation, and the place of women in the trade-union movement. After the 1920s it functioned less as a pioneer organization than as part of a broad front in support of labor standards and social legislation, and in time outlived its usefulness and was dissolved. It is worth noting, however, that between the heyday of the WTUL and the formation of the Coalition of Labor Women in 1974, the national trade-union movement focused attention on the problems of women workers only once, in 1961, when a conference on this subject was sponsored by the industrial union department of the AFL-CIO. The difficulties in communication across and within the bounds of class and sex serve to underline the significance of this joint effort to advance the cause of women workers.

Essays two through ten thus deal with one or another of the major factors and issues in the history of American industry, issues which in many instances are still unresolved. They cast rays of light into the still largely unseen lives of women workers and suggest the many directions in which further exploration needs to go. The first essay, on the systematic study of urban women, points to materials, techniques, and directions for such study.

With respect to the concepts of class and sex used as tools of analysis by the authors of these essays, it is appropriate to consider how well the concepts serve for the study of the historical situations to which they have been applied. The traditional concept of class has been used, based on the assumption of a confrontation between the owners/controllers of the means of production and those who supply the labor; horizontal solidarity within each of these opposed elements is also assumed. In this usage, "class" both indicates situation and characterizes perception. As a descriptive term, it is applied to occupational categories and power relationships. In defining a point of view, it is used in contradistinction to individualism to imply a value system in which horizontal loyalty takes precedence over individual ambition, which seeks upward mobility.

The concept of sex, in the sense of "feminism," is much less clearly established as a tool of analysis and its application is not uniform. Like "class," it is used in these essays both to describe the actual situation in which women found themselves and to refer to their perceptions and attitudes; in addition, it includes within its meaning a sense of solidarity with other women and implies a sharing in decision making through the vote and other means. Less explicit in its usage are such ideas as freedom of choice, opportunity to enter the existing labor market, and equality of pay and treatment. Still less clear is how far the concept carries a challenge to traditional family relationships and to the roles of men and women within as well as outside the home.

In the application of these two concepts to the specific situations studied, a number of questions emerge as to the relevance and possible elaboration of each and its value for the study of labor history.

In what sense is "class" applicable to the Lowell mill girls, whose basic identification was with their generally rural community, who were concerned with their status as persons and citizens, who defended themselves against the public view that mill work was demeaning, who entered the mills for temporary employment, and who looked upon immigrant labor as lowering the status of mill workers? Does it describe their resentment of the "heartless corporations," the comradeship growing out of their collective life in the boardinghouses, and their spontaneous activism? For the peasant immigrants adapting to an alien, urban, relatively open society and striving for upward mobility with some success, does "class" take proper account for the fact that ethnicity and alien background, in and of itself, created or reinforced a classlike division between those who were dominant and those who had a subordinate status?

The Cripple Creek miners marched under the banner of "class." But, it should be noted, this class consciousness derived in large part from the fact that the individual enterprise of the prospector had been replaced by corporate enterprise. Their organized attacks on the system represented, not the effort of a depressed class to rise, but the resistance of once-independent individualists to reduction to a dependent position.

In the case of the WTUL, did differences in the concepts of class held by its members contribute to the difficulties in communication experienced by women workers and their allies?

Other more general questions are suggested by these studies. What is the meaning of "class" for women who are in and out of the labor market at different periods in their lives? This is a significant question today when nine out of ten adult women are in the labor force at some time, although less than half are fully employed at a given moment. To what occupational level does the concept of "working class" extend? Does the rapid expansion of white-collar occupations and the extension of trade unionism even to professionals mean "bourgeoisization," or the creation of a working class of new dimensions, a question raised in the study of New York's Italian women? In what circumstances is it appropriate to extend the concept of "work" to labor in the home, paid or unpaid, and how does this affect the concept of a working class?

The application of the concept of feminism, in spite of the imprecision with which it is used in these essays, provides significant insights as well as prompts questions similar to those raised by the concept of class. The feminist analysis applied to the Cripple Creek mining area reveals the underlying attitudes toward the role of men and the place of women as basic to a situation which might otherwise be described simply as a very weak job market for female labor, and it highlights factors which have made and still make the trade unions bastions of male dominance rather than aggressive champions of their women members. Applied both to native and to immigrant workers, the feminist analysis brings out the extent to which the presumption that women's activities in the home are not work has led to the underestimation of women's economic contributions. It calls attention to ways in which nineteenth-century definitions of manhood and womanhood deepened the psychological resistance of men to modifications of traditional sex roles.

By the application of a modern feminist perspective to the analysis of the past, these essays suggest the need to explore further the self-image internalized by women workers in different situations as well as the kinds of "consciousness raising" and sense of sisterhood observed in the Lowell boardinghouses, in the collective support offered by the Cripple Creek mine union against the isolation of the home, and in the solidarity which the ILGWU organizers sought, and the authors of these essays looked for within the WTUL.

What presumptions are made by the feminist analysis as to the alternatives realistically available to women in relation to the economic and occupational structure of specific communities? This question is directly considered by the study of Italians in New York and is very much present in the study of the one-industry mining district of Cripple Creek. Industry has always accepted and used women when it has needed them; women who are heads of families or alone have always been driven by necessity to seek whatever work is available; competition among workers directed against any vulnerable group has tended to exist wherever jobs are scarce, as has the tendency of employers to seek lower-cost labor in times of economic stress; and new opportunities present themselves whenever and wherever employment is expanding. What light may a feminist analysis throw on women workers in these alternative circumstances? The first essay points to sources for the objective study of such varying situations. There is still need for studies of the outlook of women faced by different realities.

Several other aspects not included in any of these essays might come within the scope of a feminist analysis of the experience of women workers. How have the perceptions of women by fellow workers and bosses affected their experiences on the job, their chances of promotion against a stereotype of subordination, and their subjection to pressure from foremen and supervisors for sexual favors in order to secure good work assignments?

The situation of women workers also needs analysis in relation to child labor, for this was the alternative, from the point of view of both industry and the possible sources of family income. In the years of great industrial growth in the late nineteenth and early twentieth centuries, 18 percent of all children from ten to fifteen years of age were gainfully employed. It would be pertinent to examine how cultural attitudes toward children as well as those toward women affected work patterns. For example, was there an actual difference of behavior within the same labor-market situation betwen Italians, who traditionally considered children as a source of family support and who viewed women's work outside the home with disfavor, and Jews, whose tradition called for dedicating family resources to the advancement of their children and who had less resistance to women going out to work?

The feminist analysis may be especially illuminating in relation to the long and far-from-complete struggle to humanize industry. Although American industry continues to be organized on the principle that labor is a commodity to be purchased bit by bit, there has been a gradual shift toward treating workers as people and insisting that industry should accommodate itself to human needs rather than the reverse. Fringe benefits, proposals for a guaranteed annual wage, national legislation for occupational health and safety, and concern with the impact of industry on the environment are reflections of this trend.

While women workers have remained among the more exploited and disadvantaged groups, detrimental conditions of work have often been challenged by women or on their behalf: by Lowell mill girls asserting their dignity as people; by reformers' efforts to eliminate the sweat-shop conditions under which women worked; by workers' education for women addressed to the whole person; by union health services initiated by women's locals of the ILGWU; by current efforts to secure community facilities, such as child care and retraining, and to adjust work schedules to meet the needs of women who must carry the double load of earning and caring for their children or who return to outside employment after years of homemaking. In this context, the present volume is a timely contribution to an understanding of present issues through insights into the past.

THE SYSTEMATIC STUDY OF URBAN WOMEN

1

by Susan J. Kleinberg

In 1933, Arthur M. Schlesinger wrote *The Rise of the City*, in which he examined, among other topics, women's changing roles in urban centers. He considered the implications of domestic technology, regional variation, reform movements, and marital, fertility, and employment patterns on women's lives and on relations between women and men.[1] Despite Schlesinger's pioneering work, urban history and the history of women emerged as largely separate disciplines. The new urban history (as distinguished from urban biography) dates from the early 1960s with the publication of *Streetcar Suburbs* by Sam Bass Warner, Jr. (1962), *The Urbanization of America* by Blake McKelvey (1963), "The Politics of Reform in Municipal Government in the Progressive Era" by Samuel P. Hays (*Pacific Northwest Quarterly*, 1964), and *Poverty and Progress* by Stephan Thernstrom (1964).[2] While these works and their descendants sometimes noted the presence of women in the cities, they made no attempt to analyze the urban woman's experience systematically.

The Women's Liberation Movement sparked sustained interest in the history of women, although several significant and influential works, including *Century of Struggle* by Eleanor Flexner (1959), *Women and Work in America* by Robert Smuts (1959), and *The Ideas of the Woman Suffrage Movement* by Aileen S. Kraditor (1965), antedated the movement. As the movement emerged books on women focused primarily on women's political and cultural activities in the nineteenth and early twentieth centuries. For example, *The Grimké Sisters of South Carolina* by Gerda Lerner (1967),

SOURCE: *Historical Methods Newsletter* 9 (December 1975): 14-25.

Everyone Was Brave by William O'Neill (1969), and *The Southern Lady* by Anne Firor Scott (1970) all concentrate on women's political, social, and cultural activism and thus do not deal with most women's lives or life experiences.[3]

However, some recent scholarship on women has viewed them as members of economic, social, and ethnic groups and as urban residents.[4] It has, as a result, placed women in the mainstream of the new urban history. The application of social science methodology to the study of the city, the emergence of a history concerned with the masses, and the renewed political activism for and by women produced an interest in the effect that urbanization and industrialization had on women. The use of quantitative techniques makes it possible to examine women as a group and as members of groups without the memoirs, diaries, and letters upon which historians have relied. Most women (and indeed, many men) did not memorialize their daily lives. If these people are to be located historically, it will be done through the records kept on them rather than through those kept by them.

This paper focuses on the relationship between urbanization and industrialization and women's economic, cultural, social, and political activities. Throughout, I will explore the concept and methods useful in examining these relationships as well as women's experiences. The essay itself is divided into two parts. The first explores the determinants of female labor-force participation and the nature of women's work. The second concentrates on the methodology and tools which can be brought to bear on the study of urban women.

Historians must examine the specific contexts in which women have lived their lives. Neither industrialization nor urbanization occurred at the same pace in different regions or even within the same region. A consideration of the environment which has shaped women's lives lends insight into the patterns and actions of those women and their lives. Such considerations, of course, hold true for men as well. Environment has influenced all classes, racial and ethnic groups, and political persuasions and has been affected by them in turn. It is critical to relate changes in women's economic, social, and political activity to demographic changes, industrialization, and urbanization in each area rather than to consider them in isolation from one another and the phenomena which gave rise to them.

For example, women have always worked, that is to say, performed economically beneficial labor. The problem arises in evaluating the significance of that work, the impact of industrialization on the focus of female and male labor, and the effect of changing concepts of work upon family relationships. The focus will be primarily on the United States. Comparisons with women in Europe and the Third World are enlightening, to be sure, but must be made carefully. Moreover, there are critical differences. For example, most urban areas in the United States, unlike those of other nations or regions, contain diverse foreign-born populations as well as rural migrants. In the New World, then, the wrench from rural to urban, from preindustrial to industrial, and from subsistence to cash economy was part of the immigration as well as the migration process. Cultural legacies, however, traveled with immigrants to the United States as they did with migrants from rural to urban settings. Such carry-overs have been examined by Virginia Yans-McLaughlin (for Italians in Buffalo), Tamara Hareven (French-Canadians in Manchester, New Hampshire), Elizabeth Pleck (Italians and Afro-Americans), and Alice Kessler-Harris (Eastern-European Jews in New York City), among others. Each study basically confirmed the findings of European historians. Lynn Lees, Teresa McBride, and Joan Scott and Louise Tilly have concluded that preindustrial or rural patterns of family economy extended into the city but were changed by urban industrial economic and employment structures.[5] In almost all cases, the separation of home and workplace precluded significant sustained labor-force participation for married women. Typically, unmarried women became wage earners while married women worked outside the home only in times of financial necessity. In all settings, it became a mark of pride for a man to have a wife who did not work.[6]

Labor force participation varied by class as well as marital status. Single middle-class women began working outside the home in the later decades of the nineteenth century. Their employment tended to be in the genteel professions, many of which were extensions of women's traditional social concerns — charity, children and religion. Single working-class women worked outside the home in much greater proportions than middle-class women. They labored in the factories, shops, and homes of others.[7] More detailed studies of the employment patterns of working- and middle-class women are needed, however, before we can compare what seems to be two very different patterns of work outside the home.

This article emphasizes labor-force participation. I do not mean, however, to denigrate the significant economic and social contributions made by women who did not work outside their own homes, but to reflect a fact of the modern industrial economy — the measurement of a person's worth in terms of the money earned by the work performed. In preindustrial societies and those not organized into cash economies, wealth and importance are not functions of salary but of property, with little buying and selling occurring. In such an economy, a woman's domestic services were extensive and critical. In both the United States and Europe, the use of mechanical devices and mass-produced domestic goods made women's services to the family less critical. Lynn Lees noted this transition in her study of Irish immigrants to London in the 1850s. As women moved to the city, "their role in the family economy changed from that of production to maintenance." [8]

Throughout the nineteenth and early twentieth centuries, women's labor-force participation was ancillary, varying with circumstances, rather than obligatory as was men's. As such, it reflected the values of the immediate society and the opportunities available. Any analysis of women's work must take into account the types of job available in the community, the attitudes of racial, ethnic, and class groups toward women and women's work, the age and marital status of the women who worked and those who did not, the number and age of children in the family, and the opportunities open to men, that is, their working conditions, jobs, and wages.[9]

These factors, however, are not equally significant in terms of causal importance. Some, such as industrial/occupational structure, were universal within a given area. Others, such as marital status and number and age of children, were peculiar to individuals, although patterns emerge from individual data. The most important factor in determining whether or not a woman worked outside the home was the occupational structure within the area. It shaped the opportunities open to all members of the family, the wages paid to adult males (which determined the need for other family members to work), the availability of work that women could do and the competition for it and, similarly, the availability of work for children of both sexes who might function as ancillary wage earners in the working-class household.

Women's labor-force participation was limited to a few job categories. As JoEllen Vinyard pointed out in her paper (at the Second Berkshire Conference on Women's History), "From Europe to Urban America: Immigrant Women in 19th-Century Detroit," women were concentrated in several low-paying occupations: domestic service, sewing, laundry, and (to a much lesser extent) teaching and clerical work.[10] However, the nature of the work within these occupations varied. It was quite one thing to work in the merchanized laundries of Troy, New York, and another to take in wash and scrub it in a tub. Sewing on a machine in a tenement factory was very different from sewing jeans by hand in the coal-mining hollows near Pittsburgh. Women's job titles are misleading, hiding great variations in the nature of the work actually done.[11] Women's work became somewhat less concentrated in the early twentieth century as single women left domestic service for better-paying or more prestigious industrial and white-collar jobs.

The percentage of women in the labor force varied dramatically as a function of the industrial, social, ethnic, and racial composition of the area. In the United States, cities with narrow industrial bases characterized by heavy industry (iron, glass, steel, railroads, and mining) had a low proportion of women in the labor force (10 to 19 percent). More than half of the women workers in these urban areas were domestic servants, working at occupations of lowest prestige and pay.[12] In such cities, great competition for women's jobs existed. In one, studied in detail, this drove down the average age of working women. Married women did not compete in the labor force. They preferred working at home for their families to working for other families at low wages. Late nineteenth-century Pittsburgh had no industrial jobs for women. The iron, glass, and steel industries which dominated its economy were capital intensive, produced relatively low population densities (because the mills required so much space, they spread population over a wide area), and resulted in class-homogeneous neighborhoods. As a result, no female-oriented industries emerged, capital being occupied elsewhere and there not being a sufficiently dense female population to attract such industries.[13] Instead, young women were exported to wealthier parts of the city as domestic workers. Virtually no married women worked outside their homes. Where additional income was required to sustain the family, children provided it. Here, the exportation of females from working-class to middle-class neighborhoods was clearly visible. Some working-class communities, most notably the Black ghetto, had few young women living with their families. Their absence and the presence of black servants of the same age in middle-class homes elsewhere suggests that their exportation served family needs.[14]

Cities had different dominant occupations and industries, and different proportions of women and children working. Urban areas with a narrow industrial base dominated by light industry, particularly textiles, had a high proportion of women and children in the labor force (30 to 40 percent of the workers in such cities were women).[15] More than half the women who worked did so in industrial occupations. Since the textile industries did not pay as well as the heavy, fabricating industries, supplemental wage earners were needed. Tamara Hareven's study of textile workers in Manchester, New Hampshire, found that married women augmented the family income when their children were too young to work and tended not to work when the children were old enough to take jobs in the mills.[16] Studies of several European cities indicate that the occupational structure of the town (with wage and opportunity understood to be part of that structure) influenced the presence of women in the labor force. In Joan Scott and Louise Tilly's comparison of the textile city of Stockport, England, and the nonindustrial city of Amiens, France, they found that in Stockport, married women worked until they had children old enough to replace them in the factories. In Amiens, some married women worked, but "mothers of young children represented the smallest proportion of married working women."[17] Obviously, family structure influenced the individual woman's labor-force participation, but the industrial structure of the cities themselves set the overall parameters.

Between the two extremes were cities with mixed industrial bases, which had relatively more balanced proportions of men and women in the labor force.[18] Women had more opportunities to work if they were husbandless or fatherless or if the males could not make a living wage. They comprised 20 to 29 percent of the labor force and were about as likely to work in industry as in domestic service. The patterns of female employment in such "modal" cities need further study for they tell us much about women's work and family experiences when they are not influenced by the unbalanced economies of Lowell, Manchester, or Pittsburgh.

Southern cities, as Patricia McDonald's work on Baltimore points out, must be treated separately. They had high rates of female labor-force participation, but most women workers in southern cities were domestic servants or laundresses. Between 25 and 35 percent of the labor force in large southern cities was female. Of the women who worked in such cities, 65 to 75 percent were either laundresses or domestic servants. In these cities, it seems, a large proportion of the women workers consisted of black laundresses and domestics. While 40 percent of the entire female labor force in the fifty largest urban centers in the United States had manufacturing jobs, less than 20 percent of the female work force in southern cities were so employed. Baltimore was the only exception in this respect; here 32 percent of the women had manufacturing jobs.[19] Clearly, then, being a woman in a southern city was different, at least from the standpoint of labor-force participation, from being a woman in the urban North. Studies of women's work in the South are needed, especially those which compare black and white, native- and foreign-born women and analyze labor force participation by class. Generally speaking, we require more information about work patterns of women from different racial, ethnic, and class groups in the South as well as in the North and West.[20]

The effect of race on women's lives obviously is a complex question which would benefit greatly from comparative studies of black, Asian, Hispanic, and native-American populations. The experiences of these groups in different regions of the United States also require examination. Until quite recently these racial groups have been neglected by historians, and women have been even more neglected. The impact of racism, low wages, and uneven sex ratios on women's and men's lives, employment, and social and familial relations are areas which need further study.

Stanford Lyman, a sociologist, explored the impact of the sexual imbalance on community life among Chinese immigrants. He found that the absence of women among Chinese immigrants, due first to custom and later to United States law, meant that most men lived outside the family structure entirely. Substitutes developed in the form of powerful community organizations which performed certain familial functions. The Japanese overcame the initial sexual imbalance through the importation of picture-brides, that is, women whose photographs had been sent to their future husbands but who had no prior contact with them. Although community organizations did develop among the Japanese in the United States, they were neither as powerful nor as long-lasting as those within the Chinese community.[21]

Mary White Ovington's landmark study of blacks in New York City around 1900 dealt with the opposite sexual imbalance, more women than men. Because of it, black women were less likely than white women to marry and more likely to marry later. They were also more likely than white women to work while married. Ovington found that nearly 33 percent of the married black women in New York City had jobs, while only 4 percent of the married white women did. Moreover, black women were far more likely than white women to work at all ages. Whether married or single, they had few employment options beside domestic and laundry work. When unmarried, they typically lived in the homes of their employers, unlike white women, who customarily lived at home. They had fewer opportunities for family life, both because their employment prohibited it and because there was a shortage of marriage partners.[22] When the employment of black women is compared to that of Italian women, and marital status, husband's income, age, and number of children are held constant (in other words, when demographic characteristics are held constant), black women are still more likely to work. Certain cultures value women's labor-force participation more than others or, for reasons rooted in their values, are either willing to accept it or be actively supportive of it.[23]

As Virginia Yans-McLaughlin has shown, ethnicity and the mores of a particular group influenced whether women worked and the nature of their employment. These factors also influenced the nature of women's power within the family, although familial power was not necessarily correlated to employment outside the home. Italian women in Buffalo, New York, if they worked at all, held jobs which did not challenge the group's notions of the role of women. Their jobs did not permit contact between women and unrelated adult males; thus young Italian women did not work as servants, for such employment threatened their chastity by throwing them into contact with strange men. Italian women did not work without the supervision of their relatives either in strange households or in the factories and canneries.[24]

Ethnicity is critical in another way. Ethnic groups apparently fostered or discouraged the occupational participation of female or male children according to certain cultural values. They did this by giving longer schooling to one sex while the other went to work, by keeping one group at home while the other worked, or by holding one sex to routine, dead-end jobs while the other explored a number of positions. In the case of the French-Canadians in Manchester, girls worked at one job in the mill while their brothers traveled about, seeking better jobs and gaining valuable work experience in a variety of positions. Among Pittsburgh's Germans, the girls stayed close to home while the boys went out to work at a relatively early age. Among the Irish of that city, girls worked as domestic servants at an early age while the boys stayed in school a bit longer, presumably preparing for white-collar jobs.[25]

There is still little historical scholarship on the women of most ethnic and racial groups, particularly Eastern-European, native-American, and Hispanic women.[26] Historians of all ethnic and racial groups should keep several principles in mind. First, women's experience should be compared with that of men of the same group and of women in other racial groups. It should also be examined in its own terms — in terms of the dynamics of community life within that group. Generally speaking, we should know what is unique to each racial and ethnocultural group and what effects class, newness to the city, sex, geographical region, and economic structure have.

For some women, work had been a phase in life.[27] For others, it had been the continuing fact of their lives. This, too, has varied with the economic opportunities available in particular cities and with particular groups within the city. For researchers concerned with women's labor-force participation, I have suggested several important variables: the economic structure of the city, the family status of the women, the number and ages of their children, and their ethnic and racial backgrounds. The studies to date suggest that general economic conditions affected women's work. Women were more likely to work when times were hard, which indicates that to some extent female labor-force participation was a function of need, not choice.[28] From city to city, the structure of participation varied with the stage in the life cycle and by race and ethnicity. Through the nineteenth and early twentieth centuries, work, especially for married women, indicated inadequate income from other sources. This was not always the case, however, and some groups (notably Italians) were much less willing than others to have women work regardless of the economic circumstances. Married women generally contributed to the family economy through their labor in the home rather than their labor-force participation. It was not until the World War II that married women began participating in the labor force in great numbers.[29]

As Thorstein Veblen noted in *Theory of the Leisure Class*, late nineteenth-century men used women as a means of displaying affluence; to have a well-dressed wife and daughters meant that the man could support them well. Not working became a virtue, something which set middle-class women apart from working-class women and permitted status gradations within the working class itself.[30] In such a society, women contributed to the family economy by consuming and organizing the labor of others as well as by (or sometimes in place of) domestic production in the home. When the adult male's wage inadequately supported the household, the decisions made about who worked indicated much about family values, emerging social roles for women, and attitudes toward male and female children. Studies of cities where a variety of employment opportunities existed for unskilled women workers and where there are adequate census records would enhance our knowledge about women's role in the family economy as well as women's social roles. Such studies should, of course, examine the types of work performed, ethnic and class variations in work, and educational as well as family patterns.

Women's economic roles varied according to the demographic composition and the mores of the society. Elizabeth Pleck noted, in her study of black family structure in late nineteenth-century Boston, that the sex ratio affected women's opportunities for marriage and work. Where women had difficulty in marrying, due either to unfavorable sex ratios or the low status of their ethnic or racial group, they remained in the labor force longer and at more menial jobs. [31] The South and West, for example, had cultural values and labor-force participation rates for women which differed from those of northeastern urban centers. Nineteenth-century southern cities had larger proportions of blacks than those in the North. They had more women than men, many of whom presumably were black women working as domestics. Western cities, on the other hand, had a preponderance of males. The ramifications of such demographic patterns need further exploration, especially as they may have influenced either cultural or political activities. [32]

The methodology used to study urban women systematically can be drawn from the new urban history and modified to suit women's anonymity in certain records. The historian interested in urban women must use every resource available. Many of these sources have been neglected or not thought applicable to women. Traditional individual sources are rare. Where they exist, they can be used to illuminate trends but not to establish them. Group history needs group or collective sources and may require quantitative techniques to aid in the analysis. Those interested in the effects of industrialization and urbanization on women have utilized a number of such techniques and resources for uncovering women's past. It is important here to be open-minded in gathering data. The best sources frequently are those which other historians have neglected. Urban institutions were voracious record keepers from the middle of the nineteenth century on. If accessible, their records can be used to examine women's lives as well as the institutions themselves. In this way, the records of such diverse institutions as bureaus of public health, streets, water, marriage, death, and birth and charitable, educational, and social organizations can be used to document women's experience where others have thought it lost or unretrievable. [33]

Detailed analyses of individual cities will establish the relationships between economic structure, age, class, ethnicity, and family status and female labor-force, political, and civic participation. Case studies can be developed from the U.S. manuscript census returns for 1860-1900 and from state census returns where they are available. Other useful sources include marriage records, which, when cross-referenced with occupation information from city directories and censuses, permit an examination of voluntary social relations. They enable historians to examine female social mobility at one of the few points where it is traceable. Urban historians claim that individual females cannot be traced because they marry and change their names. The point of marriage permits examination of their marital partners. One study indicated that women lacked social capital in heavily industrialized cities and married "beneath" themselves in class, ethnic group, and race. [34] More studies of marriage are needed before any firm conclusions can be drawn. For example, do the patterns which existed in Pittsburgh hold for cities with extremely unbalanced sex ratios? How do occupational opportunities for women affect their marriageability?

Another way to trace women's occupational and geographic mobility is through cohort analysis, that is, by selecting an age group from one census and following it over time. Such an approach assumes that the group remains coherent, although not necessarily the same, through the period examined. It is a technique well suited to studying women since it obviates the need to trace individuals.

Census records have limited utility for tracing female fertility and child-rearing patterns. Since the interval between censuses is great (ten years), groups with high infant mortality rates may be underrepresented. A comparison of birth records which include occupational, racial, and ethnic information for the parents with death records which contain similar data provides accurate statistics on child bearing, infant care, and maternal and infant death rates. Cities and states kept birth and death records from the mid-nineteenth century on. They can be used to examine child bearing and death as they varied by class, ethnicity, race, and women's work experience for urban and rural women, as well as to compare these women's family experiences.[35]

Death records have several uses. They permit comparison between female and male mortality patterns, an implicit examination of both vulnerability and priorities. For example, high female mortality among young children may indicate passive infanticide through neglect.[36] Racial and ethnic differences in mortality curves give us concrete evidence regarding the handicaps or benefits of belonging to a particular group, as do occupational and residential data. The effect of rapid urbanization can be seen both in the types of diseases which caused death and in the increased death rates from industrial, home, and traffic accidents. In the reduction in deaths from infectious diseases we see the benefits of advancing medical knowledge. The differential reduction in death rates for certain diseases indicates that such knowledge was for sale: those who could afford it benefited more quickly than the poorer segments of the urban population.

Death records are useful for another reason not related to mortality patterns at all. They contain several geographic reference points, typically place of birth, residence at time of death, and previous residence, as well as length of residence. They can be used, therefore, to trace the geographic mobility of women as well as men, something heretofore claimed impossible. When the length of residence is included, it is possible to trace the frequency of the moves as well. The usefulness of death records lies in their completeness. They are by far the most accurate and inclusive of the late nineteenth- and early twentieth-century vital statistics. Since they give complete address data, they are fairly easy to link to city directories and other vital records.[37]

Historians generally underutilize city records in studying women, and those who use city records largely ignore their implications for women.[38] Health bureau, street commission, water commission, police and public safety, justice of the peace, and public charity reports contain information about women's lives and daily experiences. Urban services affected the environment in which all women lived, whether they held jobs or not. Since women coped daily, as part of their household chores, with the shortcomings of the water, street, and sewer systems, the differential provision of services immediately concerned them. Moreover, police, charity, and court records hold concrete evidence of women's activities and distress. These documents contain the voices of the inarticulate, albeit filtered by sometimes hostile interpreters or interlopers.

For example, police and court records contain information regarding women's activities. Criminal activities need examination in the light of the economic and social structures of the communities in which they occurred. What constituted criminal behavior in one community might not be so considered in another. Criminality also varied with stages of community growth. This was the case with prostitution.[39] Job opportunities, or the lack or them, and women's wages might also influence female crime. Did women comprise a lower percentage of total arrests in Lowell, where they could find work, than in Pittsburgh, where few jobs were open to them? Were women more likely to turn to prostitution in Pittsburgh, with its limited employment opportunities, than in New York, which had many? Or did the universally low wages paid to women mean than a constant percentage of women arrested were prostitutes, regardless of the economic structure of the city? What of prostitution on the frontier, where women migrated in order to provide sexual services to the large numbers of unattached men? How was prostitution regarded in the different sections of the United States? Some of the regional aspects of prostitution are examined in photographic and informal histories of prostitution. One of the best is Al Rose's *Storyville, New Orleans*, which contains Ernest Bellocq's marvelous pictures of prostitutes and their surroundings as well as other photographs, newspaper accounts, and documents of New Orlean's legal red-light district.[40]

Elizabeth Butler, in *Women and the Trades*, suggested that prostitution was the last resort for women who could not make ends meet on their meager wages. Ruth Rosen's study of prostitution in the Progressive Era suggests that prostitution attracted working-class women because it was a viable occupation with real social costs but clear economic benefits.[41] An interurban study of prostitution based on census, police, charitable, and social survey data would answer questions about the relationship between prostitution and urban economic structure, age, family status, race, and ethnicity.

Court records, especially those of neighborhood courts, provide another means of examining women's behavior. Courts represented a forum for working-class women, a neutral ground for airing minor disputes. As such, they contain a unique record of women's cares in a world which frequently ignored them. Justice of the peace, magistrate, and aldermanic court records can be used in several ways. The nature of women's complaints can be compared to men's to determine whether, in fact, the sexes used the courts differently. The accusations against women can be compared to those against men to see whether the sexes varied in their misdemeanors. The record also provide information about neighborhood and family relations and are uniquely valuable in this area, providing a window on relationships otherwise obscured. Complaints concern minor as well as major matters — the destruction of a clothes line, harassment, parents' abuse of a child, and a husband's neglect of a wife. Patterns of behavior emerge from these records, providing information about working-class perceptions of the world around them. Such patterns also indicate those occasions when families and neighbors felt the need to appeal to outside agents for the resolution of problems.[42]

Another tool for understanding attitudes toward women and women's lives, especially in the twentieth century, is oral history. The reminiscences of women and men who worked in the Amoskeag mills enrich Tamara Hareven's work on the textile workers of Manchester, New Hampshire. These reminiscences humanize the statistical information gathered from mill-employment and census records. They provide an intimate understanding of workers' feelings about their jobs, patterns of female work, child-rearing practices, and family relations. Alice Kessler-Harris's analyses of women's trade-union activities also use oral history to provide insight into the social values of women garment workers.[43]

Studies of women's trade-union activities benefit from an interurban perspective which takes into account demographic and employment variables. In one such study, Alice Clement compares the activities of the Women's Trade Union League in New York,

Chicago, and Boston in order to document working-class women's attitudes toward protective legislation and unionization.[44]

Another subject enhanced by oral history interviews is that of women's attitudes toward and practices of birth control and abortion. Unfortunately, such sources go back only to the turn of the century at best. As a result, they cannot speak directly to the controversy regarding female sexual emancipation during the first stages of modernization which Edward Shorter raised in his article "Female Emancipation, Birth Control, and Fertility in European History."[45] Interviews done in the Los Angeles area show that working-class woman at the turn of the century were ignorant of such birth-control devices as the pessary, or cervical cap. When they practiced family limitation, it was either by abstention or abortion. In fact, abortion seems to have been more widely discussed than birth control.[46] If this is borne out by other studies, it would indicate that the nation's "popular classes" had not emancipated themselves from unwanted child bearing at the beginning of the twentieth century.

Industrialization and urbanization affected women's political, religious, social, and sexual activities as well as their economic ones. Throughout the nineteenth century, American women moved into activities which took them further and further from their homes. Such activities, or the lack of them, must be placed in the economic and social context of their times rather than viewed in isolation as discrete phenomena. Was it coincidence that many leaders of the women's antislavery and women's-rights movements came from the Burned-Over District or that the western states strongly supported female suffrage? [47] It may be that the upsurge in women's political activity throughout the nineteenth and early twentieth centuries was not related to changes in technology and economic and educational opportunities, as suggested by Flexner and others. [48] This point must be examined in terms of occupational and demographic trends, the utilization of domestic servants and labor-saving devices, and improvements in the standard of living experienced by the middle and perhaps the working class.

Historians must also study the salient characteristics of the participants in these movements, the followers as well as the leaders. Richard Jensen has begun such work in his study of female political leaders, correlating their attitudes with their family and occupational characteristics.[49] More work in this area, particularly on the local level, is needed. Case studies and comparative studies of women's political, religious, and social activities should take into account class, occupation, family size, previous sociopolitical activity, religion, age, race, and ethnicity. Local church, benevolent, fraternal, social, temperance, and suffrage organization records contain much demographic information and can be cross-referenced with census and city directories. Such studies might find that variations in the ideology of different factions of the suffrage or temperance movements correlated with demographic or regional characteristics. What influenced participation, and why and how did it vary according to such demographic characteristics?

Similarly, we need to know more about the social activities of all strata. What types of informal networks existed? Does the rise of charitable and benevolent associations mean that the strong informal socio-familial networks of the London working class did not appear in American cities? Does it mean that such networks were ineffective in the face of rapid urbanization?[50] Here an examination of church and social club records would indicate who belonged, under what circumstances members had joined and whether they varied by race, ethnicity, occupation, class, age, or length of residence.

A systematic study of urban women needs to be done in terms of the economic structure of each city. Individual demographic factors such as the woman's age, her marital status, age and number of children, class, race, and ethnicity are important. Generally speaking, the economic opportunities in a city determined the nature of women's work, while economic and demographic factors determined which women would work, under what circumstances, and in what positions. There is, of course, a need for additional investigation to determine whether consistent patterns emerge and to explore the effects of modernization on the family and on women who did not work outside the home.

Such contextual studies are useful for examining women's social, political, and religious activities as well. The upsurge in women's participation outside the home was coincident with industrialization in the United States. Was there a causal link? If so, why does it appear that the frontier West favored political emancipation for women while the more urbanized and industrialized East embraced it less wholeheartedly? Do demographic and economic factors conflict with each other? How much support did the women's rights, temperance, and other crusades garner in rural eastern and southern areas as compared with rural western ones?

A comparative case-study approach provides information about the ways in which industrialization affected women. Class, age, ethnicity, race, family status, age and number of children, and economic opportunities inform us about women's labor-force participation, social relations, and sociopolitical and religious activities. Many quantitative techniques can profitably be applied to the study of women since this approach requires the manipulation of masses of data. Much of the work cited here is in progress. Still more has to be done. The history of women in the city is only now being written. Such a history must place women in the context of their times. By so doing, it will reflect the diversity of women's experiences and correlate those experiences with critical economic, ethnocultural, and demographic differences in the cities themselves. In this way, and only in this way, can we understand the impact of urbanization and industrialization on women.

NOTES

1. Arthur M. Schlesinger, Sr., *The Rise of the City: 1878-1898.* (New York, 1933), chapter 5.

2. There are several excellent bibliographies of urban history, including those in Charles N. Glaab and A. Theordore Brown, *A History of Urban America* (New York, 1967) and Bayrd Still, *Urban America* (Boston, 1974). However, none of these deals with women as a separate topic. One text which does include women as part of the history of the city is Howard P. Chudacoff, *The Evolution of Urban Society* (Englewood Cliffs, N.J., 1975).

3. Most works on women in the city prior to the 1960s were written by sociologists or social workers. These include Edith Abbott, *Women in Industry* (New York, 1909), Elizabeth Butler, *Women and the Trades* (New York, 1910), Annie MacLean, *Wage Earning Women* (New York, 1910), and Margaret Byington, *Homestead: The Households of a Milltown* (New York, 1914), which has recently been reissued by the University Center for International Studies (U.C.I.S.), University of Pittsburgh, with an introduction by Samuel P. Hays.

4. See the following papers given at the State University of New York, Binghamton Conference on Class and Ethnicity in Women's History, September 1974: Vir-

ginia Yans-McLaughlin, "Italian Women and Work: Experience and Perception";
Tamara Hareven, "Industrial Work and the Family Cycle" (later published in the
Journal of Urban History 1[May 1975]); and Alice Kessler-Harris, "Organizing the
Unorganizable: Jewish Women and Their Unions." See also the following papers
given at the Second Berkshire Conference on the History of Women, October 1974:
Thomas Dublin, "Women, Work and the Family: Women Operatives in the Lowell
Mills, 1830-1860"; JoEllen Vinyard, "From Europe to Urban America, Immigrant
Women in 19th-Century Detroit"; and Maxine S. Seller, "Immigrant Women in
Leadership Roles Within American Ethnic Communities, 1890-1924." There are
two excellent comparative studies: Laurence Glasco, "Ethnicity and Social Structure: Irish,Germans and Native-born of Buffalo, New York 1850-1860" (Doctoral
dissertation, SUNY, Buffalo, 1973); and Elizabeth H. Pleck: "A Mother's Wages:
A Comparison of Income Earning Among Urban Black and Italian Wives,
1896-1911," presented at Newberry Library Family History Seminar, November
1975. The value of Pleck's study is that it comes to grips with the difficult issue of
the ethnic and class values which determine women's labor-force participation.

   5. See Yans-McLaughlin, "Italian Women and Work"; Hareven, "Industrial
Work and the Family Cycle"; Pleck, "A Mother's Wages"; Kessler-Harris,
"Organizing the Unorganizable"; Lynn Lees, "Irish Families in the City: Work,
Power and the Life Cycle," paper presented at the Second Berkshire Conference,
1974; Teresa McBride, "Rural Tradition and the Process of Modernization: Domestic Servants in Nineteenth Century France" (Doctoral dissertation, Rutgers, 1973);
Joan Scott and Louise Tilly, "Women's Work and the Family in Nineteenth Century Europe," *Comparative Studies in Society and History* 17, no. 1 (January 1975):
36-64.

   6. See my doctoral dissertation, "Technology's Stepdaughters" (University of
Pittsburgh, 1973). The proceedings of labor union and trade union meetings contain
frequent references to the need for sufficient salaries so that women and children
would not have to work. See also, Scott and Tilly, "Women's Work and the Family," p. 64.

   7. Kleinberg, "Technology's Stepdaughters," chapter 6.

   8. Lees, "Irish Families in the City," p. 12

   9. Joan Scott's perceptive comments on my paper, "Women in the Labor Force,
Pittsburgh, 1880" (Brockport Social and Political History Conference, 1974), led
me to rethink the factors involved in women's labor-force participation.

   10. Vinyard, "From Europe to Urban America."

   11. See Abbott, *Women in Industry*, on laundry workers in Troy and the tenement factories and Elizabeth Butler, *Women and the Trades*, on sewing in the coal-
mining regions near Pittsburgh.

   12. This information was compiled from U.S. Census, *Social Statistics of Cities*,
1880 (Washington, D.C., 1885-1886), vols. 1 and 2, passim. In Denver, Kansas City,
Pittsburgh, Scranton, and San Francisco, between 10 and 14 percent of the labor
force were women. In Allegheny, Buffalo, Camden, Chicago, Cleveland, Colum-
bus, Dayton, Indianapolis, Jersey City, Milwaukee, Minneapolis, Reading, St.
Louis, St. Paul, Toledo, and Wilmington, between 15 and 19 percent of the labor
force were women.

13. Pittsburgh Regional Planning Association, *Region in Transition* (Pittsburgh, 1963), pp. 34-40. This situation changed slightly in 1910 as some women began work in the finishing processes in the mills and glass houses while others worked in tenement, food, and laundry industries. The major source for this era, Butler, *Women and the Trades*, is rather misleading. As a progressive, Butler included the entire Pittsburgh region, not Pittsburgh alone. The city had also incorporated much of its suburban territory by 1910. Butler, moreover, gives no sense of the proportion of women in the trades as compared to the proportion in domestic service, which remained the dominant occupation for women in Pittsburgh.

14. U.S. Census Manuscript (Pittsburgh, 1880).

15. U.S. Census, *Social Statistics of Cities, 1880*. Similar data are available for the 1890 and 1900 censuses, including Lowell and other textile towns.

16. Hareven, "Industrial Work and the Family Cycle," *Journal of Social History* 5 (Summer 1972): 464-490. Additional work on women textile workers has been done by Daniel Walkowitz, "Working Class Women in the Gilded Age: Factory, Community and Family Life among Cohoes, New York, Cotton Workers," *Journal of Social History*, 1973; and Dublin, "Women, Work and the Family."

17. Joan Scott and Louise Tilly, "Daughters, Wives, Mothers, Workers: Peasants and Working Class Women in the Transition to an Industrial Economy in France." Paper presented at the Berkshire Conference, 1974.

18. U.S. Census, *Social Statistics of Cities*, 1880, which includes New York City, Philadelphia, and Boston.

19. *Ibid.* Patricia McDonald, who has a dissertation in progress at the University of Maryland, was kind enough to share her findings with me.

20. As is true of urban historians generally, those who study southern cities have thus far dealt only with men. See Richard J. Hopkins, "Status, Mobility and the Dimension of Change in a Southern City: Atlanta, 1870-1910," in Kenneth T. Jackson and Stanley K. Schultz, eds., *Cities in American History* (New York, 1952); and Paul B. Worthman, "Working Class Mobility in Birmingham, Alabama, 1880-1914," in Tamara Hareven, ed., *Anonymous Americans* (Englewood Cliffs, N.J., 1971). The techniques used by Hopkins and Worthman can be applied to women (as outlined below).

The same narrowness characterizes western urban history. See Roger W. Lotchin, *San Francisco, 1846-1856* (New York, 1974), pp. 255-258, 293, and 304-310, for information on women in that city. Robert W. Fogelson, *The Fragmented Metropolis: Los Angeles, 1850-1930* (Cambridge, Mass., 1967), barely mentions women (pp. 64, 83-84, and 214), as does Earl Pomeroy, *The Pacific Slope* (New York, 1965). A general consideration of western women is to be found in Nancy Wilson Ross, *Westward the Women: The American Saga, 1804-1900* (New York, 1944; reprint 1972). See also Nannie T. Alderson and Helena Huntington Smith, *A Bride Goes West* (Lincoln, Nebraska, 1942; reprint 1969), and Elinore Pruitt Stewart, *Letters of a Woman Homesteader* (Lincoln, Nebraska, 1913; reprint 1961). Dee Brown's *The Gentle Tamers* (Lincoln, Nebraska, 1958) is flawed by condescending attitudes toward its subjects.

21. Stanford Lyman, *The Asian in the West* (Reno and Las Vegas, 1970), p. 61. On the experience of Asian women in the United States, see *Asian Women* (c/o 3405

Dwinelle Hall, University of California, Berkeley). This book, written and published by an Asian studies class at Berkeley, contains excellent illustrations and a complete annotated bibliography on Asian women in the United States.

22. Mary White Ovington, *Half a Man: The Status of the Negro in New York* (New York, 1911), chapter 6, especially pp. 77-82. See also Elizabeth Pleck, "The Two-Parent Household: Black Family Structure in Late Nineteenth Century Boston," in Michael Gordon, ed., *The American Family in Social-Historical Perspective* (New York, 1973); Herbert Gutman, *The Black Family in Slavery and Freedom, 1750-1925* (New York, 1976); W.E.B. DuBois, *The Philadelphia Negro: A Social Study . . . Together with a Special Report on Domestic Service* by Isabel Eaton (New York, 1899). The *Special Report on Domestic Service* is an analysis of the life, wages, and conditions of black domestic workers in Philadelphia at the time DuBois conducted his survey. For black women's feelings on a variety of topics, see the excellent collection of their writings compiled by Gerda Lerner, *Black Women in White America* (New York, 1972).

23. Pleck, "A Mother's Wages."

24. Virginia Yans McLaughlin, "Patterns of Work and Family Organization: Buffalo's Italians," *Journal of Interdisciplinary History 2* (1971): 299-314. For an examination of immigrant working-class women in New York City, see Katherine Anthony, *Mothers Who Must Earn* (New York, 1912).

25. Hareven, "Family Time and Industrial Time"; Kleinberg, "Technology's Stepdaughters."

26. Patricia Herrera Duran and Roberto Cabello-Argandona, *The Chicana: A Preliminary Bibliographical Study* (Chicano Research Library, University of California, Los Angeles, n.d.), contains a few historical entries. Frank B. Lindermen, *Pretty Shield* (New York, 1932), and Olivia Vlahos, *New World Beginnings* (New York, 1970), have scattered references to women. The anthropological literature is rich in references to women.

27. My thinking on this matter has been deeply influenced by Tamara Hareven's work, "Industrial Work and the Family Cycle," *Journal of Urban History* 1 (May 1975); and Laurence Glasco, "Life Cycles and Household Structure of American Ethnic Groups," *Journal of Urban History* 1 (May 1975). This volume of *Journal of Urban History*, edited by Tamara Hareven, was devoted to the study of the urban family.

28. See Robert W. Smuts, *Women and Work in America* (New York, 1959).

29. *1965 Handbook on Women Workers* (Washington, 1966), pp. 21-23.

30. Thorstein Veblen, *The Theory of the Leisure Class* (New York, 1899; New American Library edition, 1953), ch. 7, esp. p. 121.

31. Pleck, "A Mother's Wages"; Kleinberg, "Technology's Stepdaughters," ch. 6.

32. Elizabeth Jameson, "Imperfect Unions: Class and Gender in Cripple Creek, 1894-1904," paper presented at the American Studies Association Meeting, 1975.

33. For an example of the use of metropolitan records to document women's daily experiences, see Kleinberg, "Technology and Women's Work," *Labor History* 17 (Winter 1976): 58-72.

34. Kleinberg, "Technology's Stepdaughters." The possibility of using marriage records in this fashion was suggested by Joan Scott, "The Glass Workers of

Carmaux," in Richard Sennett and Stephan Thernstrom, eds., *Nineteenth Century Cities* (New Haven, 1969).

35. Daniel Scott Smith, "The Demographic History of Colonial New England," and Wilson Grabill, Clyde V. Kiser, and Pascal K. Whelpton, "A Long View," both in Gordon, *The American Family*.

36. Emily Coleman, "L'infanticide dans le Haut Moyen Age," *Annales Economies, Sociétés Civilisations* (Mars-Avril, 1974): 315-335.

37. This description is drawn from my research in progress on patterns of mortality in Pittsburgh. I used thirty years of individual death certificates, linking them to city directory entries to obtain occupational data for women and children who were not employed and using their husband's or father's occupation as an indicator of socioeconomic status. The inclusion of several addresses for each individual on the death certificates makes it much easier to trace them. As a result, socioeconomic information was found for about twice as many women listed in the death certificates as for those listed in the marriage certificates. The same procedure for tracing women's socioeconomic status was used with both sources. The death certificates contain information only about those who died within the city; they tell us little about those who left the city or died outside it. They are, nevertheless, important sources for the study of women's death and mobility patterns.

The landmark studies of mobility, including Howard Chudacoff, *Mobile Americans*, Peter Knights, *The Plain People of Boston* (New York, 1973), and Stephan Thernstrom, *Poverty and Progress*, have not included women. The death records, especially when linked to other records, make such studies feasible.

38. This was true of the otherwise excellent study of the development of municipal and social services by Sam Bass Warner in *Streetcar Suburbs* (Cambridge, Mass., 1962) and Bayrd Still (Madison, Wisc., 1965) in *Milwaukee*. Institutional studies tend to ignore the target populations of the institutions and concentrate on the dynamics of institutional development; see, for example, Roy Lubove, *The Professional Altruist: The Emergence of Social Work as a Career, 1800-1930* (Cambridge, Mass., 1965).

39. Elizabeth Jameson, "Imperfect Unions"; Egal Feldman, "Prostitution, the Alien Woman and the Progressive Imagination," *American Quarterly* 19, no. 2, pt. 1 (Summer 1967): 192-206, roots its examination of prostitution in the sociocultural milieu.

40. Al Rose, *Storyville, New Orleans* (Tuscaloosa, Alabama, 1974). Another collection of Bellocq's sensitive portraits is John Szarkowski, *Storyville Portraits* (New York, 1970).

41. Butler, *Women and the Trades*; Paul Kellog, ed., *Wage Earnings Pittsburgh* (New York, 1909), pp. 501-509. Ruth Rosen, who is writing a dissertation on prostitution in the Progressive Era at the University of California, Berkeley, was kind enough to share some of her findings with me.

42. Kleinberg, "Technology's Stepdaughter," ch. 5.

43. Hareven, "Industrial Work and the Family Cycle"; Kessler-Harris, "Organizing the Unorganizable."

44. Alice Clement, "The Women's Trade Union League: The American Federation of Labor and Efforts to Organize Working Women, 1904-1920," paper pre-

sented at the West Coast Association of Women Historians Convention, 1975.

45. Edward Shorter, "Female Emanicipation, Birth Control and Fertility in European History," *American Historical Review* 78 (June 1973): 605-640. For a rebuttal to Shorter, see Scott and Tilly, "Women's Work and the Family," pp. 55-56.

46. Sherna Gluck, "Recovering Our Past Through Oral History Interviews," tape and slide presentation at the West Coast Association of Women Historians Convention, 1975.

47. Two studies which place women in their cultural and social environments are Gerda Lerner, *The Grimké Sisters* (New York, 1967), and Anne F. Scott (Chicago, 1970), *The Southern Lady.*

48. Eleanor Flexner, *Century of Struggle* (Cambridge, Mass., 1959); William O'Neill, *Everyone Was Brave, The Rise and Fall of Feminism in America* (Chicago, 1969).

49. Richard Jensen, "Family, Career and Reform: Women Leaders of the Progressive Era," in Gordon, *The American Family.*

50. Michael Young and Peter Willmott, *Family and Kinship in East London* (London, 1957). Herbert Gans's study of Italians in Boston, *Urban Villagers* (New York, 1962), indicates that tightly-knit working-class communities in contemporary America reject outside social services or accept them only with extreme reluctance. Such communities are vulnerable to outside forces, including highways and urban renewal. The Young and Willmott study indicated that relocation weakens the old ties.

WOMEN, WORK, AND PROTEST IN THE EARLY LOWELL MILLS: "THE OPPRESSING HAND OF AVARICE WOULD ENSLAVE US"

2

by Thomas Dublin

In the years before 1850 the textile mills of Lowell, Massachusetts, were a celebrated economic and cultural attraction. Foreign visitors invariably included them on their American tours. Interest was prompted by the massive scale of these mills, the astonishing productivity of the power-driven machinery, and the fact that women comprised most of the work force. Visitors were struck by the newness of both mills and city as well as by the culture of the female operatives. The scene stood in sharp contrast to the gloomy mill towns of the English industrial revolution.

Lowell, was, in fact, an impressive accomplishment. In 1820, there had been no city at all — only a dozen family farms along the Merrimack River in East Chelmsford. In 1821, however, a group of Boston capitalists purchased land and water rights along the river and a nearby canal, and began to build a major textile manufacturing center. Opening two years later, the first factory employed Yankee women recruited from the nearby countryside. Additional mills were constructed until, by 1840, ten textile corporations with thirty-two mills valued at more than ten million dollars lined the banks of the river and nearby canals.[1] Adjacent to the mills were rows of company boardinghouses and tenements which accommodated most of the eight thousand factory operatives.

As Lowell expanded and became the nation's largest textile manufacturing center, the experiences of women operatives changed as well. The increasing number of firms in Lowell and in the other mill towns brought the pressure of competition. Overproduction became a problem and the prices of finished cloth decreased. The high profits of the early years declined and so, too, did conditions

SOURCE: *Labor History* 16, no. 1 (Winter 1975)

for the mill operatives. Wages were reduced and the pace of work within the mills was stepped up. Women operatives did not accept these changes without protest. In 1834 and 1836 they went on strike to protest wage cuts, and between 1843 and 1848 they mounted petition campaigns aimed at reducing the hours of labor in the mills.

These labor protests in early Lowell contribute to our understanding of the response of workers to the growth of industrial capitalism in the first half of the nineteenth century. They indicate the importance of values and attitudes dating back to an earlier period and also the transformation of these values in a new setting.

The major factor in the rise of a new consciousness among operatives in Lowell was the development of a close-knit community among women working in the mills. The structure of work and the nature of housing contributed to the growth of this community. The existence of community among women, in turn, was an important element in the repeated labor protests of the period.

The organization of this paper derives from the logic of the above argument. It will examine the basis of community in the experiences of women operatives and then the contribution that the community of women made to the labor protests in these years as well as the nature of the new consciousness expressed by these protests.

The preconditions for the labor unrest in Lowell before 1850 may be found in the study of the daily worklife of its operatives. In their everyday, relatively conflict-free lives, mill women created the mutual bonds which made possible united action in times of crisis. The existence of a tight-knit community among them was the most important element in determining the collective, as opposed to individual, nature of this response.

Before examining the basis of community among women operatives in early Lowell, it may be helpful to indicate in what sense "community" is being used. The women are considered a "community" because of the development of bonds of mutual dependence among them. In this period they came to depend upon one another and upon the larger group of operatives in very important ways. Their experiences were not simply similar or parallel to one another, but were inextricably intertwined. Furthermore, they were conscious of the existence of community, expressing it very clearly in their writings and in labor protests. "Community" for them had objective and subjective dimensions, and both were important in the experience of women in the mills.

The mutual dependence among women in early Lowell was rooted in the structure of mill work itself. Newcomers to the mills were particularly dependent on their fellow operatives, but even experienced hands relied on one another for considerable support.

New operatives generally found their first experiences difficult, even harrowing, though they may have already done much hand-spinning and weaving in their own homes. The initiation of one of them is described in fiction in the *Lowell Offering:*

> The next morning she went into the Mill; and at first the sight of so many bands, and wheels, and springs in constant motion, was very frightful. She felt afraid to touch the loom, and she was almost sure she could never learn to weave . . . the shuttle flew out, and made a new bump on her head; and the first time she tried to spring the lathe, she broke out a quarter of the treads.[2]

While other accounts present a somewhat less difficult picture, most indicate that women only became proficient and felt satisfaction in their work after several months in the mills. [3]

The textile corporations made provisions to ease the adjustment of new operatives. Newcomers were not immediately expected to fit into the mill's regular work routine. They were at first assigned work as sparehands and were paid a daily wage independent of the quantity of work they turned out. As a sparehand, the newcomer worked with an experienced hand who instructed her in the intricacies of the job. The sparehand spelled her partner for short stretches of time and occasionally took the place of an absentee. One woman described the learning process in a letter reprinted in the *Offering*:

> Well, I went into the mill, and was put to learn with a very patient girl . . . . You cannot think

> how odd everything seemed . . . . They set me to
> threading shuttles, and tying weaver's knots, and
> such things, and now I have improved so that I can
> take care of one loom. I could take care of two if
> only I had eyes in the back part of my head.[4]

After the passage of some weeks or months, when she could handle
the normal complement of machinery — two looms for weavers
during the 1830s — and when a regular operative departed, leaving
an opening, the sparehand moved into a regular job.

Through this system of job training, the textile corporations contributed to the development of community among female operatives. During the most difficult period in an operative's career, the
first months in the mill, she relied upon other women workers for
training and support. And for every sparehand whose adjustment
to mill work was aided in this process, there was an experienced
operative whose work was also affected. Women were relating to
one another during the work process and not simply tending their
machinery. Given the high rate of turnover in the mill workforce, a
large proportion of women operatives worked in pairs. At the
Hamilton Company in July 1836, for example, more than a fifth of
all females on the Company payroll were sparehands.[5] Consequently, over 40 percent of the females employed there in this
month worked with one another. Nor was this interaction sur-
reptitious, carried out only when the overseer looked elsewhere;
rather, it was formally organized and sanctioned by the textile
corporations themselves.

In addition to the integration of sparehands, informal sharing of
work often went on among regular operatives. A woman would occasionally take off a half or full day from work either to enjoy a
brief vacation or to recover from illness, and fellow operatives
would each take an extra loom or side of spindles so that she might
continue to earn wages during her absence.[6] Women were generally
paid on a piece rate basis, their wages being determined by the total
output of the machinery they tended during the payroll period.
With friends helping out during her absence, making sure that her
looms kept running, an operative could earn almost a full wage
even though she was not physically present. Such informal work-

sharing was another way in which mutual dependence developed among women operatives during their working hours.

Living conditions also contributed to the development of community among female operatives. Most women working in the Lowell mills of these years were housed in company boarding houses. In July 1836, for example, more than 73 percent of females employed by the Hamilton Company resided in company housing adjacent to the mills.[7] Almost three-fourths of them, therefore, lived and worked with each other. Furthermore, the work schedule was such that women had little opportunity to interact with those not living in company dwellings. They worked, in these years, an average of 73 hours a week. Their work day ended at 7:00 or 7:30 P.M., and in the hours between supper and the 10:00 curfew imposed by management on residents of company boarding houses there was little time to spend with friends living "off the corporation."

Women in the boarding houses lived in close quarters, a factor that also played a role in the growth of community. A typical boarding house accommodated twenty-five young women, generally crowded four to eight in a bedroom.[8] There was little possibility of privacy within the dwelling, and pressure to conform to group standards was very strong (as will be discussed below). The community of operatives which developed in the mills . . . carried over into life at home as well.

The boarding house became a central institution in the lives of Lowell's female operatives in those years, but it was particularly important in the initial integration of newcomers into urban industrial life. Upon first leaving her rural home for work in Lowell, a women entered a setting very different from anything she had previously known. One operative, writing in the *Offering*, described the feelings of a fictional character: ". . . the first entrance into a factory boarding house seemed something dreadful. The room looked strange and comfortless, and the women cold and heartless; and when she sat down to the supper table, where among more than twenty girls, all but one were strangers, she could not eat a mouthful."[9]

In the boarding house, the newcomer took the first steps in the process which transformed her from an "outsider" into an accepted member of the community of women operatives.

Recruitment of newcomers into the mills and their initial hiring was mediated through the boarding house system. Women general-ly did not travel to Lowell for the first time entirely on their own. They usually came because they knew someone — an older sister, cousin, or friend — who had already worked in Lowell.[10] The scene described above was a lonely one — but the newcomer did know at least one boarder among the twenty seated around the sup-per table. The Hamilton Company Register Books indicate that numerous pairs of operatives, having the same surnames and coming from the same town in northern New England, lived in the same boarding houses.[11] If the newcomer was not accompanied by a friend or relative, she was usually directed to "Number 20, Ham-ilton Company," or to a similar address of one of the other corpo-rations where her acquaintance lived. Her first contact with fellow operatives generally came in the boarding houses and not in the mills. Given the personal nature of recruitment in this period, therefore, newcomers usually had the company and support of a friend or relative in their first adjustment to Lowell.

Like recruitment, the initial hiring was a personal process. Once settled in the boarding house, a newcomer had to find a job. She would generally go to the mills with her friend or with the boarding house keeper who would introduce her to an overseer in one of the rooms. If he had an opening, she might start work immediately. More likely, the overseer would know of an opening elsewhere in the mill, or would suggest that something would probably develop within a few days. In one story in the *Offering*, a newcomer worked on some quilts for her house keeper, thereby earning her board while she waited for a job opening.[12]

Upon entering the boarding house, the newcomer came under pressure to conform with the standards of the community of oper-atives. Stories in the *Offering* indicate that newcomers at first stood out from the group in terms of their speech and dress. Over time they dropped the peculiar "twang" in their speech which so amused experienced hands. Similarly, they purchased clothing more in keeping with urban than rural styles. It was an unusual and strongwilled individual who could work and live among her fellow operatives and not conform, at least outwardly, to the customs and values of this larger community.[13]

The boarding houses were the centers of social life for women operatives after their long days in the mills. There they ate their meals, rested, talked, sewed, wrote letters, read books and magazines. From among fellow workers and boarders they found friends who accompanied them to shops, to Lyceum lectures, to church and church-sponsored events. On Sundays or holidays, they often took walks along the canals or out into the nearby countryside. The community of women operatives, in sum, developed in a setting where women worked and lived together, twenty-four hours a day.

Given the all-pervasiveness of this community, one would expect it to exert strong pressures on those who did not conform to group standards. Such appears to have been the case. The community influenced newcomers to adopt its patterns of speech and dress. In addition, it enforced an unwritten code of moral conduct. Henry Miles, a minister in Lowell, described the way in which the community pressured those who deviated from accepted moral conduct:

> A girl, suspected of immoralities, or serious improprieties, at once loses caste. Her fellow boarders will at once leave the house, if the keeper does not dismiss the offender. In self-protection, therefore, the patron is obliged to put the offender away. Nor will her former companions walk with her, or work with her; till at length, finding herself everywhere talked about, and pointed at, and shunned, she is obliged to relieve her fellow-operatives of a presence which they feel brings disgrace. [14]

The power of the peer group described by Miles may seem extreme, but there is evidence in the writing of women operatives to corroborate his account. Such group pressure is illustrated by a story (in the *Offering*) in which operatives in a company boarding house begin to harbor suspicions about a fellow boarder, Hannah, who [has] received repeated evening visits from a man whom she does not introduce to the other residents. Two boarders declare that they will leave if she is allowed to remain in the household. The house keeper finally informed Hannah that she must either depart or not see the man again. She does not accept the ultimatum, but is promptly discharged after the overseer is informed, by one of the boarders, about her conduct. And only one of Hannah's former friends continues to remain on cordial terms.[15]

One should not conclude, however, that women always enforced a moral code agreeable to Lowell's clergy, or to the mill agents and overseers for that matter. After all, the kind of peer pressure imposed on Hannah could be brought to bear on women in 1834 and 1836 who, on their own, would not have protested wage cuts. It was much harder to go to work when one's roommates were marching about town, attending rallies, or circulating strike petitions. Similarly, the ten-hour petitions of the 1840s were certainly aided by the fact of a tight-knit community of operatives living in a dense neighborhood of boarding houses. To the extent that women could not have completely private lives in the boarding houses, they probably had to conform to group norms, whether these involved speech, clothing, relations with men, or attitudes toward the ten-hour day. Group pressure to conform, so important to the community of women in early Lowell, played a significant role in the collective response of women to changing conditions in the mills.

In addition to the structure of work and housing in Lowell, a third factor, the homogeneity of the mill workforce, contributed to the development of community among female operatives. In this period, the mill workforce was homogeneous in terms of sex, nativity, and age. Payroll and other records of the Hamilton Company reveal that more than 85 per cent of those employed in July, 1836, were women and that over 96 per cent were native-born.[16] Furthermore, over 80 per cent of the female workforce were between the ages of 15 and 30; and only 10 per cent were under 14 or over 40.[17]

Workforce homogeneity takes on particular significance in the context of work structure and the nature of worker housing. These

three factors combined meant that women operatives had little interaction with men during their daily lives. Men and women did not
perform the same work in the mills, and generally did not even
labor in the same rooms. Men worked in the initial picking and
carding processes, in the repair shop, and on the watchforce and
filled all supervisory positions in the mills. Women held all sparehand and regular operative jobs in drawing, speeding, spinning,
weaving and dressing. A typical room in the mill employed eighty
women tending machinery, with two men overseeing the work and
two boys assisting them. Women had little contact with men other
than their supervisors in the course of the working day. After work,
women returned to their boarding houses, where once again there
were few men. Women, then, worked and lived in a predominantly
female setting.

Ethnically the workforce was also homogeneous. Immigrants
formed only 3.4 per cent of those employed at Hamilton in July,
1836. In addition, they comprised only 3 per cent of residents in
Hamilton Company housing.[18] The community of women operatives was composed of women of New England stock drawn from
the hill-country farms surrounding Lowell. Consequently, when
experienced hands made fun of the speech and dress of newcomers,
it was understood that they, too, had been "rusty" or "rustic"
upon first coming to Lowell. This common background was
another element shared by women workers in early Lowell.

The work structure, the workers' housing, and workforce homogeneity were the major elements which contributed to the growth of
community among Lowell's women operatives. To best understand
the larger implications of community, it is necessary to examine the
labor protests of this period. For in these struggles, the new values
and attitudes which developed in the community of women
operatives are most visible.

II

In February, 1834, 800 of Lowell's women operatives "turned-
out" — went on strike — to protest a proposed reduction in their
wages. They marched to numerous mills in an effort to induce
others to join them, and, at an outdoor rally, they petitioned others

to "discontinue their labors until terms of reconciliation are made." Their petition concluded:

> Resolved, That we will not go back into the mills to work unless our wages are continued . . . as they have been.
>
> Resolved, That none of us will go back, unless they receive us all as one.
>
> Resolved, That if any have not money enough to carry them home, they shall be supplied.[19]

The strike proved to be brief and failed to reverse the proposed wage reductions. Turning-out on a Friday, the striking women were paid their back wages on Saturday, and by the middle of the next week had returned to work or left town. Within a week of the turn-out, the mills were running near capacity.[20]

This first strike in Lowell is important not because it failed or succeeded, but simply because it took place. In an era in which women had to overcome opposition simply to work in the mills, it is remarkable that they would further overstep the accepted middle-class bounds of female propriety by participating in a public protest. The agents of the textile mills certainly considered the turn-out unfeminine. William Austin, agent of the Lawrence Company, described the operatives' procession as an "amizonian [*sic*] display." He wrote further, in a letter to his company treasurer in Boston: "This afternoon we have paid off several of these Amazons & presume that they will leave town on Monday."[21] The turn-out was particularly offensive to the agents because of the relationship they thought they had with their operatives. William Austin probably expressed the feelings of other agents when he wrote: " . . . notwithstanding the friendly and disinterested advice which has been on all proper occassions [*sic*] communicated to the girls of the Lawrence mills a spirit of evil omen . . . has prevailed, and overcome the judgement and discretion of too many, and this morning a general turn-out from most of the rooms has been the consequence."[22]

Mill agents assumed an attitude of benevolent paternalism toward their female operatives, and found it particularly disturbing that the women paid such little heed to their advice. The strikers were not merely unfeminine, they were ungrateful as well.

Such attitudes notwithstanding, women chose to turn-out. They did so for two principal reasons. First, the wage cuts undermined the sense of dignity and social equality, which was an important element in their Yankee heritage. Second, these wage cuts were seen as an attack on their economic independence.

Certainly a prime motive for the strike was outrage at the social implications of the wage cuts. In a statement of principles accompanying the petition which was circulated among operatives, women expressed well the sense of themselves which prompted their protests of these wage cuts:

UNION IS POWER

> Our present object is to have union and exertion, and we remain in possession of our unquestionable rights. We circulate this paper wishing to obtain the names of all who imbibe the spirit of our Patriotic Ancestors, who preferred privation to bondage, and parted with all that renders life desirable — and even life itself — to procure independence for their children. The oppressing hand of avarice would enslave us, and to gain their object, they gravely tell us of the pressure of the time, this we are already sensible of, and deplore it. If any are in want of assistance, the Ladies will be compassionate and assist them; but we prefer to have the disposing of our charities in our own hands; and as we are free, we would remain in possession of what kind Providence has bestowed upon us; and remain daughters of freeman still. [23]

At several points in the proclamation the women drew on their Yankee heritage. Connecting their turn-out with the efforts of their

"Patriotic Ancestors" to secure independence from England, they interpreted the wage cuts as an effort to "enslave" them — to deprive them of their independent status as "daughters of freeman."

Though very general and rhetorical, the statement of these women does suggest their sense of self, of their own worth and dignity. Elsewhere, they expressed the conviction that they were the social equals of the overseers, indeed of the mill owners themselves.[24] The wage cuts, however, struck at this assertion of social equality. These reductions made it clear that the operatives were subordinate to their employers, rather than equal partners in a contract binding on both parties. By turning-out the women emphatically denied that they were subordinates; but by returning to work the next week, they demonstrated that in economic terms they were no match for their corporate superiors.

In point of fact, these Yankee operatives were subordinate in early Lowell's social and economic order, but they never consciously accepted this status. Their refusal to do so became evident whenever the mill owners attempted to exercise the power they possessed. This fundamental contradiction between the objective status of operatives and their consciousness of it was at the root of the 1834 turn-out and of subsequent labor protests in Lowell before 1850. The corporations could build mills, create thousands of jobs, and recruit women to fill them. Nevertheless, they bought only the workers' labor power, and then only for as long as these workers chose to stay. Women could always return to their rural homes, and they had a sense of their own worth and dignity, factors limiting the actions of management.

Women operatives viewed the wage cuts as a threat to their economic independence. This independence had two related dimensions. First, the women were self-supporting while they worked in the mills and, consequently, were independent of their families back home. Second, they were able to save out of their monthly earnings and could then leave the mills for the old homestead whenever they so desired. In effect, they were not totally dependent upon mill work. Their independence was based largely on the high level of wages in the mills. They could support themselves and still save enough to return home periodically. The wage cuts threatened to deny them this outlet, substituting instead the prospect of total dependence on mill work. Small wonder, then, there was alarm that "the oppressing hand of avarice would enslave us." To be forced, out of economic necessity, to lifelong labor in the mills would have indeed seemed like slavery.[25] The Yankee operatives spoke directly to the fear of a dependency based on impoverishment when offering to assist any women workers who "have not money enough to carry them home." Wage reductions, however, offered only the *prospect* of a future dependence on mill employment. By striking, the women asserted their actual economic independence of the mills and their determination to remain "daughters of freemen still."

While the women's traditional conception of themselves as independent daughters of freemen played a major role in the turn-out, this factor acting alone would not necessarily have triggered the 1834 strike. It would have led women as individuals to quit work and return to their rural homes. But the turn-out was a collective protest. When it was announced that wage reductions were being considered, women began to hold meetings in the mills during meal breaks in order to assess tactical possibilities. Their turn-out began at one mill when the agent discharged a woman who had presided at such a meeting. Their procession through the streets passed by other mills, expressing a conscious effort to enlist as much support as possible for their cause. At a mass meeting, the women drew up a resolution which insisted that none be discharged for their participation in the turn-out. This strike, then, was a collective response to the proposed wage cuts — made possible because women had come to form a "community" of operatives in the mill, rather than simply a group of individual workers. The existence of such a tight-knit community turned individual opposition to the wage cuts into a collective protest.

In October, 1836, women again went on strike. This second turn-out was similar to the first in several respects. Its immediate cause was also a wage reduction; marches and a large outdoor rally were organized; again, like the earlier protest, the basic goal was not achieved: the corporations refused to restore wages and operatives either left Lowell or returned to work at the new rates.

Despite these surface similarities between the turn-outs, there were some real differences. One involved scale: over 1500 operatives turned out in 1836, compared to only 800 earlier.[26] Moreover, the second strike lasted much longer than the first. In 1834 operatives stayed out for only a few days; in 1836, the mills ran far below capacity for several months. Two weeks after the second turn-out began, a mill agent reported that only a fifth of the strikers had returned to work: "The rest manifest *good 'spunk'* as they call it."[27] Several days later he described the impact of the continuing strike on operations in his mills: "We must be feeble for months to come as probably not less than 250 of our former scanty supply of help have left town."[28] These lines read in sharp contrast to the optimistic reports of agents following the turn-out in February, 1834.

Differences between the two turn-outs were not limited to the increased scale and duration of the later one. Women displayed a much higher degree of organization in 1836 than earlier. To coordinate strike activities, they formed a Factory Girls' Association. According to one historian, membership in the short-lived association reached 2500 at its height.[29] The larger organization among women was reflected in the tactics employed. Strikers, according to one mill agent, were able to halt production to a greater extent than numbers alone could explain; and, he complained, although some operatives were willing to work, "it has been impossible to give employment to many who remained." He attributed this difficulty to the strikers' tactics: "This was in many instances no doubt the result of calculation and contrivance. After the original turn-out they [the operatives] would assail a particular room—as for instance, all the warpers, or all the warp spinners, or all the speeder and stretcher girls, and this would close the mill as effectually as if all the girls in the mill had left."[30]

Now giving more thought than they had in 1834 to the specific tactics of the turn-out, the women made a deliberate effort to shut down the mills in order to win their demands. They attempted to persuade less committed operatives, concentrating on those in crucial departments within the mill. Such tactics anticipated those of skilled mulespinners and loomfixers who went out on strike in the 1880s and 1890s.

In their organization of a Factory Girl's Association and in their efforts to shut down the mills, the female operatives revealed that they had been changed by their industrial experience. Increasingly, they acted not simply as "daughters of freemen" offended by the impositions of the textile corporations, but also as industrial workers intent on improving their position within the mills.

There was a decline in protest among women in the Lowell mills following these early strike defeats. During the 1837-1843 depression, textile corporations twice reduced wages without evoking a collective response from operatives.[31] Because of the frequency of production cutbacks and lay-offs in these years, workers probably accepted the mill agents' contention that they had to reduce wages or close entirely. But with the return of prosperity and the expansion of production in the mid-1840s, there were renewed labor protests among women. Their actions paralleled those of working men and reflected fluctuations in the business cycle. Prosperity itself did not prompt turn-outs, but it evidently facilitated collective actions by women operatives.

In contrast to the protests of the previous decade, the struggles now were primarily political. Women did not turn-out in the 1840s; rather, they mounted annual petition campaigns calling on the State legislature to limit the hours of labor within the mills. These campaigns reached their height in 1845 and 1846, when 2,000 and 5,000 operatives respectively signed petitions. Unable to curb the wage cuts or the speed-up and stretch-out imposed by mill owners, operatives sought to mitigate the consequences of these changes by reducing the length of the working day. Having been defeated earlier in economic struggles, they now sought to achieve their new goal through political action. The Ten Hour Movement, seen in these terms, was a logical outgrowth of the unsuccessful turn-outs of the previous decade. Like the earlier struggles, the Ten Hour Movement was an assertion of the dignity of operatives and an attempt to maintain that dignity under the changing conditions of industrial capitalism.

The growth of relatively permanent labor organizations and institutions among women was a distinguishing feature of the Ten Hour Movement of the 1840s. The Lowell Female Labor Reform Association was organized in 1845 by women operatives. It became Lowell's leading labor organization over the next three years, organizing the city's female operatives and helping to set up branches in other mill towns. The Association was affiliated with the New

England Workingmen's Association and sent delegates to its meetings. It acted in concert with similar male groups and yet maintained its own autonomy. Women elected their own officers, held their own meetings, testified before a state legislative committee, and published a series of "Factory Tracts" which exposed conditions within the mills and argued for the ten-hour day. [32]

An important educational and organizing tool of the Lowell Female Labor Reform Association was the *Voice of Industry*, a labor weekly published in Lowell between 1845 and 1848 by the New England Workingmen's Association. Female operatives were involved in every aspect of its publication and used the *Voice* to further the Ten Hour Movement among women. Their Association owned the press on which the *Voice* was printed. Sarah Bagley, the Association president, was a member of the three-person publishing committee of the *Voice* and for a time served as editor. Other women were employed by the paper as travelling editors. They wrote articles about the Ten Hour Movement in other mill towns, in an effort to give ten-hour supporters a sense of the larger cause of which they were a part. Furthermore, they raised money for the *Voice* and increased its circulation by selling subscriptions to the paper in their travels about New England. Finally, women used the *Voice* to appeal directly to their fellow operatives. They edited a separate "Female Department," which published letters and articles by and about women in the mills.

Another aspect of the Ten Hour Movement which distinguished it from the earlier labor struggles in Lowell was that it involved both men and women. At the same time that women in Lowell formed the Female Labor Reform Association, a male mechanics' and laborers' association was also organized. Both groups worked to secure the passage of legislation setting ten hours as the length of the working day. Both groups circulated petitions to this end, and when the legislative committee came to Lowell to hear testimony, both men and women testified in favor of the ten-hour day.

The two groups, then, worked together, and each made an important contribution to the movement in Lowell. Women had the numbers, comprising as they did over 80 per cent of the mill workforce. Men, on the other hand, had the votes, and since the Ten Hour Movement was a political struggle, they played a crucial part. After the State committee reported unfavorably on the ten-hour petitions, the Female Labor Reform Association denounced the committee chairman, a State representative from Lowell, as a corporation "tool." Working for his defeat at the polls, they did so successfully and then passed the following post-election resolution: "*Resolved*, That the members of this Association tender their grateful acknowledgements to the voters of Lowell, for consigning William Schouler to the obscurity he so justly deserves . . . ."[33] Women took a more prominent part in the Ten Hour Movement in Lowell than did men, but they obviously remained dependent on male voters and legislators for the ultimate success of their movement.

Although co-ordinating their efforts with those of working men, women operatives organized independently within the Ten Hour Movement. For instance, in 1845 two important petitions were sent from Lowell to the State legislature. Almost 90 per cent of the signers of one petition were females, and more than two-thirds of the signers of the second were males.[34] Clearly the separation of men and women in their daily lives were reflected in the Ten Hour petitions of these years.

The way in which the Ten Hour Movement was carried from Lowell to other mill towns also illustrated the independent organizing of women within the larger movement. For example, at a spirited meeting in Manchester, New Hampshire, in December, 1845 — one presided over by Lowell operatives — more than a thousand workers, two-thirds of them women, passed resolutions calling for the ten-hour day. Later, those in attendance divided along male-female lines, each meeting separately to set up parallel organizations. Sixty women joined the Manchester Female Labor Reform Association that evening, and by the following summer it claimed over three hundred members. Female operatives met in company boarding houses to involve new women in the movement. In their first year of organizing, Manchester workers obtained more than 4,000 signatures on ten-hour petitions.[35] While men and women were both active in the movement, they worked through separate institutional structures from the outset.

The division of men and women within the Ten Hour Movement also reflected their separate daily lives in Lowell and in other mill towns. To repeat, they held different jobs in the mills and had little contact apart from the formal, structured overseer-operative relation. Outside the mill, we have noted, women tended to live in female boarding houses provided by the corporations and were isolated from men. Consequently, the experiences of women in these early mill towns were different from those of men, and in the course of their daily lives they came to form a close-knit community. It was logical that women's participation in the Ten Hour Movement mirrored this basic fact.

The women's Ten Hour Movement, like the earlier turn-outs, was based in part on the participants' sense of their own worth and dignity as daughters of freemen. At the same time, however, it indicated the growth of a new consciousness. It reflected a mounting feeling of community among women operatives and a realization that their interests and those of their employers were not identical, that they had to rely on themselves and not on corporate benevolence to achieve a reduction in the hours of labor. One woman, in a open letter to a state legislator, expressed this rejection of middle-class patenalism: "Bad as is the condition of so many women, it would be much worse if they had nothing but your boasted protection to rely upon; but they have at last learnt the lesson which a bitter experience teaches, that not to those who style themselves their 'natural protectors' are they to look for the needful help, but to the strong and resolute of their own sex."[36] Such an attitude, underlying the self-organizing of women in the ten-hour petition campaigns, was clearly the product of the industrial experience in Lowell.

Both the early turn-outs and the Ten Hour Movement were, as noted above, in large measure dependent upon the existence of a close-knit community of women operatives. Such a community was based on the work structure, the nature of worker housing, and workforce homogeneity. Women were drawn together by the initial job training of newcomers, by the informal work sharing among experienced hands, by living in company boarding houses, by sharing religious, educational, and social activities in their leisure hours. Working and living in a new and alien setting, they came to rely upon one another for friendship and support. Understandably, a community feeling developed among them.

This evolving community as well as the common cultural traditions which Yankee women carried into Lowell were major elements that governed their response to changing mill conditions. The pre-industrial tradition of independence and self-respect made them particularly sensitive to management labor policies. The sense of community enabled them to transform their individual opposition to wage cuts and to the increasing pace of work into public protest. In these labor struggles women operatives expressed a new consciousness of their rights both as workers and as women. Such a consciousness, like the community of women itself, was one product of Lowell's industrial revolution.

The experiences of Lowell women before 1850 present a fascinating picture of the contradictory impact of industrial capitalism. Repeated labor protests reveal that female operatives felt the demands of mill employment to be oppressive. At the same time, however, the mills provided women with work outside the home and family, thereby offering them an unprecedented independence. That they came to challenge employer paternalism was a direct consequence of the increasing opportunities offered them in these years. The Lowell mills both exploited and liberated women in ways unknown to the pre-industrial political economy.

NOTES

1. *Statistics of Lowell Manufacturers,* January 1, 1840. Broadside available in the Manuscripts Division, Baker Library, Harvard Business School.

2. *Lowell Offering* I, p. 169.

3. *Ibid.* IV, p. 145-148, 169-172, 237-240, 257-259.

4. *Ibid.* IV, p. 170.

5. These statistics are drawn from the author's dissertation, "Women at Work: The Transformation of Work and Community in Lowell, Mass., 1826-1860" (Columbia Univ., 1975).

6. Harriet Hanson Robinson, *Loom and Spindle, Or Life Among the Early Mill Girls* (New York, 1898), p. 91.

7. Dublin, "Women at Work," Chapter 4. Statistics are based on linkage between company payrolls and register books of the Hamilton Manufacturing Company. The register books were alphabetically organized volumes in which operatives were signed into and out of the mills. They gave the nativity and local residence of operatives as well as additional data. For a detailed discussion of the linkage methods used see the appendices of "Women at Work."

8. Dublin, "Women at Work," Chapter 5. Statistics based on analysis of federal manuscript census listings of Hamilton boarding houses in 1830 and 1840.

9. *Lowell Offering* I, p. 169.

10. *Ibid.* II, pp. 145-155; I, pp. 2-7, 74-78.

11. *Hamilton Manufacturing Company Records,* vol. 283, *passim.* This volume, along with all the other company records cited in this article, is located in the Manuscript Division of Baker Library, Harvard Business School.

12. *Lowell Offering* IV, pp. 145-148.

13. *Ibid.* I, p. 5; IV, p. 148.

14. Henry A. Miles, *Lowell As It Was And As It Is* (Lowell, 1845), pp. 144-145.

15. *Lowell Offering* IV, pp. 14-23. Like so many of the stories in the *Offering*, this one has a dramatic reversal at its conclusion. We learn at the end that Hannah's visitor is her brother, whose identity could not be revealed because he was afraid that the woman he was courting might learn that his sister was an operative.

16. These statistics are based on the linkage of payroll and register books of the Hamilton Company as were the data on residence presented above. See Chapter 4 and Appendices of Dublin, "Woman at Work."

17. These data are based on an analysis of the age distribution of females residing in Hamilton Company boarding houses as recorded in the federal manuscript censuses of 1830 and 1840. See Dublin, "Women at Work," Chapter 4.

18. Federal Manuscript Census of Lowell, 1830.

19. Boston *Evening Transcript*, February 18, 1834.

20. *Lawrence Manufacturing Company Records*, Correspondence, Vol. MAB-1, March 4 and March 9, 1834.

21. *Ibid.,* February 15, 1834.

22. *Ibid.,* February 14, 1834.

23. Boston *Evening Transcript,* February 18, 1834.

24. Robinson, *Loom and Spindle*. p. 72; *Lowell Offering*, February 1841, p. 45. For an interesting account of conflict between an operative and an overseer, see Robinson, p. 57.

25. The wage cuts, in still another way, might have been seen as threatening to "enslave." Such decreases would be enacted by reductions in the piece rates paid women. If women were to maintain their overall earnings, given the wage cuts, they would have to speed up their work or accept additional machinery, both of which would result in making them work harder for the same pay. Opposition to the speed-up and the stretch-out were strong during the Ten Hour Movement in the 1840s, and although I have found no direct evidence, such feeling may have played a part in the turn-outs of the 1830s as well.

26. Robinson, *Loom and Spindle,* p. 83; Boston *Evening Transcript*, October 4 and 6, 1836.

27. *Tremont-Suffolk Mills Records*, unbound letters, vol. FN-1, October 14, 1836.

28. *Ibid.,* October 17, 1836.

29. Hannah Josephson, *The Golden Threads: New England's Mill Girls and Magnates* (New York, 1949), p. 238.

30. *Tremont-Suffolk Mills Records*, Unbound Letters, Vol. FN-1, October 10, 1836.

31. *Hamilton Manufacturing Company Records,* Vol. 670, Correspondence of Treasurer, March 14, 1840; Lowell *Advertiser*, June 6, 1845, gives data on 1842 wage cuts.

32. Massachusetts *House Document* No. 50, 1845. Quoted in full in John R. Commons et al. *A Documentary History of American Industrial Society* (Cleveland, 1910), Vol. 3, pp. 133-151.

33. *Voice of Industry,* November 28, 1845.

34. Based on author's examination of Ten Hour Petitions at Massachusetts State Archives, 1845, 1587/8 and 1587/9.

35. *Voice of Industry,* December 5 and 19, 1845, July 24, 1846, October 30, 1846, December 4, 1846, January 8, 1847.

36. *Voice of Industry,* March 13, 1846.

HEARTS TO FEEL AND TONGUES TO SPEAK: NEW ENGLAND MILL WOMEN IN THE EARLY NINETEENTH CENTURY

3

by Lise Vogel

> Never while we have hearts to feel and tongues to speak will we silently and passively witness so much that is opposed to justice and benevolence . . . never, while we are conscious of powers undeveloped, affections hemmed in, energies paralyzed, privileges denied, usefulness limited, influence impaired, honors forfeited, and destiny thwarted. No, never shall we hold ourselves exempt from responsibility, never shall we cease our efforts in the warfare against evil.
>
> Mehitable Eastman, speech reported in *Voice of Industry*, September 4, 1846

The establishment of New England cotton mills in the early part of the nineteenth century signaled the beginning of large-scale capitalist industry in the United States. In the mills run on the "Waltham," or boardinghouse, system — as, for example, in Lowell, Massachusetts — women made up the majority of the work force. These women were thus important participants in the formation of the American working class. Their story has been told many times, and the basic outlines are clear. What is most remarkable is that the women left extensive written and, indeed, literary material. We have, then, a rare opportunity to gain direct access to their perceptions of their experience in the factory towns.

Most accounts of the boardinghouse mills present a pastiche of partial or incomplete images. Positive aspects tend to be stressed in the early years while the 1840s are portrayed as a time of oppressively long hours, frequent wage reductions, incessant speed-up, and generally deteriorating conditions in factories and boardinghouses. One traditional stereotype depicts the mill town as an industrial paradise; poor working conditions, labor unrest, and working-class organization are reduced to disturbing intrusions. Another version overemphasizes the oppressive character of mill life and the attempts of the operatives to organize against their exploitation by the corporations. A more integrated view would try to include both the progressive aspects of life in the mill towns and the very real problems that went along with factory work. Such a perspective acknowledges that it was possible to enjoy the independence and opportunities provided by mill life and at the same time resist the oppression. It corresponds best to the actual experiences of the women operatives as depicted in writings by and about them. Four documents from the period provide an overview of the wide range of individual responses and raise a variety of questions concerning the factory women's consciousness — their self-awareness, their perceptions of social experience, their values and beliefs, their motivations for what they did, their aspirations, and their plans.

This one-page letter, dated 1840, was sent by a young woman living in a boardinghouse in Lowell to a friend, Elisebeth, back home. She has just arrived, for the first time, in the mill town.

> Dear Friend according to my promise I take my pen in hand to Write to you to let you no that iam A Factory girl and iwish you Was one idont no But thaire Will Be aplace For you in a forthnigh or three Weeks and as Soon as thaire is iwill let you no and as soon as you Can board With me We Will have first rate fun getting up mornings in the Snow Storms Susan Sends love to you you dont no how iwant to See you and ivery often think of the good times We have had together give my respects to moses tell him not to forget the Spanggles you dont no how pleasent it is here We Can See all dracut From our Window give my love to the miss gruys.

Elisebeth [there] is a lot of hansome fellows here
my mother is a going to Send me a Bundle this
Week and you Besure to Write and put the letter in
it Write me all the logick you Can think of about
every thing often ithink iwould like to have you
here toohave a good laught for pitty Sake   dond
Show this letter to any body for the girls are talking So that idont no What iWrite
So I Subscribe myself your Freind. adieu[2]

The next letter, written in September 1846 by H.E. Back, is from
a young women who was not new to factory work. Back divided
her life between a rural New England home town and the mills of
Lowell, occasionally visiting friends and relatives elsewhere. In this
long and rather literary letter, she writes from Lowell to a friend
back in New Hampshire. Although the tone is sometimes
humorously ironic, she presents herself as generally content.

Dear Harriet
With a feeling which you can better imagine
than I can describe do I announce to you the horrible tidings that I am *once more a factory girl!* yes;
once more a factory girl, seated in the short attic of
a Lowell boarding house with a half dozen of girls
seated around me talking and reading and myself
in the midst, trying to write to you, with the
thoughts of so many different persons flying
around me that I can hardly tell which are my
own; but having the organ of individuality
very prominent perhaps I can select a few ideas
which are indisputably my own and if I succeed I
shall in all probability send them to you in the
shape of a *long* letter. I received your epistle with
pleasure and was very happy to hear you were enjoying yourself so well; perhaps you would like to
hear how I enjoyed my visit to Vermont. I enjoyed
it well I assure you, I was gone three weeks and
when I came away the vines, the bare fruit trees,

and the berry bushes broken and trampled upon, showed too plainly that I had not been idle, and the scratches upon my hands and arms told in plain hieroglyphics that the berries were not without their thorns; but like all happy hours those three weeks passed quickly away and I returned home to enjoy a season of rest as I supposed for my friends and my mother had almost persuaded me to stay at home during the fall and winter but when I reached home I found a letter which informed me that Mr Saunders was keeping my place for me and sent for me to come back as soon as I could and after reading it my Lowell fever returned and, come I would, and come I did, but now, "Ah! me, I rue the day" although I am not so homesick as I was a fortnight ago and just begin to feel more resigned to my fate. I have been here four weeks but have not had to work very hard for there are six girls of us and we have fine times doing nothing. I should like to see you in Lowell once more but cannot wish you to exchange your pleasant home in the country for a factory life in this "great city of spindles."

I hope you will learn to perform all necessary domestic duties while you have an opportunity for perhaps you may have an invitation (from a certain dark eyed gentleman whom you mentioned in your letter) to be mistress of his house his hand and heart and supposing such an event should take place then I will just take a ride some pleasant day and make you a visit when I will tell you more news than I can write — but I will not — anticipate.

I almost envy your happy sundays at home. A feeling of loneliness comes over me when I think of *my home*, now far away; you remember perhaps how I used to tell you I spent my hours in the mill — in imagining myself rich and that the rattle of machinery was the rumbling of my charriot wheels but now alas, that happy tact has fled from me and my mind no longer takes such airy and visionary flights for the wings of my imagination have folded themselves to rest; in vain do I try to soar in fancy and imagination above the dull reality around me but beyond the roof of the factory I cannot rise and in my disappointment I can express my feelings in no other way but in the sublime and beautiful language of the poet

"When I was a little boy and lived by myself
All the bread and cheese I had etc."

you probably know the rest and can sympathize with me, as you no doubt did when you fell in the Merimac river I wish you would tell me in your next letter who fished you out for it was a lucky chance for some one for you must certainly have been worth catching. You told me you had been gypsying a number of times but I hope you will not turn gipsy in imitating their wandering yet *happy* life; I say happy because any one must be happy while they are free to rove when and where they will among the green fields, by the running streams, in the debths of the forest, and in the pleasant valley with none to molest or make them afraid, so different from a city life. But enough of this now, for the very good reason that I have no room to write it; do not think I am unhappy because I cannot wish you here; far from it; but I think you are happier *there*.

I forgot to tell you that Sarah Burton has left our dress room in old No. 2 to be married. I believe she is going to reside in Maine. I have no more that you would be interested in, to write. When you receive this letter I shall expect that *long* one you promised me. So write it wont you.

Your friend H.E. Back

Excuse all the blunders for I have written it all upon a band box cover. I only put this last line in to help fill up. Do burn it up wont you. [3]

These two letters draw a picture of The Happy Mill Girl — homesick but excited by the opportunities to be independent, to live in an urban setting, and to explore new experiences. The dates — 1840 and 1846 — span a period of rapidly deteriorating conditions in the mills, increasing working-class resistance, and the formation of labor organizations. Should we consider the authors of these letters to be typical of the Yankee textile operatives, enthusiastically enjoying a rare and temporary freedom before assuming the burdens of marriage? Why do these women seem to ignore the worsening conditions of factory work? Are they perhaps the victims of some so-called false consciousness?

The third document is a newspaper account of an incident that took place in the small factory town of Newburyport, Massachusetts, in January 1846.

> The Police Court was the scene of quite an excitement on Tuesday, caused by a suit brought against an overseer of the Carding Room in the James Mill, for an assault on a girl who had recently been employed in that mill. The friends of the overseer and agent of the mill, say that for want of *proper order and discipline* in that room, the work of the mill was suffering and a few weeks ago a new overseer was placed in the room, with directions to enforce *proper order and discipline.* Several of the girls, who were not pleased with this movement, were discharged; on Monday, one of them calling at the mill, was directed by the overseer to leave the room, and not leaving immediately, he took her by the arm to lead her out. This is statement of the friends of *order* [and] *discipline,* but by the witnesses it appeared that she *did* move towards the door, and not keeping pace with his wishes, he laid hold of her to hurry her along, thereby tearing her clothes; but she being stout, and strong, like a woman of spirit, resisted, so that he was obliged to give it up "as a bad job"—hence this suit was brought.

> Considerable feeling was manifested by people
> living in the vicinity of the mill, so much so, that
> the overseer was pelted with snowballs in the street
> . . . . From what we have heard, we believe that
> had the girl belonged to our town, more serious
> acts would have followed.[4]

By her actions this woman seems to have been angrily expressing
a kind of generalized discontent. Was she simply an isolated militant? Was she hoping to precipitate a turn-out of the mill women?
Does she accurately represent the developing dissatisfaction of
thousands of female textile operatives as they confronted the
worsening situation in the mill towns?

Finally, there is an address presented before a meeting of the
Manchester Industrial Reform Association in September 1846. The
speaker was Mehitable Eastman, a leader of the Female Labor Reform Association in Manchester.

> The evils and abuses of the present system of
> factory labor, have accumulated too rapidly to be
> passed by in silence. I have been employed by a
> manufacturing company, for eight years, — have
> been subject to its increasing heartlessness and
> cruelty, and from bitter experience can affirm that
> a change cannot be effected too soon. And who
> can speak the truth upon this subject, if the opera-
> tive cannot, who has dragged out a miserable exis-
> tence within the prison walls of a factory? We have
> witnessed from time to time the cruelties practiced
> by brutal Overseers and selfish agents upon de-
> fenceless operatives, while they dare not speak in
> self-defence lest they should be deprived of the
> means of earning their daily bread.
>
> Much has been written and spoken in this coun-
> try in woman's behalf, yet a large class are destined
> to a servitude as degrading, as unceasing toil can
> make it. How long can this state of things exist?
> Many have already said "What can the opera-

tives do to change the conditions of industry and reduce the hours of daily labor?'' We answer, "what cannot the operative do?'' Our oppressors well know our strength. Ask the capitalist, if you please, what the operatives have done for him. Then we will ask what cannot we do for ourselves?

We feel determined to know what we can do, and to leave no means untried that will serve to bring about the great reform so devoutly to be wished. And if we do not realize its benefits at once, we will hope, and work on. Let us remember that the children of Israel did not arrive at the promised land, save through a journey of forty years in the wilderness. Operatives! let us not be discouraged! Our cause is a righteous one, and we have every reason to believe it must triumph.

And since in this reform movement our aid has been solicited, and our influence is so much needed, shall they be withheld from the side of truth and right? No! never while we have hearts to feel and tongues to speak will we silently and passively witness so much that is opposed to justice and benevolence: — never, while a wretched being is crying to us for succor, from the alleys and dens of our cities — from our crammed manufactories, and work-shops, from poverty stricken garrets and cellars, — never, with the awful facts of female degradation, under our present system of industry, staring us in the face; never, while we are conscious of powers undeveloped, affections hemmed in, energies paralyzed, privileges denied, usefulness limited, influence impaired, honors forfeited, and destiny thwarted. No, never shall we hold ourselves exempt from responsibility, never shall we cease our efforts in the warfare against evil.[5]

Mehitable Eastman's speech reflects a commitment to women's and to human liberation. She stresses the importance of united and disciplined action, shared responsibility within the organization, perseverance over a long period of time and solidarity with a larger movement of the exploited and oppressed. Is Eastman to be considered a utopian reformer whose visions of the struggle and of the future were shared by only a few? Or was hers the authentic voice of the masses of class-conscious mill women?

These documents, and the many others like them, suggest several conclusions. First, *all* of the voices are authentic. Each responds to at least one aspect of the self-awareness of one woman at a particular instant. Any given individual possesses a complex consciousness which cannot be simplified and which is always changing according to the moment, the mood, and the context.

Second, the documents are typical in that each represents a sizable sector of the women working in the mills. There is, in fact, no conflict between the view of mill work as an opportunity for independence as well as self-improvement and the recognition that that same work is oppressive, accompanied by the determination to resist — individually or collectively. The issue concerns which of these responses was dominant in the experience of a given mill woman, what she did about it, and how many others felt and did likewise. In other words, the consciousness of individuals does not conform in any simple way to the usual categories of political analysis.[6] At no time were the women operatives a monolithic mass sharing a single consciousness. On the one hand, factory work was the principal way these women could be independent and as such was highly valued by many, despite any difficulties that they might encounter. On the other hand, life as an operative was not an idyllic boarding-school existence which somehow became disagreeable to numbers of mill women in the 1840s.

It is clear that, from the start, there were discontent and resistance in the mills, although the records are fragmentary, certain kinds of events are completely undocumented, and it is often impossible to find our just what happened and what the results were. For example, the Hamilton Company of Lowell had been incorporated in 1825, and by 1826-1827 women were already being discharged for a variety of reasons, including "misconduct," "captiousness," "disobedience to orders," "impudence to overseer," "[dissatisfaction] with wages," and something called "mutiny."

One woman "had written after her name emphatically, 'regularly discharged *forever*.' "[7] In December 1828, less than two years after the mill in Dover, New Hampshire, was incorporated, three or four hundred women turned out in what was the first recorded strike of female textile operatives; they were protesting the imposition of "obnoxious regulations" in the factory.[8] Sporadic strikes, as well as other expressions of discontent, continued through the thirties and intensified in the forties. What happened, of course, is that as the conditions of factory life deteriorated, more and more women experienced it as oppressive; among those who stayed in the mills, an increasing number began to fight back. Thus it was that one operative could make light of "the rattle of machinery" and the "dull reality" of the factory while another was signing her letters with, "Yours until death in the cause of Labor Reform." [9]

Third, this approach to the consciousness of the mill women suggests a more adequate way to understand and evaluate their experience of oppression. The women textile operatives were facing the problem that first-generation wage workers always have to face: how best to respond to the new patterns of work, time, and leisure that they encountered in the industrial setting as opposed to the farm environment from which they had come.[10] At the same time, the situation of the female operatives was very specific. The organization of industry on a capitalist basis was new and special to conditions in the United States. The operatives were native-born Americans from rural New England backgrounds. And they were women. These facts shaped the particular quality of their experience.

The New England textile manufacturers had devised the boardinghouse system as an experiment. They wanted to obtain an adequate supply of labor and, at the same time to prevent the formation of the kind of working class they saw when they visited England. This was not simply a question of some American ideological tradition or of good intentions on the part of the New World capitalists. The American observers correctly perceived that the English proletariat was physically exhausted, culturally demoralized, politically desperate, and dangerously rebellious. The new boardinghouse system was, in large part, an attempt both to ensure a cheap and productive labor force and to circumvent the development of a permanent factory population which might combine into labor organizations or even rise up against the owners.[11] In particular, the system of company-supervised boardinghouses suggested that parental discipline would simply be transferred to factory life. The manufacturers hoped that the women would be cooperative and uncomplaining workers — just as, presumably, they were obedient daughters.

To the extent that the new plan did not work, it was largely because the textile entrepreneurs did not sufficiently allow for the complexity of the women's responses once they arrived in the factory towns and began to work in the mills. Many characteristics made the young Yankee farmwomen potentially hardworking, productive, and docile factory workers, as the New England manufacturers had very astutely estimated. Each such characteristic had, however, another side which, in the right circumstances, could result in discontent, anger, and resistance. The energy and alertness that made the operatives so different from their British counterparts could also make them ready and very able to fight back. Just as the owners hoped to avoid the rebelliousness and low productivity of British workers, so the mill women had no intention of enduring the oppression experienced by their sister operatives across the Atlantic. When confronted with exploitative conditions, the strong and independent operatives might recall their traditions as native-born Americans and turn quickly to the ideology of righteous republicanism. Moreover, as women, the operatives were subject to a variety of well-known ideological assumptions and imperatives; these they sometimes accepted and sometimes turned around, according to the goal and the context.

Work as a textile mill operative was, at the time, one of a number of possible female occupations, paid and unpaid. For most women, the stay in the factory town was temporary. The women expected to continue working after leaving the mills, most probably in an unpaid household role. The opportunity to be financially and socially independent was therefore rare and very precious — even if, in the long run, the pay was too low for permanent independence. Any encroachment on that sense of autonomy was liable to spark outrage and determined opposition. For example, when editor Harriet Farley reported in the *Lowell Offering* that there was "a special

and earnest call here for about five thousand good-looking, in-
dustrious, and sweet-tempered young women" to go out to Iowa as
wives for 5,000 bachelors, the response among the operatives was
quite heated:

> Some of our operatives did not like our assertion,
> on the cover of the last number, that they would go
> to Iowa, &c. Many of them do not believe in matri-
> mony, and the others think they will wait till
> the *"Iowas"* come for them. We shall henceforth
> consider it one of the disputed questions, with
> which the Offering hath nothing to do.[12]

Harriot F. Curtis, co-editor, with Farley, of the *Offering*, raised
the issue of independence in a spirited argument for both equal pay
and equal jobs:

> Woman must be content *to live* and *suffer* upon a
> cup of water and crust of bread; and not only suf-
> fer herself, but see the wants of those she loves and
> cannot relieve, because, forsooth! independence of
> means, unless *married*, or inherited, is not con-
> sonant with "female delicacy!" It matters not
> what her tact, talents, or energy may be. She may
> teach urchins their A B Cs for one-third that a man
> would receive for the same labor; she may make a
> coat or vest for one-half that the male "shears"
> asks for the same work; or she may make a shirt
> for sixpence to pay her rent, and eat and drink her
> tears for sustenance; but if she dares to exercise her
> knowledge or talents wherein she *must* receive an
> *equal* remuneration with man, "indelicacy,"
> "boldness," "presumption," and "has unsexed
> herself," will be the universal *viva voce*.
>   If a man has health, energy, integrity, prudence
> and sense, it is his prerogative to gain property,
> and secure his own independence. A woman may
> possess all of these in a superior degree, and she is

graciously permitted to be dependent — if she has
anyone to depend upon; or, if she has not, it is
peculiarly her prerogative to want, suffer and toil
for a pittance which will just keep soul and body
together while her health continues good. And if
she loses that, she may seek a support at the "public crib," the *alms-house*. This may be a superior
delicacy, but it is also very near the *acme* of injustice. Time is time, labor is labor, and *to live* is
an equal necessity with woman as with man; and
we never could understand why a man's time and
services were, in fact, more valuable than
woman's, when the labor was equally as well performed by one as the other. Nor why every employment which was the more lucrative, must also
be masculine.[13]

In the long run, the lack of an adequate wage and the deteriorating conditons of factory work were the most serious threats to the
mill women's independence. Once decided on a course of resistance, the women could be extremely militant. The fact that their
time in the mills was essentially temporary meant that they might
decide they had little to lose. The War of Independence often in-
spired them to experience their oppression in revolutionary terms,
as in this resolution of 1836: "As our fathers resisted unto blood
the lordly avarice of the British ministry, so we, their daughters,
never will wear the yoke which has been prepared for us."[14] The
rhetoric of republicanism was frequently tied to the concrete details
of a mill woman's daily experience. A New Hampshire operative
calling herself "Octavia" put it this way in 1843:

What are we coming to? I can hardly clear my way,
having saved from four week steady work, but
three hundred and ninety-one cents! And yet the
time I give to the corporation, amounts to about
fourteen or fifteen hours. We are obliged to rise at
six, and it is about eight before we get our tea,
making fourteen hours. What a glorious privilege

we enjoy in this boasted republican land, don't
we? Here am I, a healthy New England Girl, quite
well-behaved, bestowing just half of all my hours
including Sundays, upon a company, for less than
two cents an hour, and out of the other half of my
time, I am obliged to *wash, mend, read, reflect, go
to church*!!&c. I repeat it, what are we coming to?
What is to make the manufacturing interest any
better? [15]

The labor reform associations of the 1840s tried to provide organizational form to such outbursts of discontent and resistance.
They fought to reduce the length of the working day and to limit
speed-up; and they opposed the blacklist and the oppressive behavior of overseers. Rallies, petitions, and strikes were the principal
tactics. The labor associations also recognized the need to establish
and maintain a network of communications among the various
factory towns. They issued organizing pamphlets, sent traveling representatives out, and, above all, supported the labor newspapers.
For a brief period there was a vision of an association of textile mill
operatives that would unite workers from Maine to western Pennsylvania. Consonant with this spirit, Huldah J. Stone, the secretary
of the Lowell Female Labor Reform Association, expressed her
heartfelt enthusiasm in a letter to the newly formed Female Labor
Reform Association of Manchester, New Hampshire, in December
1845:

Sisters in the cause of human improvement and
human rights — to your sympathies — to your
sense of duty and justice, would we at this time appeal. You have now manifested a good degree of
zeal and interest in the work of "Labor Reform,"
and we hope and trust that you will continue to in-
vestigate the subject and take such efficient
measures as shall assist in accomplishing the great
object of this our noble and philanthropic enterprise, viz: — the elevation and promotion of the
real producers of our country to that station and

standing in society which they were by a benificent
God designed to occupy! Too long have the virtu-
ous poor been looked down upon as a lower race
of beings, while vice and crime of the darkest hue,
rolled in luxury and splendor through our streets
— too long have our females been treated like as
many senseless automotons in the kitchens of the
purse-proud aristocrats of our Republic — and as
a *part* of the machinery in our manufacturing
towns and districts throughout the Union. It is
now for the working men and working women of
these United States to say whether this state of
society which debases the masses to a level with the
serfs of the old countries shall continue; or
whether a new and brighter era shall dawn on the
republican shores, giving to all equal rights and
true liberty. To effect this glorious work of reform
we believe a complete *union* among the worthy
toilers and spinners of our own nation so as to
have a concert of action, is all that is requisite. By
organizing associations and keeping up a
correspondance throughout the country, and
arousing the public mind to a just sense of the
claims of humanity, we hope to roll on the great
tide of reformation until from every fertile vale
and towering hill the response shall be echoed and
re-echoed: — *Freedom* — freedom for *all*!

Operatives of Manchester, you have begun well,
may God grant that you persevere united, faithful-
ly, triumphantly! You have now an Association
organized and consisting of a goodly number already, and hundreds more are ready to join your
ranks, I doubt not, if you prove active and vigi-
lant, — true to yourselves and faithful to the noble
enterprise in which you are now engaged. We shall
be extremely happy to correspond with you and
meet with you in your meetings as often as possible. Let us seek to encourage and strengthen each
other in every good word and work.

If discouragements arise as they surely will, will you yield to despair and falter? God forbid! Rather, take the simple motto of your sister Association of Lowell, and let its spirit fire your every heart with NEW ZEAL and unwavering hope — *"We'll try again!"* Let us aim in all that we do, to increase the intelligence and knowledge of all — to raise higher the standard of moral and intellectual worth among us — then shall we become stronger and stronger, throwing around us that protecting power which is, and ever will be invincible, the power of knowledge!

Let your regular meetings be fully attended. Do not leave all the duties resting on the association, to be performed by a few who are spirited and zealous enough to be at their posts whether tempests frown or sunshine gilds the horizon. No, we beseech you to "act well your parts," for on this your success depends.

We have now a paper owned and edited in and by our associations, devoted entirely to the Laborer's cause — the cause of humanity and human rights, which it is only necessary to say is emphatically the workmen and women's paper, in order to have every one who feels the least interest in the cause, subscribe for and support. Just forward one dollar to W.F. Young, Editor, Lowell, Mass., and you will receive it one year free of postage. Communications, also, for the paper from any who shall feel disposed to write will be thankfully received. Shall we not hear from Manchester, often, of your success and perseverance. Let *Excelsior* be the motto, which shall nerve us on to the conquest.

In a word, let us be active, firm and united in every good work, until righteousness shall be established throughout the length and breadth of Columbia's land.

Yours until death in the cause of Labor Reform.[16]

Despite all their energy and efforts, the activists in the labor reform movements could not maintain their organizations in opposition to the corporations. A letter to the editor of the *Voice of Industry*, on the possibility of marriage, summed up the situation as it
appeared to an individual participant:

> At one time I would almost resolve to live single
> through life, that I might devote myself more ex-
> clusively to the cause of humanity; because there
> are so few willing to labor for the good of the
> whole . . . .
> I must tell you I am a Factory Girl, tired enough
> of this slave like life, seeing no prospect of a reduc-
> tion of the hours of labor. My education is better
> than that of factory girls in general, — am very
> fond of books, and must tell you I am turned out
> of the mill, for reading in the mill, and my name
> has gone to all the Black Lists kept at the counting
> rooms. I have no home, and know not what to
> do.[17]

Against such tactics, the new labor organizations had no resources.
A woman operative had few alternatives, and marriage was chief
among them. The companies were not just powerful; they took
shrewd advantage of the contradictions inherent in the experience
of their workers as women. Here, as on other questions, the labor
reform movements of the 1840s were unable to develop an adequate strategy, and even the stronger movements of subsequent
years did little more in this area.[18] Indeed, similar problems still
face those who are today seeking to mobilize women workers in
some modern version of Huldah Stone's "complete *union* among
the worthy toilers and spinners of our own nation so as to have a
concert of action" to gain "*Freedom* — freedom for *all*!"

NOTES

1. See, for example, Edith Abbott, *Women in Industry* (New York, 1910), especially chs. 6, 7, and 12; Helen L. Sumner, *History of Women in Industry in the United*

States in *Woman and Child Wage-Earners in the United States* (Washington, D.C., 1910), vol. 9, ch. 2; Norman Ware, *The Industrial Worker, 1840-1860* (Boston, 1924), chs. 8-10; Caroline Ware, *Early New England Cotton Manufacture* (New York, 1931), especially chs. 8-10; Vera Shlakman, *Economic History of a Factory Town, Smith College Studies in History* 20, nos. 1-4 (Northhampton, 1935); Philip S. Foner, *History of the Labor Movement in the United States* (New York, 1947), vol. 1, ch. 11; Hannah Josephson, *The Golden Threads: New England Mill-Girls and Magnates* (New York, 1949); Ray Ginger, "Labor in a Massachusetts Cotton Mill, 1853-1860," *Business History Review* 28 (1954): 67-91; and H.M. Gitelman, "The Waltham System and the Coming of the Irish," *Labor History* 8 (1967): 227-253. More recent works include: Thomas Bender, *Toward an Urban Vision: Ideas and Institutions in Nineteenth-Century America* (Lexington, 1975), especially chs. 2-4; Thomas Dublin, "Women, Work, and Protest in the Early Lowell Mills: 'The Oppressing Hand of Avarice Would Enslave Us,' " *Labor History* 16 (1975): 99-116, and reprinted in this volume; and "Women, Work, and the Family: Female Operatives in the Lowell Mills, 1830-1860," *Feminist Studies* 3 (1975): 30-39; and Lise Vogel, "Their Own Work: Two Documents from the Nineteenth-Century Labor Movement," *Signs 1* (1976): 787-802; John Kasson, *Civilizing the Machine: Technology and Republican Values in America, 1776-1900* (New York, 1976), pp. 53-106. Forthcoming are: Vogel, "Humorous Incidents and Sound Common Sense': More on the New England Mill Women," in *Labor History*; " 'What Factory Girls Had Power to Do': Writings by and about New England Mill Women in the 1840s" in *Signs*; and *Women of Spirit, Women of Action: Mill Workers of Nineteenth-Century New England* (Somersworth: The New Hampshire Publishing Company). This essay is based on a paper, "Woman of Spirit: Content, Discontent, and Resistance among New England Operatives," presented at the Second Berkshire Conference on the History of Women, Cambridge, Massachusetts, October 1974. A grant from the Louis M. Rabinowitz Foundation in 1973 partially supported the author's work on the New England mill women.

2. Unsigned letter to Elisebeth A. Sachman, Lowell, 1840 (Lowell Historical Society, Lowell, Massachusetts).

3. Letter from H.E. Back to Harriet Hanson, September 7, 1846 (Schlesinger Library, Radcliffe College, Cambridge, Massachusetts).

4. *Newburyport Advertiser*, January 23, 1846; reprinted in the *Voice of Industry*, February 6, 1846.

5. *Voice of Industry*, September 4, 1846.

6. For example, a typical approach to working-class activity describes it as moving sequentially from submission through individual resistance and primitive rebellion to collective and then class action. This progresion has a particular reality at the level of general political analysis, but each historical situation has a specificity that must also be analyzed carefully. To what extent is the general sequence revealed in the given situation? What are the nature and source of any peculiarities? How do they develop and express themselves? Most important, from the perspective of the present essay, is the relationship between these overall trends in the situation and the responses of the individuals involved in it.

7. Hamilton Company Papers, quoted by Caroline Ware, *Early New England Cotton Manufacture*, pp. 266-267.

8. For an account of the strike, see John B. Andews and W.D.P. Bliss, *History of Women in Trade Unions* in *Woman and Child Wage-Earners in the United States* (Washington, D.C., 1911), vol. 10, pp. 23-25.

9. Back letter, cited above in text and note 3; letter from Stone, cited below in text and note 16.

10. See E.P. Thompson, "Time, Work-Discipline, and Industrial Capitalism," *Past and Present* 38 (1967): 56-97; Keith Thomas, "Work and Leisure in Pre-Industrial Society," *Past and Present* 29 (1964): 50-62; and Sidney Pollard, "Factory Discipline in the Industrial Revolution," *Economic History Review* 16 (1963): 254-271. Herbert Gutman surveys the American material in "Work, Culture, and Society in Industrializing America, 1815-1919," *American Historical Review* 78 (1973): 531-588. Joan Scott and Louise Tilly attempt to generalize the experience of women in Europe in these terms in "Women's Work and the Family in Nineteenth-Century Europe," *Comparative Studies in Society and History* 17 (1975): 2-35. For some critical comments on this approach, see Elizabeth Fox Genovese, "The Many Faces of Moral Economy: A Contribution to a Debate," *Past and Present* 58 (1973): 161-168, and Lise Vogel, "Rummaging through the Primitive Past: A Note on Family, Industrialization, and Capitalism," The Newberry Papers in Family and Community History (Chicago: The Newberry Library, 1976).

11. Good discussions of the origins and development of the boardinghouse system are included in Bender, *Toward an Urban Vision* and Kasson, *Civilizing the Machine*. Robert F. Dalzell, Jr., presents a more rosy view of the motivations of the Boston associates in "The Rise of the Waltham-Lowell System and Some Thoughts on the Political Economy of Modernization in Ante-Bellum Massachusetts," *Perspectives in American History* 9 (1975): 229-268.

12. *Lowell Offering*, new ser., vol. 3, nos. 6 and 7 (March and April 1843), inside back covers.

13. *Lowell Offering*, new ser., vol. 5, no. 1 (January 1845), inside front cover.

14. *National Laborer*, October 29, 1836; cited in Andrews and Bliss, *History of Women in Trade Unions*, p. 30.

15. *The Factory Girl* (Exeter, N.H.), March 1, 1843.

16. *Voice of Industry*, December 26, 1845.

17. *Voice of Industry*, December 11, 1846.

18. For the labor reform movement's attempts in the direction of a strategy, see the discussion in Vogel, "Their Own Work." For some examples from later periods, see James Kenneally, "Women and Trade Unions, 1870-1920: The Quandary of the Reformer," *Labor History* 14 (1973): 42-55; Alice Kessler-Harris, " 'Where Are the Organized Women Workers?' " *Feminist Studies* 3 (1975): 92-110, and Nancy Schrom Dye, "Feminism or Unionism? The New York Women's Trade Union League and the Labor Movement," *Feminist Studies* 3 (1975): 111-124.

"SHE EARNS AS A CHILD; SHE PAYS AS A MAN": WOMEN WORKERS IN A MID-NINETEENTH-CENTURY NEW YORK CITY COMMUNITY

4

by Carol Groneman

Little is known about the mid-nineteenth-century urban immigrant poor. The image of a disorganized and brutalized lower class portrayed by contemporary middle- and upper-middle-class observers, essentially a reflection of their own ethnic, class, and religious prejudices, colors present-day accounts of the period. Many immigration, labor, and urban historians continue to posit this distorted picture either because they accept the stereotype or because sources leading to any other view have been ignored.[1] Based on an invaluable and hitherto neglected source, the 1855 New York State census manuscript schedules, this paper begins to reexamine this unknown world by focusing on a brief moment in time and a single subgroup within this large heterogeneous population: Irish immigrants living in New York City's Sixth Ward in the 1850s.[2]

Several questions must be asked. Since contemporary evidence indicates that a single income was often insufficient to support a working-class family in the mid-nineteenth century, how did these immigrants cope with the daily struggle for survival? Traditional historical sources which provide information only on individual incomes cannot adequately answer this question and in fact obscure the real patterns of work in a poor immigrant community. Evidence from the census manuscripts indicates that in almost one-half of Irish households in the Sixth Ward, at least two members of each household, most often husband and working wife, contributed to the family income. Because women assumed the major burden of supplementing family income, it is important to establish not only how many women worked but what effect Irish women's economic function had on traditional family patterns and relationships. Did the profound changes these preindustrial peasants faced in indus-

SOURCE: Richard Ehrlich (ed.), *Immigrants in Industrial Society.* Charlottesville: University of Virginia Press, 1977.

trializing America cause, as many American social historians have concluded, the breakdown, disruption, and disorganization of immigrant families, values, and culture? Finally, was the work pattern we find in the Sixth Ward unique to the Irish or did it cut across ethnic lines to include other working-class groups? An examination of the relationships between family and work roles can shed some light on this larger issue of immigrant adaptation to new work processes and life styles in America's urban centers.

The neighborhood chosen for study was New York City's Sixth Ward, a traditional Irish working-class area. Bounded by fashionable Broadway and the colorful Bowery, the Sixth Ward was itself home to the notorious Five Points slum. While predominantly Irish, a heterogeneous mixture of nationalities, races, and religions mingled on the streets of the ward. Native-born whites and blacks and earlier Irish immigrants shared the neighborhood by the late 1840s and 1850s with recently arrived Irish famine victims, as well as Germans, Dutch, Italians, and Polish and Russian Jews. Over 25,000 people crowded into this small ward. Availability of work in the factories, foundries, shops, docks, hotels, publishing industry, and building, transportation, and clothing trades attracted immigrants to this and other lower Manhattan wards. For working-class families faced with the problem of irregular and seasonal male employment, areas like the Sixth Ward offered a solution to this dilemma by providing work for wives and children.

We have a general, though inadequate, picture of mid-nineteenth-century wages, prices, and rents in New York City's immigrant neighborhoods from contemporary newspapers, government reports, and census statistics.[3] For example, John Mitchell, the editor of the *New York Citizen*, estimated in 1854 that rent took one-half of a poor man's income and that food and fuel prices had risen over 30 percent that year.[4] Both the *New York Times* and the *New York Tribune* suggested that a moderate income for a family of four required approximately eleven dollars per week in the early 1850s.[5] But many men and women earned far less: factory operatives and common laborers averaged less than five dollars per week and the lowest-paid seamstresses earned only about two dollars per week. Although some unionized workers increased their wages by periodic strikes in the early fifties, even these wages hardly kept pace with the rising cost of living. Women's wages, consistently lower than those of their male counterparts, rose little during the 1840s and 1850s and, in some trades, actually declined. The depressions of the 1854-1855 and 1857, combined with seasonal and irregular employment throughout the period generally, left the individual worker's income far below the minimum standard suggested by the *Times* and the *Tribune*.[6]

Sixth-Ward Irish families responded to these economic conditions by supplementing the income of the head of the household through the earnings of other family members, usually the wife. But more than economic need affected both a woman's decision to work and the type of work she performed. Age, family relationships, and availability of work influenced Sixth-Ward Irish women in a variety of ways which require careful analysis. We can begin by examining the numbers of working women in relation to their ages and the kinds of work they performed.

No less than 44 percent of the 4,200 Sixth-Ward Irish women aged 15-49 were gainfully employed. As might be expected, the percentage of employed women decreased with age, but the decrease was not marked since 35 percent of all women over forty years of age still worked. The most common employment for young Irish women in the area was domestic and personal service, including hotel maids, waitresses, and cooks as well as personal servants, housekeepers, and laundresses. Forty-five percent of women under thirty years of age were employed in these occupations (Table I). Servants in private households worked as many as fifteen hours per day, oftentimes seven days per week, in dark unventilated kitchens. They occupied overcrowded sleeping quarters and received between four and eight dollars per month in addition to room and board. Although living conditions might be overcrowded and food often consisted of the leftovers from the family table, servants' physical needs were probably better filled than those of other working women who had to pay rent and buy food out of their meager salaries. Servants complained most about the long hours, lack of free time, and the disdainful and haughty attitude of employers.[7]

Besides domestic service in individual households, numerous women worked as chambermaids, waitresses, cooks, and laundresses for the many hotels of the Sixth Ward. Twenty-five Irish

TABLE 1

Occupations of Irish Women in the Sixth Ward by Age, 1855*

	15-19	20-29	30-39	40-49	50 AND OVER
Sewing Trades	40.5%	29.3%	16.9%	16.4%	14.1%
Domestic Service	50.6	39.9	26.4	27.3	28.5
Taking Boarders	.9	25.5	49.9	47.9	47.5
Petty Enterprises	.3	.5	1.8	3.1	3.5
Store Keepers	0	.8	2.8	3.1	4.4
Other Manuf. and ind.†	7.5	3.0	.9	1.0	1.9
Professionals	0	1.0	.9	1.0	0
	99.8%	100.0%	99.6%	99.8%	99.9%
Total Number	333	828	435	242	160

*Compiled from the manuscript schedules of the 1855 New York State Census.

†Upholsterers, type polishers and cutters, printers, book binders, and folders, confectioners, makers of ink, pianos, cigars, cards, and boxes.

women, for example, were employed at the Carlton House on Broadway and thirteen at Pat Garrick's Sixth-Ward Hotel. In an investigation conducted in 1857, a New York State committee found that four-fifths of the servants, even in first-class hotels, slept in overcrowded garrets, receiving compensation comparable to that of domestic workers in private households. Unlike private domestics, however, hotel workers had more time to escape the drudgery of housework because they were not expected to be available beyond required working hours.[8]

The next largest occupation for young Irish women, the sewing trades — including dressmaking, tailoring, cap and vest production, millinery, and artificial-flower manufacture — accounted for 35 percent of the jobs held by young working women. Many Sixth-Ward needle trades' workers shared the conditions described by the 1853 *New York Tribune's* investigation, "Needle Women of New York." Shops located in the lower wards gave out piece work to seamstresses who were paid eight cents, and often as low as four cents, per shirt. Since finishing three shirts was a hard day's work, the *Tribune* estimated that some needlewomen could conceivably have earned fifty cents for an entire week's labor: this figure included the time spent in obtaining and returning the goods, as well as in traveling to secure their pay. Though thousands of milliners, dressmakers, and other needle trades' workers earned betwen $3.50 and $6.00 per week, according to the *Tribune*, there were hundreds of tailoresses and seamstresses who, due to irregular and seasonal employment, earned less than two dollars per week. "A woman," the *Tribune* commented, "may be defined to be a creature that receives half price for all she does, and pays full price for all she needs . . . . She earns as a child; she pays as a man."[9]

Young Irish women also labored in other areas of manufacture, such as type cutting, printing, book binding, and making ink, cigars, cards, and boxes. Women in these industries were concentrated at the lowest levels of skill and received about one-half to one-third the wages of men doing comparable work. Apprenticeships for women in most industrial occupations lasted from a few days to a few months, and most of the labor required, above all, manual dexterity and stamina. Conditions varied greatly from the light and airy workshop of the Bible House and Tract Society Publishing Company to the dangerous, chemical-filled factories of the ink makers. Wages were usually paid by the piece and a contemporary study, Virginia Penny's *Employments of Women*, suggests an average wage of $3.50 to $6.50 per week.[10]

Peddling was not an important source of employment for young women, but this activity became increasingly common in each succeeding age category. The older woman who sold fruits, vegetables, or candies was a familiar and sometimes colorful figure in the immigrant neighborhoods. For example, when the City Hall Park "apple woman" was threatened in July 1845 by a policeman and told to move on, "being a full-blooded Sixth Warder, and consequently somewhat accustomed to little scenes of tumult," she pummeled him unmercifully, much to the amusement of the passing crowd.[11] Throughout the city about 1,300 huckster women, mostly older Irish women, sold fruits and vegetables on the fringes of the New York markets. Around City Hall Park, Printing House Square, and near the Bowery, women and some young girls peddled flowers, newspapers, candy, and fruit to the hundreds of passers-by.[12]

Store keeping was also the province of a relatively few older women: Mary Cavanagh ran a dry-goods store on Pearl Street; in an adjacent shop, Ann Welsh sold fancy goods; the gold balls of the pawnbroker hung outside Bridget Costello's shop on the Bowery; and Catherine Sweeney sold candy in a rear shop on Baxter Street. A few women were involved in large-scale enterprises. For example, Ann Furgus, a thirty-five-year-old widow, ran a boardinghouse on Center Street, housing over fifty boarders and employing a staff of six domestics. Most women classified here as store keepers, however, managed small grocery and liquor stores. Up by 4:00 A.M. to buy the fruits and vegetables brought by the farmers to market, one proprietress in the late 1850s described how she opened her store at 5:00 A.M. and did not close until 10:00 at night. Even with those long hours, she could not make more than three or four dollars per week after deducting the weekly rent of six or seven dollars and the cost of fuel and candles.[13]

Age was an important factor in determining the kinds of work at which Sixth-Ward Irish women were employed, but in order to understand the larger issue of the effects of women's work on the family, we must discuss working women in relation to their position within the household. How did a woman's role within the family, as wife, daughter, or widowed head of the household, affect both her decision to work and the type of work she would perform? The great majority of women working outside the home in domestic service, factories, and some sewing trades were young single women whose role within the household as daughter, relative, or boarder did not depend on remaining at home throughout the work day. This was not the case with married women. When forced by economic necessity to provide supplementary income for their families, they did so by working within their homes, thereby minimizing the strains on family life.

The major occupation of these married women was one which has been ignored by historians relying exclusively on the compiled census statistics: namely, taking in boarders (Table 2). While "boardinghouse keeper" was an occupational classification in the

TABLE 2

Total Irish Working Wives by Age, Sixth Ward, 1855*

20-29	30-39	40-49	50 and over
28.4%	30.8%	25.5%	25.4%
(No.) 258	227	95	43
Working Wives Other Than Those Who Took Boarders			
6.3%	3.0%	2.4%	3.6%

*Compiled from the manuscript schedules of the 1855 New York State Census.

census, it encompassed only a small proportion of the many households renting space to one or more boarders. Women taking a few boarders into their homes were simply not counted by census takers as gainfully employed although they received an average $1.25 per week for each boarder.[14] Since this work was carried on in the home, it was looked upon as an extension of women's traditional work role even though it was a money-making occupation. The arbitrary application of the definition of gainful employment by census takers, perhaps the unwillingness of women to list an occupation, and the dependence on the compiled statistics by later historians have resulted in the exclusion of fully 25 per cent of the

Sixth-Ward married women from the statistics of the gainfully employed.

It is interesting to speculate on the amount of possible income these women sacrificed by working in the home. The Sixth-Ward factories, for example, paid an average of $5.50 per week to women workers.[15] Since most industrial trades were easily learned with a few weeks' apprenticeship, skill probably had little influence on the limited number of married women working outside the home. The lower wards also offered other employment opportunities outside the home, and many single women worked in the local hotels, department stores, and laundries. Therefore, it is reasonable to hypothesize that Sixth-Ward married women's work in the home reflected more than limited opportunities, namely, an element of conscious choice. Women who chose this particular occupation very likely did so because it allowed them to continue to function in their roles as housewife and mother while also contributing to the family's support.

This is not an insignificant suggestion. A considerable body of historical literature insists that immigration and the alienation of the large city led to disruption and breakdown of the family. The evidence presented here concerning married women's work role within the home suggests the need to reevaluate the alleged disorganization of America's immigrant communities. This evidence, coming from a poor working-class area like the Sixth Ward, is all the more revealing since its residents, many of whom had fled the Irish famine, would have been particularly vulnerable to these supposed processes of family disintegration. Contrary to the hypothesis, however, the family-centered Irish peasant women adapted to the economic pressures of urban life in such a way as to preserve their traditional role in the family. They did this by combining their economic activity with the functions of child rearing and housekeeping. The large number of the Sixth Ward married women who took in boarders suggests that this was a central means of coping with the multiple demands placed upon immigrant women in America. Even when forced by necessity to work, they did so in ways which would reinforce, rather than disrupt, their traditional familial values.[16]

This point can be demonstrated further by a comparison of the structure of Sixth-Ward households headed by Irish, German, and white native-born Americans. We find that the great majority of immigrant households were kin-related while a relatively insignificant proportion was composed of nonrelated adults or adults living alone.[17] Table 3 compares the type of household of Irish, German, and native-born white inhabitants of the Sixth Ward. The native-born significantly had the lowest percentage of kin-related households. If the immigration process had been as disorganizing and disintegrating as is often suggested, it is highly unlikely that the

TABLE 3
Type of Household, Sixth Ward, 1855*

	Irish	German	Native-Born
Kin-Related	94.6%	90.5%	86.9%
Irregular	3.6	6.1	6.9
Single	1.5	3.2	6.0
	99.7%	99.8%	99.8%
Number of Households	2,736	943	346

*Compiled from the manuscript schedules of the 1855 New York State Census.

immigrants in this poor working-class ward, especially those who had fled the Irish famine, would have exhibited such a stable structural pattern in the reconstitution and creation of their households in America. Furthermore, native Americans had not been affected by the "disorganizing" process of immigration across the Atlantic (only one-quarter of the individuals had migrated from outside New York City), and yet the percentage of kin-related households among them was considerably lower than among the German and Irish.

Dividing kin-related households into nuclear, augmented, and extended households demonstrates that the majority of Irish, Ger-

man, and native-born white Sixth-Ward residents lived in households composed only of nuclear family members (Table 4). Slightly
higher percentages of Irish and native-born white Americans, compared to Germans, took relatives and boarders into their house-

TABLE 4

Composition of Irish, German, and Native-Born White
Kin-Related Households, Sixth Ward, 1855*

	Irish	German	Native-Born
Nuclear	62.9%	65.3%	60.8%
Augmented	28.5	27.1	28.3
Extended	8.6	7.6	10.9
	100.0%	100.0%	100.0%
Number of Households	2,589	854	301

*Compiled from the manuscript schedules of the 1855 New York State Census.

holds. The higher proportion of extended households among the
native-born whites perhaps reflected the fact that they were more
likely than the Irish or German immigrants to have had relatives in
the city with whom to share their households. Fully 37 percent of
the total Irish, German, and native-born American households
shared their living quarters with other than nuclear family members. That almost identical proportions in each group found it
necessary to do so suggests that Sixth Warders, regardless of ethnic
origins, responded in similar ways to poverty, the needs of relatives, and the lack of available housing. While an argument based
on household structure obviously tells us nothing about the tensions and conflicts within those immigrant families, it does suggest
that the larger outlines of the picture should emphasize cohesion
rather than breakdown.[18]

We can further illustrate the attempts of married immigrant working women to reduce the strain of their dual roles by looking at those wives who worked in occupations other than taking boarders. The evidence suggests that availability of work in the home, and not simply the income level of the husband, determined whether or not a wife worked. If we divide the occupations of Irish male heads of households into the two most numerous, artisans and laborers, we find that artisans' wives were more likely to work than laborers' wives (Table 5). At first glance, this might seem

TABLE 5

Irish Working Wives by Occupations of Heads of
Households and by Age, Sixth Ward, 1855*

	Age		
	20-29	30-39	40-49
Artisans' Wives	32.3%	40.6%	25.0%
Laborers' Wives	30.4%	25.9%	27.5%

*Compiled from the manuscript schedules of the 1855 New York State Census.

surprising since laborers, on the whole, tended to receive lower wages than many artisans. Since irregular employment affected both artisans and laborers, it cannot account for this apparent anomaly. By analyzing artisans' occupations more closely, however, we find that tailors' wives working in the sewing trades with their husbands, and oftentimes with their children, accounted for most of the difference. The opportunity to work at home and thus combine family and work roles seemed to be the decisive factor in determining whether or not wives would work.

However difficult it was for a married woman to provide needed income for the family, the problems of the widowed head of household were infinitely greater. According to the New York City Inspector's Reports, large numbers of the foreign-born laboring population, chiefly male heads of households, died in the prime of life, between twenty-five and forty years of age.[19] While the wages of a needle woman, in combination with a husband's or a father's

TABLE 6

Households of Irish Artisans, Laborers, and Widows
with Two or More Workers, Sixth Ward, 1855*

Age of Head of Household	20-29	30-39	40-49	50 and Over
	ARTISANS' HOUSEHOLDS			
Workers:				
Husband and Wife	32.3%	39.3%	20.1%	19.3%
Husband, Wife, and Child	0	1.3	4.9	7.0
Husband and Child	0	2.2	18.5	26.3
Husband and Relative	1.5	1.2	3.4	0
Households with Two or More Workers	33.8%	44.0%	46.9%	52.6%
Husband Only	66.2	55.9	53.1	47.4
	100.0%	99.9%	100.0%	100.0%
No. of Households	130	229	81	57

earnings, might have produced a subsistence wage, a widow who
had to support a family on this limited income lived on the brink of
disaster. Sheer necessity forced widowed heads of households to
work in a greater variety of occupations than married women.
About 25 percent of all employed widows, a figure roughly comparable to the percentage of wives, kept boarders. Most other
widows were concentrated in domestic and personal service or in
the sewing trades. Younger widows worked as seamstresses, milliners, and cap makers, while those over forty years of age turned to
laundering and housekeeping. Very few wives worked in domestic
and personal service, but over 20 percent of the widows did. As
chief support of the household, these widows, unlike the Sixth-

TABLE 6 (cont.)

LABORERS' HOUSEHOLDS

Workers:				
Husband and Wife	30.4%	25.9%	20.2%	14.9%
Husband, Wife and Child	0	0	7.3	7.3
Husband and Child	0	1.6	8.4	20.6
Husband and Relative	1.7	5.1	2.6	1.1
Households with Two or More Workers	32.1%	32.6%	38.5%	43.9%
Husband Only	67.9	67.3	61.5	56.1
	100.0%	100.0%	100.0%	100.0%
No. of Households	240	365	262	262

WIDOWS' HOUSEHOLDS

Workers:					
Widow Only	68.6%	55.7%	26.7%	11.8%	
Widow and Relative	7.7	6.6	.2	1.5	
Widow and Child	0	16.9	27.7	30.1	
Child Only	0	1.9	20.2	36.8	R
Relative Only	0	2.8	0	0	
No Workers Listed	23.7%	16.0	25.2	19.8	
	100.0%	99.9%	100.0%	100.0%	
No. of Households	38	106	119	136	

*Compiled from the manuscript schedules of the 1855 New York State Census.

Ward wives, were forced to work outside their homes, performing the difficult manual labor of a laundress or charwoman.[20]

Comparisons of the households of Irish artisans and laborers with both parents living to those headed by widows also reveal significant differences in patterns of family employment created by the absence of a male breadwinner (Table 6). For example, in households headed by widows between the ages of 20 and 29, fewer persons contributed to the family income simply because these households lacked a second employable adult. Also, a higher percentage of these same households included working relatives. More significant, however, was the tendency, given the extremely low wages paid women workers in the mid-nineteenth century, for widows to send their children to work. Between the ages of 30 and 59, 13 percent of the artisan-headed households, 14 percent of the laborer's households, and 47 percent of the households headed by widows included working children. At each age interval, the children of widows worked in considerably higher percentages that did laborers' or artisans' children.

The death of a husband and father in this period meant both that widows would be more likely to work than women in general and that their children would be forced to work at a younger age and remain in their mothers' households longer than the children of working fathers. We can assume that these offspring responded to the greater need for their earnings created by female-headed households and stayed at home to provide that support. That twenty-five- and thirty-year-old sons and daughters, in general, remained within their parents' households suggests far more than the family's need for their income. The children's willingness and desire to continue to contribute to the survival of the family unit indicates the tenacity and endurance of strong family ties within this Irish community.

As we have seen, age, family relationships, and availability of work in the home affected both the kinds of work Sixth-Ward Irish women performed and the likelihood that they would be employed. Did these patterns represent a peculiarly Irish adaptation to a new environment or did other ethnic groups respond in similar ways? Comparison with the second largest Sixth-Ward immigrant group, the Germans, shows that approximately the same percentage of German and Irish women worked (Table 7). This confirms what the Irish statistics suggested, namely, that in a poor working-class community like the Sixth Ward, women's work was necessary for their own and their family's survival. It further suggests that the work patterns we have been discussing do not necessarily reflect responses based on ethnicity but rather cut across ethnic lines. Working-class women, whether German or Irish, responded in similar ways to the need to secure an adequate family income.

Similar to their Irish counterparts, many young, unmarried German women in the Sixth Ward worked as domestic servants. This is surprising since an analysis of New York City as a whole indicates that a greater percentage of Irish women worked as servants than

TABLE 7

German and Irish Working Women by Age, Sixth Ward, 1855*

	15-19	20-29	30-39	40 and over
German	50.2%	50.4%	34.7%	31.1%
(No.)	89	327	118	55
Irish	47.9%	46.9%	39.3%	37.4%
(No.)	333	828	435	402

*Compiled from the manuscript schedules of the 1855 New York State Census.

did Germans or any other immigrant group. This differential is usually attributed to the German family's tendency both to emigrate as a household and to stay together in America. The Irish, on the other hand, allegedly emigrated as individuals. Contrary to this assumption, the majority of Sixth-Ward Irish families emigrated as a unit, and a higher percentage (71 percent) of young Irish women lived with parents, husbands, children, or other relatives than did young German women (65 percent). In fact, the stereotype notwithstanding, a higher percentage (51 percent) of young Sixth-Ward German women worked as servants than did their Irish neighbors (43 percent). Because there were numerous large German boardinghouses in the Sixth Ward requiring domestic staff, the language barrier, which existed in the rest of the city and probably contributed to the small overall percentage of German servants, did not prevail. Thus, in the Sixth Ward, the general assumptions concerning the low proportion of German servants and the family-oriented explanation for this low percentage did not hold true.

Fully one-third of the German wives between the ages 20 and 49 worked — a higher percentage in each age category than the Irish. Assuming that both groups had similar economic needs, how can we account for the greater tendency of German wives to work? Although the percentage of German working wives is greater, we can see that the pattern of adaptation to the demand for their labor is similar to that of Irish wives. Approximately the same proportion of German and Irish wives took boarders into their households. Since more Sixth-Ward German than Irish men were tailors, it was the greater availability of needle work in the home which accounted for the higher overall percentage of German working wives.

Thus, young unmarried women, whether German or Irish, worked outside the home when opportunities such as domestic service existed. Married women of both nationalities maintained their function as wife and mother by working within the home when work was available. This observation reinforces the conclusion that both German and Irish families adapted to economic conditions of mid-nineteenth-century New York City in similar ways. It can be posited, therefore, that work patterns of the urban poor cannot be understood simply by studying aggregate occupational statistics. They must be analyzed within the context of the neighborhood and the employment opportunities it offered.

Many women in a poor working-class neighborhood like the City's Sixth Ward worked at some point, if not all of their lives. In order for their families to survive, wives and daughters often had to supplement the income of the head of the household and many widowed households depended on women as the major breadwinner. The ways in which women responded to their families' need for income indicate that facile assumptions concerning family disorganization and breakdown in America's urban centers must be discarded. This is not to suggest the substitution of a roseate picture of immigrant life in America. Grinding poverty, overcrowded and unsanitary housing, and high disease and death rate plagued the poor neighborhoods. But despite the physical deprivation which immigrants suffered, strong family and kin ties provided an internal coherence to their daily lives which must be recognized. The relationship between family and work roles discussed in this paper suggests the dynamics of immigrant adaptation to the pressures both of a new environment and an industrializing society. Even when dealing with the basic problems of survival, these immigrants found ways to minimize the strains of their new world and to reinforce their traditional familial values. Only by recognizing and reexamining this process of adaptation can we begin to understand the mid-nineteenth-century urban immigrant poor.

NOTES

1. Oscar Handlin, *The Uprooted* (New York, 1951), pp. 154-157; Oscar Handlin, *Boston's Immigrants*, 2nd. ed. (Cambridge, Massachusetts, 1959), p. 120; Nathan Glazer and Daniel Patrick Moynihan, *Beyond the Melting Pot*, 2nd. ed. (Cambridge, Massachusetts, 1970), p. 239; Douglas T. Miller, *Jacksonian Aristocracy: Class and Democracy in New York, 1830-1860* (New York, 1967), p. 184; Robert Bremner, *From the Depths* (New York, 1956), p. 58; James Richardson, *The New York Police: From Colonial Times to 1901* (New York, 1970), p. 27; Alexander Callow, Jr., *The Tweed Ring* (New York, 1966), pp. 55-62.

2. The manuscript schedules of the 1855 New York State Census are located at the County Clerk's Office, New York City. The 1855 state census was chosen rather than the 1850 federal census for two reasons: the 1850 census did not enumerate women's occupations and did not include the major German and Irish immigration of the early 1850s. Historians, such as Robert Ernst, in *Immigrant Life in New York City, 1825-1863* (New York, 1949), have previously used the manuscripts to enumerate, for example, carpenters, or Italians, or shopkeepers, but the wealth of material on household and family relationships provided by the manuscripts has been entirely neglected.

3. See, for example, J. D. B. DeBow, *Statistical View of the United States . . . A Compensium of the Seventh Census of 1850* (New York, 1970); U.S., Eighth Census, *Statistics of the United States in 1860* (Washington, D.C., 1893); N. W. Aldrich, *Wholesale Prices, Wages and Transportation*, U.S. Report No. 1394, 52nd Congress, 2nd Session (Washington, D.C., 1893); U.S. Dept. of Labor, Bureau of Labor Statistics, Bull. No. 499, "The History of Wages in the United States from Colonial Times to 1928" (Washington, D.C., 1929); U.S. Industrial Commission on Immigration, *Reports*, vol. 15, (Washington, D.C., 1901); Edith Abbott, "Wages of Unskilled Labor in the United States, 1850-1900," *Journal of Political Economy*, 13 (June 1905), 321-367. For contemporary newspaper accounts, see the investigations reported in the *New York Tribune*, August 14, 19, 29, September 3, 5, 9, 11, 17, 1845; May 27, June 8, 17, 29, July 20, 28, 1853; and in *America's Own*, April 14, July 7, September 1, 1849.

4. *The Citizen*, February, March 18, 1854; also *New York Tribune*, February 21, 1854. Greeley estimated an increase of 50 percent in the cost of provisions in New York City between 1843 and 1850. See *New York Tribune*, November 14, 1850.

5. *New York Times*, November 8, 1853; *New York Tribune*, May 27, 1851.

6. Stanley Lebergott, *Manpower in Economic Growth: The American Record Since 1800* (New York, 1964), p. 150; Norman Ware, *The Industrial Worker, 1840-1860*, 2nd. ed. (Chicago, 1964), p. 31; John R. Commons et al., *The History of Labour in the United States* (New York, 1919), vol. 1, p. 488; Carl Degler, "Labor in the Economy and Politics of New York City: A Study of the Impact of Early Industrialism" (Ph.D. dissertation, Columbia University, 1952), pp. 175-176.

7. *New York Tribune*, November 6, 1845, September 16, 1846; William Burns, *Life in New York* (New York, 1851); U.S. Senate, Doc. No. 645, 61st Congress, 2nd Sess., *Report on the Condition of Woman and Child Wage Earners in the United States*, vol. 9, Helen Sumner, *History of Women in Industry in the United States*

(Washington, D.C., 1910), pp. 177-185; Virginia Penny, *The Employments of Women: A Cyclopedia of Women's Work* (New York, 1863), pp. 423-433; Lebergott, *Manpower in Economic Growth,* pp. 278-284.

8. New York State Assembly, Document No. 205, "Reports of the Select Committee to Examine into the Condition of Tenant Houses in New York and Brooklyn" (Albany, 1857), vol. 3, p. 87. See also Sumner, *History of Women in Industry,* p. 179; Penny, *Employments of Women,* pp. 428-433; Burns, *Life in New York.*

9. *New York Tribune,* June 8, 1853. The statement from the *Tribune* was quoted in Virginia Penny, *Think and Act* (Philadelphia, 1869), p. 84.

10. Virginia Penny sent out questionnaires to employers and visited many establishments, particularly in New York City, between 1859 and 1861; Penny, *Employments of Women.* See also Sumner, *History of Women in Industry,* pp. 195-230; Edith Abbott, *Women in Industry* (New York, 1924), pp. 246-261.

11. *The Subterranean,* July 19, 1845.

12. Penny, *The Employments of Women,* p. 159; *New York Tribune,* September 14, 1845; *Young America,* November 1, 1845; James MacCabe, *Secrets of the Great City* (Philadelphia, 1868), p. 504; Burns, *Life in New York.*

13. All individuals are taken from the manuscript schedules of the census. See also Penny, *The Employments of Women,* pp. 121-122. Women who ran stores, boardinghouses, or family businesses jointly with their husbands were not listed as gainfully employed in the 1855 census. They are enumerated in the present-day censuses, however, in a category called "unpaid family worker."

14. *New York Tribune,* March 7, 1845.

15. The average wage is based on the wages given in the 1855 New York State Census Manuscript, Manufacturing Statistics, Sixth Ward.

16. These conclusions are not unique to the Irish or to mid-nineteenth-century New York City. For recent studies of women's work experience and its relationship to family structure in other nineteenth- and early twentieth-century communities, see Virginia Yans-McLaughlin, "Patterns of Work and Family Organization: Buffalo's Italians," in Theodore K. Rabb and Robert I. Rotberg, *The Family in History: Interdisciplinary Essays* (New York, Harper Torch Books, 1973), and Daniel J. Walkowitz, "Working-Class Women in the Gilded Age: Factory, Community and Family Life Among Cohoes, New York, Cotton Workers," *Journal of Social History,* (Summer 1972): 464-490.

17. Households are composed of nuclear family members only, nuclear family members and relatives (extended households), or nuclear family members, relatives, and boarders (augmented households).

18. For a further analysis of family and household structure, immigration patterns, and occupational structure in this community, see my dissertation, "The 'Bloody Ould Sixth': A Social Analysis of a New York City Working-Class Community in the Mid-Nineteenth Century" (Ph.D. dissertation, University of Rochester, 1973).

19. *Annual Report of the City Inspector of the Number of Deaths and Interments in the City of New York for the Year 1851* (New York, 1852), pp. 448-450.

20. Compiled from the manuscript schedules of the 1855 New York State Census.

21. See, for example, Ernst, *Immigrant Life in New York City,* p. 66.

ITALIAN WOMEN AND WORK: EXPERIENCE AND PERCEPTION

5

by Virginia Yans-McLaughlin

American historiography has generally accepted contemporary cultural definitions of productive work, and this acceptance has implicitly involved a devaluation of work performed by women. Only recently have historians widely recognized women workers within and outside the home as important contributors to the nation's economy. This revisionism itself reflects our culture's changing definitions of what productive work is and the higher value currently ascribed to domestic toil. The time has come to move beyond this basic recognition to more sophisticated hypotheses and methodological techniques. The central task before us is to define clearly and categorically what we mean by "women's work" and to construct a specific methodology for understanding it.

Much of the current excitement in women's history, I believe, results from the fact that several scholars, setting out from very different directions, are moving toward a resolution of major methodological difficulties.[1] I think we might benefit from a clarifying pause: we must make certain implicit, and perhaps unconscious, assumptions explicit and conscious. I would like to fill one small gap in that pause by arguing that a methodological breakthrough cannot occur until a more precise operational definition of "women's work," a definition cognizant of cultural variations, is provided.

My own work and Louise Tilly's astute criticism of it convinced me of the need for clarification of theoretical assumptions concerning relationships between women, work, and culture.[2] The model I have employed for understanding immigrant Italian families and woman's position within them assumes, as Tilly correctly points out, that "cultural traditions . . . mediate or modify strictly economic roles." On the other hand, she believes that "values must be consonant with actual experience," more specifically, with economic experience. While I am willing to attribute the Italian woman's power within the family at least partially to certain Sicilian cultural traditions, she argues that "this is certainly a case of selling short the economic importance of the wife and mother in peasant and working-class families." Shopping, mending, food preparation, and other household tasks, Tilly states, were important contributions to the family economy. A problem with my model, according to her, is that I define "economic role in terms of the market place, in which 'work' is the production and distribution of goods or services in return for wages. Peasant and working-class women made enormous contributions to their families that they, their husbands and their children recognized." [3]

The crucial issue, as Tilly points out, is the definition of "women's work." Her critique forced a realization of hidden assumptions in my model, which does indeed implicitly assign different values to economic contributions made by male and female Italians. But the assumptions originated with Italian immigrants and peasants, not with me. South Italians themselves placed a lower value upon women's work, and it was their definition of work I accepted, not my own. This seems to me an entirely defensible position. To place a higher value upon women's work than Italians themselves ascribed to it is to distort their cultural reality. Such a distortion, I think, emerges from an ethnocentric bias reflecting current, more positive reevaluations of women's household contributions.

Here lies the crux of the matter. Whose definition and evaluation of work should the historian accept: his or her own, or those of the culture under consideration? Granted this dichotomy is too clear-cut; no matter how strong the commitment to objectivity, current values and concerns find expression in historical writings. If, however, objectivity is the ideal, the continuing dialectic between history and polemics, a dialectic highly apparent in the current historiography of women, must be made explicit. And if empathetic understanding of past cultures is our goal, cross-cultural and historical differences in definitions of women's work must be recognized.

I find any model which focuses almost exclusively upon economic causation and excludes culture as a mediator insufficient to explain social change, including shifts in women's work roles. The economic model is entirely appropriate if one wishes to understand how a society's wealth is produced and allocated. But the history of women's work involves another basic human problem — how biological sex differences work themselves out within different economic contexts into different cultural roles. The focus upon economic causation, perhaps rooted in the historian's and the sociologist's tendency to study broad societal change, tends to draw attention away from sexual differentiation as an explanatory variable. We cannot explain the history of working women solely on the basis of their inferior class status; we must explore their position as women vis-à-vis the men in their class and ethnic groups. Certainly, when intraclass behavior is being analyzed, that is, when class position is held constant, sex-role differentiation becomes extremely important. We have already begun writing history from the bottom up; it is time for women's historians to begin writing it from the inside out.

I am arguing, in this essay, for a kind of *gestalt* approach, not one that would exclude objective conditions or economic causation, but one which would give due recognition to differences in perception between long-dead individuals and contemporary historians. Perceptions of women as workers embedded in past cultures frequently seem to distort what, with hindsight, we see as their actual contributions to economic life. This apparent lack of congruence between perceived and objectively defined experience itself offers important insights to historians attempting to study and to define women's work.[4] The lack of congruence also leads me to emphatic disagreement with the notion that "values must be consonant with actual experience,"[5] economic or otherwise.

These theoretical considerations and my own study of immigrant Italian women in Buffalo, New York, convince me of the necessity for definitions of women's work which both reflect ethnic and cultural variations and for a highly eclectic methodology capable of defining such objective conditions as economic, demographic, and occupational structures and changes in these structures over time.

The gap between women's actual work experience and cultural perceptions of those experiences has other important methodological implications; its analog exists in historical sources themselves. A recent interview I conducted with a Buffalo immigrant illustrates both the importance of cultural perceptions and the lack of congruence between values and experience. I asked Mr. D., a Sicilian immigrant, if his wife worked. "My wife did not work after we were married," he said. "Why should she work?" Later on I asked him to explain how he, a struggling immigrant, managed to purchase a home for his family. He replied that he and his wife converted a newly purchased home into a rooming house and used the profits to pay their mortgage. As a casual aside he added, "We had a lot of people [as boarders] . . . to make money . . .; my wife used to take care of that . . . . I didn't pay any attention to it."[6] Within eleven months of their marriage, his wife gave birth to their first child; ten more followed. Yet in Mr. D.'s eyes, childbirth eleven times over and running a boardinghouse to pay off a mortgage was not "work.' If Mrs. D. were alive, she, like hundreds of other Buffalo immigrant women, would probably also reply that she did not work after marriage. But a little probing by the interviewer would often reveal that she cared for boarders, made arttificial flowers, sewed, or engaged in some other kind of homework, and perhaps worked at a nearby country cannery during the summer.

The gap between women's actual work experience and perceptions of it finds its way into other kinds of historical sources. Italian women did not report part-time seasonal occupations such as summer cannery work and a variety of income-producing tasks performed within the home as "work" to census canvassers; Italians instructed them to write "housewife" in the column designated "occupation." A historian using only manuscript censuses and oral history interviews might well conclude that Italian women did not work. Yet newspaper, factory, and tenement investigations as well as middle-class charity workers tell us otherwise.[7]

Upon presenting these apparent contradictions to an anthropologist as an important methodological problem for historians, Vincent Crapanzano provided a practical panacea. "Perhaps," he said, "you must do an ethnology of women's work before you do a history of women's work."[8] The sequence he prescribed is less important than the task; by this point it should be clear that I strongly agree that such an ethnology is needed. Its application would extend far beyond the study of Italian women, perhaps to women in all of western culture. Polish immigrant women who worked as domestic servants and did the laundry of middle-class families in their homes rarely reported their occupations to census canvassers.[9] Yet written sources indicate that they frequently took such jobs. In his study of Lancashire, England, Michael Anderson observes that women who worked in their husbands' shops and a variety of additional part-time positions did not report their occupations formally. Sam Bass Warner informs us that "colonial tax lists did not report the contributions of female domestic labor although such labor constituted an important fraction of . . . [Philadelphia's economic] output."[10] It should come as no surprise that historical sources merely reflect the devaluation of women's work, even income-producing work, characteristic of most western cultures.

I do not wish to imply that census canvassers, immigrant husbands, and colonial tax-list compilers engaged in a conscious conspiracy, in which women colluded, to undervalue women's work. The underestimation of women's work, it seems to me, points in a different direction. Anthropologist Margaret Mead sees the depreciation of both women's work and her domestic roles as an antidote to a universal human problem: all human cultures face the task of conditioning men to be nurturing fathers. The male must be conditioned to work and to share the product of his toil with his wife and children: "Men have to learn to want to provide for others . . . . Women may be said to be mothers unless they are taught to deny their childbearing qualities."[11]

This socialization process hinges upon acceptance of sex roles. The female's sexual identity is confirmed by immediate biological ties to her young, the experience of carrying, giving birth, and nursing them. The male must turn to the outside world "to reassert . . . [and] to redefine his maleness."[12] Each society has its own way of socializing males to accept their fathering roles; depreciation of women's work in and outside the home seems to be the common ploy used to assuage the male's pride and to reward him for his productive activities and nurturing function.

In her book *Male and Female*, Mead explains why the depreciation of women's work frequently accompanies male sex role socialization:

> In every known human society, the male's need for achievement can be recognized. Men may cook, or weave or dress dolls or hunt humming-birds but if such activities are the appropriate occupations of men, then the whole society, men and women alike, votes them as important. When the same occupations are performed by women, they are regarded as less important. In a great number of human societies men's sureness of their sex role is tied up with their right, or ability, to practice some activity that women are not allowed to practice. Their maleness, in fact, has to be underwritten by preventing women from entering some field or performing some feat. Here may be found the relationship between maleness and pride; that is, a need for prestige that will outstrip the prestige which is accorded to any woman . . . . Cultures frequently phrase achievement as something that women do not or cannot do, rather than directly as something which men can do well. The recurrent problem of civilization is to define the male role satisfactory enough — whether it be to build gardens or raise cattle, kill game or kill enemies, build bridges or handle bank-shares — so that the male may . . . reach a solid sense of irreversible achievement, of which his childhood knowledge of childbearing have given him a glimpse. [13]

Using this anthropological perspective, we can begin to make sense of the lack of congruence between female work experience and cultural perceptions of that experience. Male immigrants like Mr. D., who did not see his wife as a working woman, defended themselves psychologically against female encroachments either by depreciating women's work or by seeing it as an extension of usual female household functions. For Italian immigrants, work within woman's traditional sphere, — the home — was not recognized as work, even if the enterprise produced profits. Part-time work for some family-related goal (saving for a home, for example) or seasonal work outside the urban market place with other family members at the canneries could be legitimized in similar fashion.[14]

The depreciation of woman's work had important practicality in an immigrant community where male unemployment was extremely high. Italian laborers and dock, railroad, and construction workers found themselves out of work five or six months annually. I have written elsewhere about the conservatism of Italian female employment patterns.[15] These patterns and immigrant perception of women's work provide evidence for continuing patriarchal control among Italian-Americans. The Italian woman's economic contributions made family survival possible, yet she apparently remained a silent partner in the marital economic relationship; Italians did not admit their women worked, even to themselves. The wife retained a good peasant woman's acceptance of male control. Even when she did work and her husband could find no job, her sense of her own importance was not inflated.[16] Devaluation of women's work helped to maintain this precarious balance of family power between males and females.

As we construct our work ethnologies for various immigrant groups, no doubt some overlap will occur between one group and another. This should come as no surprise since many came from European peasant cultures which had much in common. Many immigrant women — Poles, Italians, and Jews among them — took boarders into their homes. A logical extension of their traditional household routines, the practice permitted them to stay at home to care for their children. The same group might engage in slightly different occupations in different cities or, due to a variety of conditions, it might surrender traditional attitudes toward work in one city more quickly than in another. Neither should this surprise us, for pressure for change varied with the context. New York City Italian women, for example, seem to have more readily entered the work world outside the home than their sisters in other cities did.[17] This may have been due to a variety of conditions which make New

York an atypical metropolis. No matter what the cultural background, economic, demographic, and occupational peculiarities and the biological peculiarities of the female life cycle must be taken into consideration in any model attempting to explain women's work. But the model I propose does not assume a determinist relationship between the development of material conditions and cultural values. The cultures these groups brought with them was neither so passive nor so brittle. The work choices immigrant women made are better understood as a product of reciprocal interactions between traditional values and new social contexts. Reciprocity implies adaptation of Old World culture, not its destruction. Although the immediate historical context and occupational structure limited work choices for women, I believe that within this context, ethnic groups chose work styles and occupational modes which permitted minimal family strain. In short, immigrants constructed and interpreted their social reality in terms of past experience.

The work experience of south Italian women in Buffalo provides an example of how this model works. What kind of work did these women engage in and why? What role did culture play and how did culture intersect with changing socioeconomic circumstances?

Since I am arguing that the past influenced work choices and perceptions of work options, we must make a detour back to nineteenth-century southern Italy to determine what those work patterns were.[18] A wife's clearly defined household responsibilities included childbearing and child rearing, overseeing family resources, preparing and purchasing food, mending, spinning, sewing, and directing children in household tasks. Most of the southern peasants looked disdainfully upon those wives who left their homes to work, and few did so unless poverty required it. Sicilians held very strictly to this rule. One Sicilian immigrant recalled, "It was almost a crime for women to work."[19] But in many parts of the *Mezzogiorno*, an expected part of a wife's year-round labors included joining the family in crop harvesting. Seasonal migrations also drew entire peasant families away from their villages, but females rarely worked in nonagricultural occupations, partly because few factory towns existed in southern Italy. Also, because family honor was invested in a girl's virginity and a women's purity, females usually did not leave their homes unchaperoned. This requirement put obvious restrictions on work options.[20] Women who left home to labor generally worked as members of a family unit, earning a portion of the family wage. They did not regard themselves (nor were they regarded) as independent wage earners. Women did not derive their status within the family from their position as wage earners, nor did the wages they earned challenge the husband's positions as chief breadwinner.

Returning to the city of Buffalo, we can see how these work routines fared in a new context. We divide our analysis into work performed within and outside the home. Early twentieth-century census returns indicate that less than 2 percent of Italian wives reported full-time employment which could have taken them from their domestic concerns; some involved themselves in family enterprises which did not draw them from the home or give them the status of independent wage earners.[21] Most women (12 percent) who contributed to the family budget did so by providing housekeeping services to roomers and boarders. The remaining wives reported no occupation at all, but we know that many engaged in part-time cannery work or homework. Italian women and girls rarely left their homes unsupervised by relatives or friends to work as domestics or as factory laborers.

Polish families revealed strikingly different attitudes toward women entering the work world. Very soon after their initial settlement, Polish women eagerly sought work as factory hands.[22] Because women did not report such occupations to census representatives, we do not know exact proportions, but literary sources unanimously confirm that Irish, German, and especially Polish women sought domestic service jobs in Buffalo's middle-class homes. Mothers or married women liked the flexible routines such employment allowed, being reluctant to engage in full-time factory labor.[23]

Apparently, once in America, Italians did not conceive of women's work in exactly the same way as other groups. True, Italian women shared a preference for homework and boarders with other immigrant women. Their shared experiences as women—childbearing and child rearing— contributed to these mutual preferences. Yet it is also true that Italian women tended to gravitate more heavily to some occupations than to others and that some kinds of work were more acceptable to them than others. Three criteria seem to have governed their work choices, all derivatives of their cultural past. Work performed within the home, such as homework or caring for boarders, was acceptable because it did not take women away from their young and also because it represented a comfortable extension of traditional household routines. Italians also found positions permitting the continuation of strict sexual and familial controls upon women to be appropriate. Part-time or seasonal work was acceptable because women would not be assaulting male pride by working more steadily than their frequently unemployed husbands.

Homework and cannery work filled many of these requirements. The former provided a transitional step for recently arrived peasant groups and cushioned the introduction to industrial society. A New York State Factory Investigating Commission report on 300 New York City families emphasized the peculiar preference Italians seemed to have for this work style:

> The large proportion of Italians engaged in homework is significant of the fact that their home traditions lend themselves with peculiar readiness to the homework system. The Germans accept homework as a trade and adapt themselves to specific phases of it at which they may become expert. They do not do finishing, but do fine custom tailoring, making vests complete or fine hand-made button holes . . . . The Irish and American adopt homework only as a last resort. They do it only when they are poverty stricken and driven to it by necessity. The Italians come usually from rural districts and know little about factory work and organized industry. The men become laborers and fall into seasonal trades where the wages are small and irregular and must be supplemented. As a rule they have strong home associations, they expect their girls to marry young, and they do not like them to go out into factories. Accustomed in Italy

> to depend upon the labor of their children in the
> fields, they expect them in this country to yield a
> financial return at the earliest possible moment
> and are, therefore, ready to have them adopt
> homework, a system that lends itself to the ex-
> ploitation of women and children. [24]

In both homework and cannery industries, the family continued
as the basic productive unit, and the organization of work, if not its
substance, closely resembled Italian practices. The mother's role as
arbiter of household tasks and disciplinarian of children was reinforced by her economic position as work manager, be it artificial flower making, sewing, or canning. She maintained her inferior position to her husband because she had not become the
chief breadwinner. As in Italy, these families viewed income earned
by wives and children at the canneries or at home as a supplement
to the father's wages, not a replacement.

In neither case did the Italian male relinquish his obligation to
support his family, nor did he forfeit his control and authority.
And women and children who worked at the canneries or at home
did not drift as separate individuals into the labor market. They
were recruited, lived, worked as family members under the close
scrutiny of other Italian-Americans, many of whom were *paesani*
and kin. Social controls, including those which insured traditional
sexual attitudes, operated as effectively in the canning factory as
they did in the neighborhood. The visible and public nature of
work and of living conditions partially explains why such controls
functioned so effectively. Finally, like the household, the migrant
labor camp permitted close integration of living and working
quarters and therefore did not separate the family's productive and
child-rearing capacities. A close association of economic and
family functions similiar to that which existed in Italy prevailed in
both situations. Italians found such arrangements agreeable because they brought income in but minimized sex-role conflict. [25]

In contrast, Italians regarded factory work and domestic service
more negatively than did other groups. Stricter notions of female
chastity caused them to perceive such employment as sexual en-
counters as well as economic arrangements. Jealous Italian
men would not permit their wives to work under another man's

roof, no matter what the family's economic circumstances. Efforts of various organizations in Buffalo and elsewhere to interest Italian women in such work failed; even second-generation Italians did not find service occupations as agreeable as other second-generation groups did. A National Federation of Settlements survey, characterizing Italian parents as especially hesitant to permit daughters to enter factories, cited parental concern for their children's morality as a reason. The report also stressed the sexual aspects of the factory situation which were particularly disturbing to Italian parents:

> Though the factory is morally more protected than certain other employments, conditions are far from what they should be. In many places girls work side by side with, or in the near vicinity of men. They sometimes become careless in their conduct, slack in manners and conversation, immodest in dress, and familiar to a degree that lays them open to danger.[26]

Many Italian women, upon becoming factory workers, internalized parental values. Those in New York State canneries warned co-workers of "fresh" timekeepers. One issued a special caveat concerning men of her own nationality: "One must be careful not to get fresh with the Italian boys because they are dangerous."[27]

Italian women avoided both domestic and factory work for other reasons entirely consistent with their cultural background. By avoiding domestic service, Italian women also shunned the one position available to unskilled workers which could have given them steadier employment than their husbands. They were also more cautious about leaving their homes for factories than other women were. Emphasizing cultural differences between Italian and Polish women in Pittsburgh, Butler explained the relative unimportance of Italians in the city's industrial life as follows: "The Polish women have not the conservatism which keeps the Italian girl at home. They have not the same standard of close-knit family relations. There is a flexibility in their attitude toward life and their part of it."[28] In 1909 Tobenkin compared Chicago's Italian,

Polish, Jewish, and Lithuanian girls and came to similar conclusions regarding Italian conventionality.[29] One married Buffalo
Italian cited other reasons for staying at home. She indicated her
cultural bond to Italian males, who also preferred accustomed pre-
industrial work routines: "You go to factory, you have to work
just as hard as at home. Boss say 'Hurry up! Hurry up!'" At home,
no one say 'Hurry up!' I figure out."[30]

Given the stringent and controlling attitudes of Italian males, it
seems strange that most women contributing to family income did
so by caring for boarders. While this occupational choice kept
women at home, it also exposed them to intimate contact with men.
But morality was not jeopardized for money, no matter how
serious the economic need. J.A. recently told how "everybody had
boarders in their homes at one time or another. It would not cause
problems. It was not like that in those days. The sense of family
was too strong for anything like today, especially if the boarders
were *paesani.*"[31] Normally overprotective husbands allowed such
men in their homes because many sought only temporary residence
while seasonal work was available or until they established their
own households. The brevity of their stay limited opportunities for
indiscretion. Kinship and village ties which bonded Italian neighborhoods also discouraged infidelities. With minimized risks, then,
a family could increase its income by housing boarders.

This discussion of Italian attitudes towards women's work must
be placed in a broader context: community's economy, work opportunities, and demographic structure require examination, for
these define the possible perimeters of behavior and the context in
which cultural adaptation occurred.

The work choices of Buffalo's Italian women occurred within the
changing context of early twentieth-century supply and demand.
Although both the proportion and demand for female labor increased, married, unskilled, foreign-born women did not reap the
major benefits. The greatest expansion of female opportunities occurred in clerical and communications jobs, operations requiring
literacy and familiarity with English. Heavy immigration to
American cities at the turn of the century produced a supply of
women exceeding employer demand. Moreover, two typical employers of married immigrant women, domestic industry and the

nonfactory clothing industry, declined in importance.[32] Demand
for domestic servants and for women willing to do laundry in their
Buffalo homes remained heavy. In 1910 foreign-born women (42
percent) entered domestic service almost as readily as native-born
women did (58 percent).[33] With the exception of Italians, many
immigrant wives took such positions because they represented an
extension of traditional household routines.[34] They did not conflict with norms assigning higher priorities to child rearing and
other wifely functions than to full-time work outside the home. Before World War II, employer preferences for young, single working
women supported such priorities.[35] The second-generation daughters of immigrant women flocked to available jobs in clothing, pa-
per-box, and soap factories. Others found work in the laundry and
publishing industries. Employer demand only partly determined
their decision. Ability to speak English, lack of child-rearing obligations, and diminished acceptance of traditional attitudes toward
women's work also help to explain their presence in factories.[36]

Demographic characteristics of Buffalo's Italian women may offer further clues regarding their decision to forego factory work
and domestic service. A preponderance of Italian females were
young married women. In 1905, 45 percent of married Italians were
between 15 and 30 years of age, the peak child-rearing years when
women were least likely to work. But age and life-cycle stage do not
fully explain why married Italians were much less likely to work
than Poles. A 10 percent sample of 1905 Polish households revealed that 36 percent of all married Polish women were under 30.[37]
Poles, then, had only about 10 percent more married women past
peak child-rearing years who could more easily engage in occupations outside the home. This 10 percent difference is not substantial
enough to account for varying employment patterns of married
Italians and Poles.

Demographic differences do explain why Buffalo factories employed proportionately more single Polish women than Italian. The
Polish population was substantially larger, and Polish women married considerably later. In 1905 each group had roughly the same
proportion of women under 30 — 50 percent for the Italians and 47
percent for the Poles. Yet only 35 percent of Italian women under
30 remained single; 59 percent of Polish women of that age group

remained unmarried.[38] Free of familial obligations, a larger proportion of Polish women could seek work. But to overemphasize demographic variables is to oversimplify. The decision to marry or work was itself, of course, culturally informed; Italians, for example, merely continued the Old World custom of relatively early marriage. Both groups had more men than women in their communities, so abnormal sex ratios do not explain differences in their marriage patterns.

Demographic differences between Poles and Italians, specifically the possibility of a lower proportion of Italian females, might explain why Italian women less readily entered domestic service. Because Italian males outnumbered Italian females (a sex ratio of 144.4 in 1910), Italian women would eschew domestic service, finding a ready market for their household skills among unattached men seeking room and board. Comparable figures pertaining to the Polish sex ratio are not available, but Polish males almost certainly predominated as males did among most "new immigrant" groups, excluding Jews. We know, moreover, that thousands of Polish families supplemented their incomes with boarders' fees.[39] Lack of demand for these services, therefore, cannot explain why Polish wives opted for domestic service.

Because neither labor-market conditions nor demographic characteristics fully explain differences between Polish and Italian female employment preferences, the cultural basis for such decisions deserves reemphasis. Italians in other industrial cities, like Buffalo, made similar choices.[40] When occupational structure is held constant, therefore, cultural preferences seem to play themselves out in similar ways. But the cultural argument is further sustained upon examining Italian female employment patterns in cities with highly differentiated occupational structures. Although Philadelphia's textile factories offered opportunities to unskilled Italians, the women preferred to continue working at home in their own neighborhoods. Philadelphia Italians were more likely than any other group to engage in homework, and most of the city's homework production centered in Little Italy. A 1929 survey revealed that Italians ranked highest in percentage (70 percent) of women who had not worked since marriage.[41] Figures for working women in 1909 in Passaic, New Jersey, where thousands found employment in worsted mills, revealed that only 7 percent of a sample of south Italian women worked. But the percentages for other ethnic groups were Ruthenian, 47 percent; Magyar, 45 percent; Slovak, 27 percent.[42] Studies of other cities, including Pittsburgh and Boston, reveal that single and married Italian women tended to avoid domestic service while Polish women depended heavily upon it.[43] A search of the 1905 manuscript census for New York City revealed that almost no Italian women reported employment after marriage.[44] In New York, Italian girls left domestic and personal service to other ethnic groups, but they did enter factories. Still, they viewed factory labor chiefly as an opportunity to learn skills, such as sewing, which they could continue at home after marriage.[45]

In conclusion, cultural backgrounds played a role in influencing work choices and also in determining what female work experiences meant to immigrants. The fact that immigrant women worked was perhaps less important than their interpretation of the situation. A New York social worker's comments illustrate this point. Observing that Italian females did not achieve as much independence as those of other nationalities, she explained that their men saw women's labor as an "inevitable evil induced by conditions of American life which did not in any way alter their dependent position . . . . In this way the women are kept in the paradoxical position of simultaneous wage-earning and dependence."[46] Here is a clear example of a lack of consonance between values and experience. Immigrant attitudes toward women's work appear inconsistent only if we forget that they comprehended new circumstances in terms of an Old World gestalt. In this sense, perhaps the dichotomy I have suggested between experience and perception is real only for historians, not for the immigrants who lived the lives we are studying.

NOTES

1. Two examples of important recent contributions are Joan W. Scott and Louise A. Tilly, "Women's Work and the Family in Nineteenth-Century Europe" (unpublished paper, October 1973), and Alice Kessler-Harris, "Between the Real and the Ideal: Conflict in the Lives of American Working Women at the Turn of the Century" (unpublished paper presented to the Organization of American Historians, April 1974).

2.Louise A. Tilly, "Comments on McLaughlin and Davidoff Papers" (Anglo American Conference on Comparative Labor History, April 27, 1973). A revised and condensed version of Tilly's comments and a paper by the author were subsequently published in the *Journal of Social History*; see Virginia Yans-McLaughlin, "A Flexible Tradition: South Italian Immigrants Confront a New York Experience," *Journal of Social History* (Summer 1974): 429-445 and Louise A. Tilly, "Comments on the Yans-McLaughlin and Davidoff Papers," ibid., pp. 452-459.

3. Tilly, unpublished version of "Comments on Yans-McLaughlin," pp. 1-2.

4. I am not here making philosophical and psychological assumptions concerning a dichotomy between objective and subjective experience; the dichotomy is a useful heuristic device, and that is the sense in which I intend it.

5. Tilly, "Comments on Yans-McLaughlin," *Journal of Social History*, p. 452.

6. Interview with C.D., Buffalo, New York, April 16, 1974.

7. Virginia Yans-McLaughlin, "Patterns of Work and Family Organization: Buffalo's Italians," *Journal of Social History* 2 (Autumn 1971): 299-314, discusses Italian women and work.

8. Vincent Crapanzano at City College of New York conference on oral history and oral traditions, May 1974.

9. A search of the New York State Manuscript Census, 1905, and the U.S. Federal Manuscript Census, 1900, for Buffalo, New York, revealed this to be true. Caroline Golab, "The Impact of the Industrial Experience on the Immigrant Family: The Huddled Masses Reconsidered" (unpublished paper, University of Pennsylvania, November 1973): p. 30, emphasizes that many married Polish women worked as domestics. Golab points out that it is difficult to estimate the percentages of women in domestic work because of "irregular, unregulated . . . private arrangements between women and their employers."

10. Michael Anderson, *Family Structure in Nineteenth Century Lancashire* (Cambridge, England, 1971): 71; San Bass Warner, "If All the World Were Philadelphia: A Scaffolding for Urban History, 1774-1930," *American Historical Review* 84, no. 1 (October 1968): 31.

11. Margaret Mead, *Male and Female: A Study of Sexes in a Changing World* (New York, 1949), pp. 194-195, 140.

12. Ibid., p. 168.

13. Ibid.

14. On the canneries, see Yans-McLaughlin, "A Flexible Tradition."

15. See Yans-McLaughlin, "Patterns of Work and Family Organization."

16. Male unemployment was not an entirely new experience for immigrants any more than it had been for them as agricultural laborers in Italy. The Italian family withstood it as well in the New World as it had in the Old. For a discussion of this point, see Yans-McLaughlin, "Patterns of Work and Family Organization," pp. 303, 312.

17. See, for example, Louise Odencrantz, *Italian Women in Industry: A Study of Conditions in New York City* (New York, 1919). Still, most of these women were single.

18. On women's work patterns in Italy, see Yans-McLaughlin, "Patterns of Work and Family Organization."

19. Interview with V. DeB., Buffalo, New York, April 16, 1973.

20. Leonard Covello, "The Social Background of the Italo-American School Child: A Study of the Southern Italian Family Mores and Their Effect on the School Situation in America" (Ph.D. dissertation, New York University, 1944), pp. 321ff; Phyllis H. Williams, *South Italian Folkways in Europe and America* (New Haven, 1938), p. 81; Celina Baxter, "Sicilian Family Life," *The Family* 14 (May 1933): 84.

21. New York State Manuscript Census, 1905.

22. Yans-McLaughlin, "Patterns of Work and Family Organization," p. 309.

23. John Daniels, "Polish Laborers and Their Needs," *Buffalo Express*, March 13, 1910; see Golab, "The Impact of the Industrial Experience on the Immigrant Family," p. 29, on Poles in Philadelphia.

24. New York State, *Second Report of the Factory Investigating Commission*, vol. 2, Appendix IV, "Manufacturing in the Tenements," (Albany, 1913), pp. 684-685.

25. On the canneries and work, see Yans-McLaughlin, "A Flexible Tradition."

26. Robert A. Woods and Robert J. Kennedy, *Young Working Girls: A Summary of Evidence from Two Thousand Social Workers* (Boston, 1913), pp. 59, 23.

27. Testimony of Mary Chamberlain, quoting Italian factory workers, Nov. 26, 1912, *Second Report of the Factory Investigating Commission*, vol. 2, p. 10014.

28. Elizabeth Beardsley Butler, "The Working Women of Pittsburgh, *The Survey* 23 (1910): 573.

29. Elias Tobenkin, "The Immigrant Girl in Chicago," *The Survey* 23 (1909): 190.

30. Interview with M.C., Buffalo, New York, April 16, 1973.

31. Interview with J.A., Buffalo, New York, April 16, 1973.

32. Scott and Tilly, "Women's Work and the Family in Nineteenth-Century Europe," also emphasize the importance of domestic work, home industry, and light manufacturing as entry points into the urban industrial labor force for women from traditional cultures.

33. Derived from U.S. Government, Department of Commerce and Labor, *Thirteenth Census of the United States*, vol. 4, *Occupational Statistics* (Washington, D.C., 1914), p. 543.

34. Scott and Tilly, "Women's Work and the Family in Nineteenth-Century Europe," also point to these occupations as an extension of traditional household routines.

35. See Valerie Kincaid Oppenheimer, "Demographic Influences on Female Employment and the Status of Women," *American Journal of Sociology* 78, no. 4 (January 1973): 946-961, and Robert W. Smuts, *Women and Work in America* (New York, 1959), p. 19ff.

36. Eleanor G. Coit, "An Industrial Study, Buffalo, New York" (unpublished paper, Business and Industrial Department, Young Women's Christian Association, 1922), p. 45, notes that few non-English-speaking women worked in Buffalo factories.

37. The following figures are from the New York State Manuscript Census, Buffalo, New York, 1905.

38. Actually, the proportion of single Polish women is underestimated because the 1905 sample included only single women living in family households. All Buffalo Italians are used as the basis for comparison.

39. See John Daniels, "Americanizing 80,000 Poles," *Charities and the Common Good* 24 (June 4, 1910): 379.

Because Poland was not a nation-state at the time, early twentieth-century census figures do not distinguish between Austria, German, and Russian Poles, but 1910 sex ratios for these nations — respectively, 169.8, 102.3, 180.8 — suggest that Polish males predominated. The figures are from U.S. Government, *Thirteenth Census of the United States, Population*, vol. 1, p. 871. The German ratio is low; many of Buffalo's Germans came early in the nineteenth century and had been settled in the city for some time. These non-Polish Germans probably explain the relatively balanced ratio.

40. See, for example, Amy Bernardy, "L' Emigrazione delle donne e dei fanciulli italiana," *Bolletino dell' Emigrazione* no. 1 (1909): 8ff.

41. Barbara Klaczynska, "Why Women Work?: A Theory for Comparison of Ethnic Groups," *Labor History* 17 (Winter 1976): 73-87.

42. Personal communication from Michael Ebner.

43. Golab, "The Impact of the Industrial Experience on the Immigrant Family," p. 29; Odencrantz, *Italian Women in Industtry*, p. 33; Bernardy, "L'Emigrazione delle donne," pp. 8ff.

44. Personal communication from Herbert G. Gutman, based on New York State Manuscript Census, New York, New York 1905. This probably is an underestimate since we know that Italian women did not always report their part-time occupations to census canvassers.

45. Mary van Kleeck, *Artificial Flower Makers* (New York, 1913), pp. 32, 38.

46. Odencrantz, *Italian Women in Industry*, p. 176.

ITALIAN-AMERICAN WOMEN IN NEW YORK CITY, 1900-1950: WORK AND SCHOOL

6

by Miriam Cohen

There are two major premises underlying my analysis of Italian women in New York from 1900 to 1950. The first is that we must use the family unit as the context for examining Italian female behavior patterns.[1] It is generally true for all racial and ethnic groups that women's most important roles have been played out within the family unit as daughters, sisters and wives; certainly this has been true of Italian women.[2] Therefore, we must look at changing family needs to understand changes in the social behavior of Italian women. The second premise is that the changes in the family's needs and wants must be understood in the context of the changing social, economic, and political life of New York City.

To illustrate the connection between these two premises, discussion will focus on changes in the work and school patterns of first- and second-generation Italian-American women over the course of fifty years. Toward the end of the Great Depression, young Italian-American women began to attend school for a longer period of time and with greater regularity then their mothers and older sisters had. Why was this so? Historians have generally assumed that an increase in school attendance reflected aspects of behavioral and attitudinal changes that occurred as immigrants abandoned Old-World familial values and adopted American values, such as individualism, and American middle-class family styles, which emphasize the needs of children rather than those of adults. Certainly, social workers and reform advocates at that time assumed that such value changes were necessary in order for Italian families to change their attitude about the education of girls. My research suggests that Italian families did not have to adopt the views of the middle or upper classes in order for the increase in female school atten-

SOURCE: *Labor History* 16, no. 1 (Winter 1975).

dance to take place. Instead, we must look to important demographic and social changes which took place in New York City and within the Italian community for explanations.[3] There are, in fact, connections between changes in family size, infant mortality rates, job opportunities, and perhaps income levels, which affect family decisions about schooling. Much further research is needed in order to understand these linkages. I am going to deal with only one of those factors here, namely, how changes in the female employment structure affected the attitudes of Italian families toward female education. To do this, I will first describe the work and school patterns of Italian-American women during the first few decades in New York, then survey the changes in those patterns which had taken place in mid-century and, last, offer some explanations for those changes. Since the research for this project is still in progress, any conclusions I can draw at this point are necessarily tentative. They do, however, suggest areas for further investigation and revised ways of thinking about the acculturative process.[4]

In order to understand the work patterns of Italian immigrant women, we must realize that most of them emigrated from an agrarian society which was in large part organized around household production.[5] All members of the family contributed to the family's income in one way or another. In every place but Sicily, it was normal for women to work in the fields. They generally did their work in groups and worked separately from men. Even in parts of Sicily, women helped their husbands and adolescent sons pick grapes during harvest time. Women also contributed to family production through spinning, weaving, dress making, and embroidery. They tilled gardens, tended animals, and threshed wheat. In addition, married women had full responsibility for supervising the children during the day while their husbands were working away from home. In the early period of Italian immigration to America, males predominated. During those years, Italian women, left behind in Italy, managed both domestic and economic activities for long periods of time without their husbands' aid.[6]

When families were reunited in New York, familial priorities survived; all were expected to, and did, contribute to the maintenance of the family. However, as the century progressed, the ways in which Italian women contributed to this maintenance changed with the changing demands of the urban environment.

Italian women who arrived in New York City during the first two decades of the twentieth century usually joined family groups in which the earning capacity of the male members was quite low. A large number of Italian men worked as hod carriers, tailors, and cobblers, but the greatest proportion did unskilled labor, which included street cleaning, painting, digging, shoveling, dock labor, and unskilled factory and construction work.[7] Such labor not only commanded low wages but also was irregular. Most of the outdoor jobs were dependent on the weather while much indoor employment varied with seasonal demand. Under these circumstances, many Italian men were unemployed several months of the year. Seventy-six percent of Italian household heads earned less than $600 annually, with the average income being $519, one of the lowest figures among all the immigrant groups surveyed.[8] (See Table 1.) Thus Italian families were faced with a strong financial motive for sending women to work.

Complementing Italian economic needs, New York City provided enormous employment opportunity for women, offering many jobs in small-scale industries, which have been traditional employers of women throughout the world. In addition, it was the center of the garment industry and also important for the manufacturing of other consumer's goods, such as candy, tobacco, and artificial flowers. All of these industries were heavy employers of female workers. Such labor did not require knowledge of English and made use of traditional skills that were easily learned or were extensions of household skills which Italian women brought with them from Europe. Moreover, many male and female relatives who had arrived earlier already worked in these enterprises and were able to help newcomers to secure employment.

And so Italian females flocked to work. Italian adult women made up 68 percent of the female work force in the men's garment industry in New York.[9] (See Table 2.) South Italian women made up the largest number, 36.2 percent, of the female work force of the entire garment industry (both men's and women's clothing).[10] South Italian women also dominated the artificial-flower and feather industries, representing 72 percent of the occupational force. Large numbers also worked in custom dress making as well as in paper-bag and tobacco factories.[11]

TABLE 1

Average Earnings per Year of Male Heads of Families (foreign-born)		Percentage of Women 16 Years Old and Over at Work (foreign-born)	
Negro*	$439	Negro*	65.6%
Slovak	$507	Bohemian and Moravian	62.8
Hebrew, other	$508	Italian, southern	45.5
Italian, southern	$519	Slovak	41.2
Hebrew, Russian	$520	German	41.0
Magyar	$580	Magyar	36.5
Bohemian and Moravian	$612	Hebrew, Russian	34.0
German	$676	Hebrew, Other	31.1
Irish	$676	Irish	22.9

*Includes native and foreign-born.

SOURCE: U.S. Congress, Senate, Immigration Commission, *Immigrants in Cities*, vol. 1 (Washington, 1911), pp. 228, 220. A Spearman's Rho coefficient of 0.39 indicates an inverse association between the income of male household heads and the percentage of women working in their respective communities. Spearman's Rho is an elementary rank order coefficient. In this particular case, a coefficient of 0.36 or greater would be necessary in order to indicate that a pattern exists. See Charles Dollar and Richard J. Jensen, *Historian's Guide to Statistics* (Huntington, New York, 1971), chapter 3.

Turning to the Italian female population of New York City as a whole rather than to the employment structure of certain industries, 45.5 percent of Italian women over sixteen years of age were gainfully employed, a higher percentage than all other ethnic groups surveyed, except for Bohemian and Moravian women (considered as one category), and almost double the national figure for all women recorded as working during this period.[12] (See Table 1.)

Like most white women, the majority of Italian married women stayed at home to care for children and keep house while their single sisters and daughters went to the factories. However, the city's demand for female labor was so great and the economic need often so critical that large numbers of Italian married women, particularly those without children, worked outside the home in garment shops.[13] In 1910 the percentage of married Italian women who worked in the men's clothing industry was far greater than that of any other immigrant nationality. Of a group of 249, as many as 32 percent worked away from home in shops.[14]

Thousands of Italian wives also contributed to the family income by working at home. During the early years of the twentieth century, many industries offered women such work because production processes were decentralized and required little or no machinery. Seventeen percent of all women employed in the men's garment industry were home workers, almost all being Italian wives and mothers.[15] Home work was done in approximately 25 percent of the apartments occupied by Italians; in almost all cases, it was done by wives, who often had help from other members of the household.[16] Finally, many married women contributed to the family income by taking care of boarders.[17]

Italian women, like most females employed in manufacturing jobs, were engaged in seasonal work. Nevertheless, unlike Italian females in Buffalo (in Virginia Yans-McLaughlin's findings), those in New York City and their families apparently did not consider women's work as supplementary to men's.[18] When evaluating the importance of women's income for the family, it is important to remember that males also faced the problems of irregular earnings. As soon as New York City women were fired from one job, they began to search for other employment: of a group of 279 working women, over one-third had held at least two jobs, and one-fourth had held more during the preceding year.[19]

Throughout the first few decades of the twentieth century, Italian-American women continued to respond to the demand for female labor which was so characteristic of New York City. Be-

cause the nature of industrial employment changed so little in New
York during those decades, women were able to work in the same
kinds of jobs. They continued to labor in small clothing factories
and workshops, hat factories, and artificial-flower shops. Grad-
ually, in family units in which the males received a steady income
and there were children (both male and female) of working age,
their combined earnings could bring wage stability and, eventually,
better housing as well as an overall improvement in living conditions. [20]

However, low wages, unemployment, and inability to move out
of unskilled labor categories continued to be a problem for the
Italian community, particularly among those who remained in the
inner city. [21] Data for them indicate the extent to which even young
children and mothers were employed to help the family survive in
face of dire economic conditions. A 1920 survey of Italian women
conducted in the Mulberry Street District, in the heart of Little
Italy, found that approximately 50 percent of those between fourteen and twenty years old were gainfully employed; 29.1 percent of
those between twenty-one and forty-four were working; and 21
percent of all housewives had jobs, 16 percent in factories, stores,
and domestic service, and 5 percent in home work. [22]

Because New York's apparel industry remained decentralized
married women and young children continued to help their families
during economic crises by doing home work. During the height of
the Great Depression, surveys of the Mulberry Street neighborhood
showed that while younger women were having an increasingly
hard time finding factory work, older women were returning to the
ranks of gainful employees as home workers. [23] During the early
and middle thirties, home work flourished in the men's garment
and the artificial-flower industries. [24] The increase in home work
was so noticeable that it engendered labor agitation on the part of
the city's garment unions and eventually led to stiffer state and
federal labor legislation.

Beside being gainfully employed, which made great demands on
her time, the married woman was also occupied with her family as
child rearer and housekeeper. If she had boarders, there were
added duties as cook and cleaner. To aid in both domestic duties
and industrial employment, she naturally turned to her offspring,

who helped to make flowers or put hooks on pants as soon as they were physically able to do so. (See Table 2.) As they grew older, boys usually did odd jobs, such as selling newspapers or helping their father peddle goods. Daughters continued to assist their mothers in home work and also to care for younger children, thereby enabling mothers to work at home or, if necessary, in the factories. There are countless personal descriptions of these activities.

> I am a little girl, eleven years old. I live on Jones St. in a tenement. I have many sisters and brothers and we all help do the work in our house.
>
> Every morning before school, I sweep out three rooms and help get breakfast. Then I wash the dishes.
>
> After school I do my homework for an hour, then I make flowers. All of us, my sisters, my cousins, my aunts, my mother work on flowers. We put the yellow centers into forget-me-nots. It takes me over an hour to finish one gross and I make three cents for that. If we all work all our spare time after school, we can make as much as two dollars between us.
>
> In the mornings, on the way to school, I leave finished flowers at the shop, and stop for more work on the way home.
>
> In the summer, we do not make flowers. But I mind Danny, my baby brother, all the time. My mother says she would rather work in a shop than have to mind bad kids. But she does not go to work, she stays at home and I do lots of housework for her. Sometimes I do the washing.
>
> In the summer I don't have much time to play because always I must mind Danny. All during vacation, I carry lunch to my father. He works at a barber shop on 23rd Street and every day in summer I walk there and back for him.
>
> Sometimes I go to play a little while at night with

TABLE 2

Number and Percentage of Employees of Each Ethnic Group,
Men's Garment Industry (1910)

Females 16 years and over	No.	%
American	52	1.8
Bohemian	1	
German	220	7.5
Hebrew	510	17.0
Italian	1,996	67.7
Lithuanian	37	1.3
Polish	25	.8
Scandinavian	1	
Other groups	114	3.9
All groups	2,956	100.0%
Females 16 years and under		
American	1	2.6
Bohemian		
German		
Hebrew	6	15.3
Italian	30	76.9*
Lithuanian		
Polish		2.6
Scandinavian		0
Other groups	1	2.6
All groups	38	100.0%

*The large percentage of Italian children is in large part due to the numbers of Italian mothers doing home work.

SOURCE: U.S. Congress, Senate, Bureau of Labor, *Report on Conditions of Women and Child Wage Earners,* Part 6 (Washington, 1911), pp. 45, 46. This table is based on a survey of eighty-eight establishments in New York City. The data was compiled from both the records of employers and investigations of employee families.

the other children but I must mind Danny there because he does not like to go to bed until we do.
Then he gets so tired he goes right to sleep on my
lap and I carry him up. I think my brother is very
nice but I get tired minding him sometimes.[25]

With so many chores, it is not surprising to find that
Italian-American girls attended school for only a minimal period of
time, if at all. As soon as girls turned fourteen, they were eligible
for working papers, but if they had not completed the eighth grade
by then, they were required to wait until they were fifteen and had
completed sixth grade.[26] The New York City Census of 1920 indicates a marked drop-off in school attendance for Italian girls in
Little Italy at the age of fifteen: of fourteen-year-old girls, 84 percent of the foreign-born who lived in the heart of Little Italy and 85
percent of the native-born were recorded as attending school. By
contrast, of the fifteen-year-old girls, only 48 percent of the
foreign-born and 51 percent of the second generation* were in
school.[27]

Moreover, while official records indicated that Italian families
were obeying the law by sending their female children to school until they were fourteen, social workers and school officials knew
otherwise, and they were very concerned about the Italians' lack of
appreciation of schooling. Numerous investigations indicated a
high level of truancy, and families would often pull their children
out of school for two or three days a week or have their chidren
attend school for half-day periods.[28] Naturally, this problem was
most acute in the neighborhoods where industrial home work was
prevalent.[29]

The effects of truancy showed up in official records which recorded the amount of grade retardation, as it was called, experienced by Italian children. Approximately 63 percent of the Italian-
American children aged ten to twelve were below the proper grade
for their age, a good 15 to 20 percent more than for almost all other
immigrant groups. Another study done in 1909 indicated that the
"retardation" rate of Italians was the highest of any ethnic
group.

*Foreign-born are considered first generation, and their native-born children second
generation.

In 1950, the U.S. Census Bureau asked first- and second-generation Italian females in the New York metropolitan area how many years of schooling they had completed and reported the statistics by age categories. [31] Four categories of Italian women had reached the age of fifteen by 1940: those foreign-born who were (1) twenty-five to forty-four and (2) forty-five and over, and those native Americans who were (3) twenty-five to forty-four and (4) forty-five and over. In all categories except native-born women of Italian parents aged twenty-five to forty-four, the median number of school years completed by the groups was 8.2 years or less. Among the foreign-born over forty-five, only 7 percent had finished at least one year of high school. Among native-born women forty-five and over, only 20 percent had finished at least one year of high school. Among foreign-born women aged twenty-five to forty-four, 27 percent had completed the ninth grade, and 14 percent had completed the twelfth grade. Only in the younger American category (native-born women aged twenty-five to forty-four) do we see the median number of years of completed education increase to 1½ years of high school; in this group, 55 percent had completed at least one year of secondary education and 29 percent had graduated. [32] (See Table 3.)

By the 1940s, indeed, Italian-American women were attending school on a more regular basis, and larger numbers were staying on into the high-school years. In the late thirties, a decline in truancy took place both in the poorest neighborhoods and in the more economically stable communities, although the decrease occurred more slowly in the poor areas. [33] The surveyors who returned to the Mulberry Street District during the depression found that between 1930 and 1932, the percentage of adolescents who were attending high school, although still quite low, was on the increase even in this poor district. [34] In 1950 the median number of years of schooling completed by native-born Italian women aged fourteen to twenty-five was 11.2; 80 percent had completed at least one year of high school, and 39 percent had graduated. The percentage for women over the age of eighteen, if such data were available, would certainly be even higher. (For foreign-born women aged fourteen to twenty-five — only 1 percent of the female population in 1950 — the median number of years of school completed was 9.4). [35] (See Table 3.)

TABLE 3

Schooling, First- and Second-Generation Italian Families
New York — Northeastern New Jersey Standard Metropolitan Area, 1950

FOREIGN BORN

	Age		
	45 +	25-44	14-24
Total number females in group	177,210	41,505	6,735
Number completing one year high school or more	13,400	11,140	3,610
Percent completing one year high school or more	7%	27%	54%
Number completing four years high school or more	8,250	5,715	1,850
Percent completing four years high school or more	5%	14%	27%
Median number school years completed	4.3	8.2	9.4

Why did the increase in schooling take place at this time? That Italian-American daughters as a group were able to insist upon education is an intriguing but unrealistic thought. They did not, much like the vast majority of teen-age girls who lived with their parents, have that kind of control over such important decisions. Therefore, we must look to a changing trend in family decisions. After all the years of failure, had social reformers finally convinced Italian families that educating women was worthwhile? Or had the Italian community been exposed to American ideas and values for so long and so intensely that they finally got the message? Such questions are difficult to answer with hard evidence and they avoid the real

TABLE 3 (cont.)

NATIVE BORN, FOREIGN PARENTAGE

	Age		
	45 +	25-44	14-24
Total number females in group	58,045	292,955	126,325
Number completing one year high school or more	11,460	162,535	106,640
Percent completing one year high school or more	20%	55%	80%
Number completing four years high school or more	5,820	83,520	49,345
Percent completing four years high school or more	10%	29%	39%
Median number school years completed	8.2	9.6	11.2

SOURCE: U.S. *Census of Population,* 1950, vol. 4, *Special Reports,* Part 3A (Washington, 1954) p. 284.

inquiry, namely, why were the Italian families ripe for the message in the late thirties and forties and not earlier? We can begin tackling the problem by analyzing how the development of New York's employment structure helped to change attitudes toward female education among Italians.

New York City was a major center for the production of consumer goods after 1900, but as the century progressed, the tertiary sector of the economy, rather than manufacturing, showed the largest growth.[36] The city was, and still is, the center of business and sales operations of many major corporations. As modern corporations expanded during the century so, too, did clerical jobs for women. Communications work and mercantile establishments also grew rapidly in New York, providing many jobs for the female population. While manufacturing had dominated the female employment structure in New York at the turn of the century, by 1930 clerical work was the largest single category of female labor, occupying 30 percent of the city's female work force. Indeed, this percentage was almost twice that of the rest of the country, which indicates the dominance of office work in New York City.[37] By 1950, clerical and communications work accounted for 35 percent of the female work force in New York, sales another 6 percent, while manufacturing accounted for 23 percent. The last figure indicates that New York still offered a large number of factory jobs for women, but the dominance of the white-collar sector is obvious.[38]

Tertiary occupations, unlike factory labor, require education. To be a clerical worker, a bookkeeper or saleswoman, one must at least know how to read and write with some fluency and be competent at simple arithmetic. For more advanced secretarial skills, special courses in shorthand and typing were required. In short, a high-school education was necessary.

After 1920, Italian families sent women to work in industrial occupations. Even as late as 1940, 86 percent of the female workers in one neighborhood in Little Italy worked as factory operatives.[39] Therefore, investment in a daughter's education beyond minimal reading and writing skills was unnecessary.[40] To allow a young girl to stay in school was impractical, especially if she was needed to help at home while her mother worked. But this approach became less convincing as the Depression wore on. During the 1930s, a variety of political and social events began to converge which made a change of attitude toward education understandable.

First, during the Roosevelt years, it became increasingly more difficult for older women and their young children to contribute to family earnings through home work. High unemployment and low wages increased the agitation, on the part of the well-organized garment unions, for tighter legal restrictions on home work, including the prohibition of child labor in the home-work phase of the industry. During the early decades of the century, laws regulating home work as well as female child labor were loosely enforced and, moreover, were inadequate to meet conditions during the Depression.[41] In the 1930s, however, the combination of union pressure and the government's realization that such laws were necessary — to counteract high adult unemployment and cutthroat competition provided a powerful incentive for change. Eventually, by the end of the decade, both state and federal agencies passed and enforced protective legislation which significantly undermined the practice of home work.[42]

In addition, during the New Deal, the state took a much more active role in making sure that children attended school regularly and for as long as possible. In earlier years, social workers had despaired because, despite official statements, truant officers were lax about rounding up children in poor neighborhoods and enforcing the compulsory school attendance law. Indeed, welfare workers reported that children were brought in by officials only to find that no desks or chairs were available for them.[43] During the Depression decade, however, when the government determinedly began to root out the child and youth labor from New York manufacturing, school construction and attendance both increased, attendance violations were enforced, the age for compulsory education was raised, and it became more difficult for underage students to receive employment certificates or to work illegally.[44]

State pressure to remain in school found reinforcement in the altered perspective of Italian families. There was little alternative. Since no jobs were available, children might as well spend the time in school, hoping that the future will be better.[45] During the Depression, consequently, the city's high-school attendance went up in general and among Italians in particular (just as we are finding an increase in college attendance during the current recession). But there was another factor which also accounted for rising education curves: Italian families were orienting their daughters toward white-collar work because the future there looked better than in factory labor. This was not necessarily because more money could be earned in office work, but because such work, requiring greater education, appeared to be more secure. During the Depression, unemployment hit factory operatives first and hardest. A community like the Italian, heavily dependent on blue-collar work suffered severely. Clerical work which developed later was less affected. [46]

New York officials understood that white-collar employees suffered less than industrial workers during the Depression. In fact, the Superintendent of Schools believed that city schools ought to adjust their educational training accordingly. For years they had extensive evening-school programs designed to train young working-class adults to fill manufacturing jobs, but that no longer seemed a viable strategy. "The unemployed were those who fitted in with the old order of things," the Superintendent concluded in his annual report of 1937-1938. "Too much stress had been placed [in the schools] on the so-called specialized trades . . . . Broader vocational training appeared to be the solution to the problem." The New York evening schools were therefore becoming more like general high schools, "replacing the more obvious subjects usually associated with evening schools with English, Journalism, Math and French." He hoped that students would acquire more flexible job skills in this way and would be better able to fit the needs of the job market. [47]

Did Italian families understand the need for a general education and did this affect decisons made within their families? Certainly they could look about them and see, from the evidence of their own neighborhoods, that clerical workers were somewhat better off, as figures from the 1932 Mulberry Street District survey indicate. [48] Much more proof still must be collected on this question, but it seems likely that Italians were beginning to understand the changing situation and acted accordingly by keeping their daughters in school so that they could train for white-collar work.

A change in strategy, of course, would make sense if white-collar jobs were opening up for Italian-American women in New York. In fact, prejudice against hiring ethnic women in offices, so prevalent in the 1900s, was decreasing by mid-century, particularly prejudice against second-generation females. With second-generation Americans beginning to set up their own businesses, it became easier for ethnic women to obtain white-collar jobs. State and local government bureaucracies also grew appreciably during this period, offering a further source of clerical work for females. Finally, after World War II, the demand for office workers was so great that ethnic women readily obtained positions with large corporations. [49] (By contrast, blacks and Puerto Rican women experienced deeper and stronger forms of prejudice and were effectively blocked from white-collar jobs so they took up the jobs in manufacturing and service occupations.)

By 1950, the second generation of Italian-American females had entered the ranks of clerical workers in large numbers. While only 8 percent of the first generation of Italian female workers were employed in clerical labor, 40 percent of the second generation were in those occupations. Among the youngest group of second-generation workers, females aged fourteen to twenty-four, 58 percent had clerical jobs. [50]

Interestingly, the shift in the female employment pattern took place faster than that for Italian-American males. In 1950 a breakdown of occupations by categories for second-generation Italian males shows that only 17 percent were employed in clerical jobs. If we add those who worked in professions or business, we find 33 percent of the second-generation males in white-collar jobs, compared with 47 percent of the females. For the youngest age cohort, ages fourteen to twenty-five, we find that 24 percent of the men were employed in clerical jobs; adding the other white-collar jobs, we get 31 percent of the men in such occupations as opposed to 62 percent of the females (see Table 4, pp. 136-137). [51] Clearly, the increase in clerical jobs accounts for the rapid change in the female employment structure.

The change was not accompanied by any comparable shift of Italian families out of working-class ranks. Therefore, we must perceive the changes in female work and school patterns for New York's Italian-American women not as part of the process of *embourgeoisement* of American ethnics but as a shift in working-class family strategies which were made necessary by the changes in the city's employment structure. [52] Italian-American women emerged after World War II a little more educated than their mothers and skilled enough to take a place in the new white-collar working class, so much of which was female in 1950.

TABLE 4

Percentage Occupational Distribution, First- and Second-
Generation Italians

New York — Northeastern New Jersey Standard Metropolitan Area, 1950*

Male

Age	Foreign-Born				Native-Born, Foreign Parents			
	Total	45+	25-44	14-24	Total	45+	25-44	14-24
Professional	3	3	5	3	6	7	7	4
Managerial	13	14	12	4	10	16	11	3
Clerical	6	5	9	10	17	14	16	24
Craftsmen	24	24	25	21	22	22	22	18
Operatives	24	24	27	35	29	23	28	34
Private Household	—	—	—	—	—	—	—	—
Service	14	15	10	9	6	10	7	4
Laborers	14	15	10	16	6	7	8	11
Not Reported	1	1	—	—	1	—	—	1
Total Number	196,775	153,405	39,475	3,895	369,405	49,650	254,520	65,435

Female

Age	Foreign-Born				Native-Born, Foreign Parents			
	Total	45+	25-44	14-24	Total	45+	25-44	14-24
Professional	2	2	4	3	5	4	5	4
Managerial	4	4	3	1	2	5	3	—
Clerical	8	4	12	28	40	19	31	58
Craftsmen	2	3	2	1	2	3	3	1
Operatives	77	80	73	62	44	58	51	31
Private Household	1	1	—	—	—	1	—	—
Service	4	4	3	2	4	7	4	3
Laborers	—	—	—	1	—	—	—	—
Not Reported	1	1	1	1	1	1	1	1
Total Number	51,720	33,510	14,925	3,285	177,260	14,955	97,910	64,395

*Numbers constituting less than 1 percent are recorded as blank (—). This table also does not include farming categories, which also include well under 1 percent of the population.
SOURCE: U.S. *Census of Population*, 1950, vol. 4, *Special Reports*, Part 3A (Washington, 1954), p. 284.

NOTES

1. Thanks to Anne Bobroff, Donna Gabaccia, Michael Hanagan, Robin Jacoby, Leslie Moch, Elizabeth Pleck, Charles Tilly, the University of Michigan History Department Women's Caucus, and as always, to Louise Tilly, for comments and criticisms on an earlier version of this paper.

2. For a discussion of the different roles women played in the public and private spheres, see Michelle Rosaldo, "Women, Culture and Society: A Theoretical Overview," in Michelle Rosaldo and Louise Lamphere, *Women, Culture and Society* (Stanford, California, 1974), pp. 17-42.

3. Charles Tilly discusses the problems of attributing changes in peasant family behavior and attitudes towards children to the absorption of bourgeois values. See "Population and Pedagogy," *History of Education Quarterly* 13 (1973): 113-128. For the traditional view, see Caroline Ware, *Greenwich Village, 1920-1930* (New York, 1935).

4. This paper stems from dissertation research on Italian-American women in New York City, 1900-1950.

5. The vast majority of Italian immigrants to the United States came after 1880. The peak years were between 1900 and 1910; most came from southern rather than northern Italy. See Robert Foerster, *The Italian Emigration of Our Times* (Cambridge, 1919), and the Federal Writers Project, WPA, *The Italians in New York* (New York, 1938).

6. On southern Italian society, see Charlotte Gower Chapman, *Milocca: A Sicilian Village* (Cambridge, 1971); Sydel Silverman, "Agriculture Organization, Social Structure and Values in Italy: Amoral Familism Reconsidered," *American Anthropologist* 70, no. 1 (1968): 1-20; and "Life Crisis as a Clue to Social Function," *Anthropological Quarterly* 40, no. 3 (1967): 127-138. Also see Leonard Moss and Walter H. Thompson, "The Southern Italian Family: Literature and Observation," *Human Organization* 18, no. 1: 35-41, and Louise A. Tilly, "Comments on the Yans-McLaughlin and Davidoff Papers," *Journal of Social History* 7, no. 4 (1974): 452-459. On the peasant economy see Eric Wolf, *Peasants* (Englewood Cliffs, New Jersey, 1966) and Basile Kerlslay, "Chayanov and the Theory of the Peasantry as a Specific Type of Economy," in Theodore Shanin, *Peasants and Peasant Society* (Middlesex, England, 1971), pp. 150-160.

7. See Foerster, *The Italian Emigration of Our Times*; Louise C. Odencrantz, *The Italian Women in Industry* (New York, 1919). Also see John J. Alesandre, *Occupational Trends of Italians in New York City, Casa Italiana Educational Bureau Bulletin* No. 8 (New York, 1935).

8. U.S. Congress, Senate, Immigration Commission, *Immigrants in Cities*, S. Doc. 5665, 61 Congress, 2nd session, 1911, vol. 1, (Washington, 1911), p. 234.

9. U.S. Congress, Senate, Bureau of Labor, *Report on Conditions of Women and Child Wage Earners*, S. Doc. 5685, 61st Congress, 2nd Session, vol. 2 (Washington, 1911), p. 46.

10. U.S. Congress, Senate, Immigration Commission, *Immigrants in Industries*, S. Doc. 5672, 61st Congress, 2nd Session, 1911, vol. 10, part 6, (Washington, 1911), p. 372.

11. See Mary Van Kleeck, *Artificial Flower Makers* (New York, 1913), p. 30.

12. U.S., Immigration Commission, *Immigrants in Cities,* vol. 1, p. 22

13. Valerie Kincaid Oppenheimer, in her article "Demographic Influences on Female Employment and the Status of Women" in the *American Journal of Sociology* 78, no. 4 (1973): 946-961, discusses the importance of understanding the demand for female jobs as a factor in determining the numbers of women who work. Elizabeth Hafkin Pleck suggests that Italian married women worked in New York City because the wage structure there was higher than elsewhere in the country. See "A Mother's Wages," unpublished paper (1975). Also see Miriam Cohen, "Italian-American Women in New York City, 1900-1903," unpublished paper, 1973, and Louise Tilly and Joan Scott, "Married Women's Work in England and France," unpublished paper, 1974.

14. Odencrantz, *The Italian Women in Industry*, p. 152.

15. U.S. Bureau of Labor, *Report on Conditions of Women and Child Wage Earners*, Part 6, pp. 35, 221.

16. U.S. Immigration Commission, *Immigrants in Cities*, vol. 1, p. 204.

17. Ibid., vol. 1, p. 231.

18. See Virginia Yans-McLaughlin, "Patterns of Work and Family Organization: Buffalo's Italians," *Journal of Interdisciplinary History* 2, no. 2 (1971): 299-314.

19. Odencrantz, *The Italian Women in Industry*, p. 20.

20. For a description of such families living in the Italian section of Greenwich Village during the 1920s, see Ware, *Greenwich Village, 1920-1930*, p. 73.

21. See Alesandre, *Occupational Trends of Italians in New York City*, pp. 6-10.

22. John J. Gebhardt, *The Health of a Neighborhood: A Social Study of the Mulberry District*, (The New York Association for Improving the Conditions of the Poor, 1924), Russell Sage Collection, City College of New York, p. 9.

23. Gwendolyn H. Berry, *Idleness and the Health of a Neighborhood: A Social Study of the Mulberry District*, (The New York Association for Improving the Conditions of the Poor, 1933), pp. 10, 17.

24. New York State, Department of Labor, *Homework in the Artificial Flower and Feather Industry in New York State* (1938), Special Bulletin No. 199. Also see Jacob Luft, "Workers in the New York City Men's Clothing Industry: Report of a Preliminary Sample Study," *Jewish Social Studies* 133, and Amalgamated Clothing Workers of America, *Fiftieth Anniversary Souvenir History of the New York Joint Board, Amalgamated Clothing Workers of America, AFL-CIO, 1914-1964*, ACWA Archives, New York City, New York.

25. Greenwich House, *Thirteenth Annual Report*, 1913-1914, Russell Sage Collection, City College of New York, p. 18.

26. On New York State school law, see U.S. Department of Labor, Children's Bureau, *States and Child Labor*, Publication No. 13 (1919). Also see Jeremy Felt, *Hostages of Fortune, Child Labor Reform in New York State* (Syracuse, 1965).

Census for New York City is recorded in Walter Lindlaw, *Statistical Sources for Demographic Studies of Greater New York* (New York, 1920).

27. U.S. Department of Commerce, Bureau of the Census, *United States Census of Population: 1950*, vol. 4, *Special Reports*, Part 3A, p. 284. The New York metropolitan area includes New York City and its immediate surrounding areas in New York State and New Jersey. Such a report biases the results slightly upwards because Italians living in New Jersey tend to be better off economically than those in the city proper. However, in the cases of the older age cohorts, it is most likely that the women grew up and were educated in New York City. Even if the figures are biased, they do indicate a trend which allows us to compare the experience of New Yorkers and their slightly more mobile daughters. Aggregate census data must be used because the manuscript census schedules after 1900 are unavailable to the public.

28. See Kelly Durand and Louis Seswin, "The Italian Invasion of the Ghetto," *University Settlement Studies* 1, no. 4 (1908): Lillian Betts, "Italians in New York," *University Settlement Studies* 1, no. 3, (1908): Greenwich House, *Annual Reports, 1900-1925*. Also see the New York State Factory Investigating Committee, *Minutes of the Public Hearings in New York City, October 1912*, second series, reprint from the *Preliminary Report, New York State Factory Investigating Committee* (March 1912), p. 1739, testimony of Lillian Wald.

29. See New York State Factory Investigating Committee, *Minutes of the Public Hearings in New York City*, pp. 1735-1747, testimony of Lillian Wald, and pp. 1593-1602, testimony of Florence Kelley. Also see Odencrantz, *Italian Women in Industry*.

30. U.S. Congress, Senate, Immigration Commission, *The Children of Immigrants in Schools*, S. Doc. 5874, 61st Congress, 2nd session, 1911, vol. 4, p. 614.

31. U.S Department of Commerce, Bureau of the Census, *United States Census of Population: 1950*, vol. 4, *Special Reports*, Part 3A (Washington, 1954), p. 284. The New York City metropolitan area includes the immediate surrounding urban and surburban areas in New York State and New Jersey. Therefore, the data reported can be used only to approximate the change in school patterns for New York Italians. The 1950 census is used here because the information on schooling patterns by age cohorts for two generations offers the best data yet available. The state and federal manuscript census schedules for the mid-twentieth century are unavailable to the public. The completed study will make use of available records of individual high schools in New York. However, for purposes here, it was decided that the value of the information offered by the published U.S. Census of 1950 outweighed its problems. We can take comfort in knowing that the female occupational structure in the New Jersey area approximated the New York experience throughout the period. It is unlikely that a different social experience in the outlying regions would greatly alter the pattern among those Italians living outside the city proper. While Italians living in the suburban areas tend to be better off economically than those in the city proper, it is most likely that in the case of the older age cohorts, the women grew up and were educated in New York City or other urban areas in the region.

32. The discrepancy in school achievement between first- and second-generation

females aged twenty-five to forty-four is probably due to several factors. First, there were greater difficulties in overcoming language barriers among the foreign-born. The discrepancy can also be explained, in part, by the difference in the age distributions within the two categories. In the foreign-born category, the majority of women were closer to the age limit, forty-four, while in the native-born group, more women were closer to age twenty. (For the age structure of the female population, see Massimo Liui Bacci, *Gli Italiani negli Stati Uniti Secondo le Statische Demographiche Americae* (Milano, 1961), pp. 44, 92.) Hence, among the foreign-born, more women would have reached age fifteen before the end of the Great Depression when the increase in female school attendance took place.

33. Leonard Covello, *The Social Background of the Italo-American School Child* (New York, 1967), p. 286. Also see Selma Berrol, "Education and the Italian and Jewish Community Experience," in Jean Scarpaci, ed., *The Interaction Between Italians and Jews in America* (The American Italian Historical Association, 1975), pp. 31-41.

34. Berry, *Idleness and the Health of a Neighborhood*, p. 21.

35. U.S. Department of Commerce, Bureau of the Census, *United States Census of Population: 1950*, vol. 4, *Special Reports*, Part 3A (Washington, 1954), p. 284.

36. The tertiary sector of the economy refers to all those occupations other than agriculture (the primary sector) and manufacturing (the secondary sector). It includes white-collar and service and sales jobs.

37. Personnel Research Federation, *Occupational Trends in New York City: Changes in the Distribution of Gainful Workers* (New York, 1935), Charts 1 and 2.

38. U.S. Department of Commerce, Bureau of the Census, *Census of Population: 1950*, vol. 2, *Characteristics of the Population*, Part 32, New York State (Washington, 1952), pp. 266, 267, 269, 272, 273, 275. (The figures quoted in the text are for the city proper: for the metropolitan area, we find that 34 percent of the female workers were engaged in clerical work, while 24 percent were operatives.)

39. U.S. Department of Commerce, Bureau of the Census, *Sixteenth Census of the United States, 1940: Population and Housing, Statistics for Health Areas, New York City*, (Washington, 1942), p. 135.

40. Lillian Brandt pointed to this phenomenon as early as 1904. In her study of Italian school children, she contrasted the attitudes of Italian parents and American parents, stating that American families kept their children in school so that they could fill clerical jobs. See "A Transplanted Birthright," *Charities* 2 (1904): 494-497. A rereading of Covello indicates that he too felt that there was at least some connection between Italian attitudes toward education and the employment structure. See Covello, *The Social Background of the Italo-American School Child*.

41. See New York State, Department of Labor, *Report on Manufacturing in Tenements Submitted to the Commission to Examine the Laws Relating to Child Welfare* (New York, 1924), and New York State, Department of Labor, *Homework in the Artifical Flower and Feather Industry in New York State*. Also see Lazare Teper and Nathan Weinberg, "Aspects of Industrial Homework in the Apparel Trades," International Ladies Garment Workers Research Paper, 1941, Russell

Sage Collection, City College of New York: Russell Lindquist and Donald K. Smith, "Industrial Homework," *Minnesota Law Review* 29 (1944-1945): 295-317; Donald Martha, "Wage, Hour and Child Labor Legislation in the Roosevelt Administration," *Lawyers Guild Review* 5, no. 3 (1945): 185-191.

42. See Teper and Weinberg, "Aspects of Industrial Home Work," and Martha, "Wage, Hour and Child Labor Legislation." The Roosevelt Administration tried to wipe out home work as early as the NRA era; when the NRA was declared unconstitutional, agitation to eliminate home work continued on the state and federal levels. The Fair Labor Standards Act of 1938 did in fact provide the strongest federal measures to date except for the NRA provisions. The ILGWU apparently felt that the FLSA would not abolish home work but would serve to encourage subterfuge operations (see Teper). But by 1945, apparently thanks to government enforcement on the state and federal levels, the problem had been fairly well routed out of the garment industry. (See Martha and Lindquist and Smith, "Industrial Homework.")

43. See N.Y. State Factory Committee, *Minutes of the Public Hearings in New York*, second series, pp. 1735-1747, testimony of Lillian Wald, and Betts, "The Italians in New York," p. 100.

44. See Works Progress Administration Historical Records Survey, "New York Teams," Catalogue No. 3597, Article 19, Municipal Archives, New York City; and New York City Board of Education, *Youth in School and Industry, The Continuation of Schools and Their Problems* (1933-1934). Also see Felt, *Hostages of Fortune.*

45. See Berry, *Idleness and the Health of a Neighborhood*, p. 21. Also see WPA Historical Records Survey, Catalogue No. 3597.

46. In 1930, the U.S. Census Bureau found that in New York City, 15.6 percent of the men and 10.0 percent of the women in manufacturing were unemployed. They found that 6 percent of the males and 4.6 percent of the females in the clerical category were unemployed. From *Fifthteenth Census*, vol 2, *General Reports*, recorded in *Occupational Trends in New York City*, Index. On Italian economic and social conditions, see U.S. Department of Commerce, Bureau of Census, *Fifteenth Census of the United States, 1930: Special Report on Foreign Born White Families* (Washington, 1942), pp. 133-193. Also see Massimo Livi Bacci, *Gli Italiana negli Stati Uniti*, p. 58.

48. *Thirty-Ninth Annual Report of the Superintendent of Schools, 1936-37*, quoted in WPA Historical Records Survey, Catalogue No. 3597, Article 19, p. 19.

48. The Mulberry survey indicated, on the basis of a bar graph, that in 1930 approximately 50 percent of the clerical and 85 percent of the clothing workers were either idle or underemployed. In 1932, the figures jumped to 75 percent for the clerical and 85 percent for the clothing workers. See Berry, *Idleness and the Health of a Neighborhood*, p. 21.

49. Oppenheimer points out that the demand for office workers in the U.S. has become so large that even the traditional prejudice against hiring married women has been abated. See "Demographic Influence on Female Employment and the

Status of Women." Similarly, in New York City, discrimination against ethnic women had to decline in order to fill the need for female office workers.

50. U.S. Department of Commerce, Bureau of the Census, *United States Census of Population: 1950*, vol. 4, *Special Reports,* Part 3A, p. 284. See Note 31 above.

51. Ibid. Interestingly, the differences in the male and female occupational distributions appear to be reflected in the educational patterns of the two sexes. Whereas in the first generation, Italian women were less educated than men, the gap decreased in the second generation, particularly among younger people. In the youngest cohort of the second generation, females were slightly better educated than their male counterparts. Eighty percent of the females aged fourteen to twenty-four completed at least one year of high school, compared with 75 percent of the males. Since more women were working in white-collar positions, it makes sense that as a group, the females were more educated than their male counterparts.

52. Louise Tilly has also warned historians of the danger in assuming that the various changes in the behavior of working-class women in the nineteenth century are indications of the *embourgeoisement* of the working class. "Married Women's Work in England and France," Lecture given at the University of Michigan Colloquium on Comparative History, September 1975.

ORGANIZING THE UNORGANIZABLE: THREE JEWISH WOMEN AND THEIR UNION

7

by Alice Kessler-Harris

Women who were actively engaged in the labor struggles of the first part of this century faced a continual dilemma. They were caught between a trade-union movement hostile to women in the work force and a women's movement whose participants did not work for wages. To improve working conditions for the increasing numbers of women entering the paid labor force, organizers painstakingly solicited support from labor unions that should have been their natural allies. At the same time, they got sympathetic aid from well intentioned women with whom they otherwise had little in common. The wage-earning women who undertook the difficult task of organizing their co-workers faced yet another problem: they had to reconcile active involvement in labor unionism with community traditions that often discouraged worldly roles for women.

Understanding how women who were union organizers experienced these tensions tells us much about the relationships of men and women within unions and throws into relief some of the central problems which unionization posed for many working women. It also reveals something of what feminism meant for immigrant women. Evidence of conscious experience, frequently hard to come by, exists in the papers of three women who organized for the International Ladies Garment Workers Union (ILG): Pauline Newman, Fannia Cohn, and Rose Pesotta. All were Jews working for a predominately Jewish organization. Their careers spanned the first half of the twentieth century. Their lives, taken together, reveal a persistent conflict between their experiences as women and their tasks as union officers. Their shared Jewish heritage offers insight into the ways in which women tried to adapt familiar cultural traditions to the needs of a new world.

SOURCE: *Labor History* 17, no. 1 (Winter 1976).

Like most of the women whom they represented, Newman, Cohn, and Pesotta were born in Eastern Europe. Cohn and Newman emigrated as children before 1900, Pesotta as a teenager in 1913. Poverty drove them to the East Side's garment shops to work in the dress and waist industry, a rapidly expanding trade in which Jewish workers predominated until the 1930s and in which women made up the bulk of the work force. [1]

Their experiences were in many ways typical. Among immigrant Jews in New York, Philadelphia, Boston, and other large cities, only the exceptional unmarried woman did not operate a sewing machine in a garment factory for part of her young adult life.[2] In the old country, where jobs were scarce, daughters were married off as fast as possible. In America they were expected to work, for the family counted on their contributions. Many girls immigrated as teenagers, and they would seek out an uncle or older sister who might help them to find work so that some part of their wages could be sent back to Europe.[3] The wages of other young girls helped to pay the rent, to buy food and clothing, to bring relatives to America, and to keep brothers in school. The first job of the eldest daughter might mean a larger apartment for the family, "a dream of heaven itself accomplished."[4] When they married, young women normally stopped working in the garment shops. But much as in the old country, they were still expected to contribute to family income. Married women frequently took in boarders, ran small shops, or helped in the businesses of their husbands.

A combination of factory or sweatshop work before marriage and the expectation of a different kind of paid labor afterwards presented problems for Jewish women who, like Newman, Cohn, and Pesotta, wanted to take advantage of the possibilities offered by life in the new world. Young women who worked for wages could dream of self-sufficiency. [5] They could hope that the transition to America would bring about a heretofore unknown independence and offer them new and different roles. Seventeen-year-old Rose Pesotta (the name had been changed from Peisoty) left Russia because she could "see no future for [herself] except to marry some young man . . . and be a housewife. That [was] not enough . . . . In America a decent middle class girl [could] work without disgrace."[6]

Expectations of independent self-assertion were frustrated when marriage intervened and women were confined to more restricted roles. But aspirations toward upward mobility may have provided the deathblow. Jewish families moved up the ladder of economic success with legendary rapidity. As they did so, it became less necessary for wives to help out financially, and they were deprived of even the limited economic roles that marriage permitted. Their subsequent involvement in children and food soon became known as the "Jewish mother" syndrome. Yet the hard physical labor required of women who worked for wages around 1900 led them to seek escape from the work force as soon as possible. A folk song, reportedly first sung in Eastern Europe at the turn of the century and later heard in New York's sweatshops, records one woman's wish for a husband:

> Day the same as night, night the same as day.
> And all I do is sew and sew and sew
> May God help me and love come soon
> That I may leave this work and go.[7]

Women who hoped that they would soon marry and leave the shops joined trade unions only reluctantly, and male union leaders thought them poor candidates for membership.[8]

To choose a militant and active future among a people who valued marriage and the family as much as did most Eastern European Jews must have been extraordinarily difficult.[9] Women who decided to be continuously active in the labor movement knew consciously or unconsciously that they were rejecting traditional marriage. In her autobiography, Rose Schneiderman, just beginning a career in the Woman's Trade Union League, recalls her mother warning that being so busy, she would never get married![10] One woman organizer, who did marry, made the following comment when asked about children: "I wouldn't know what to do with them. First of all I never . . . we were very active, both of us, and then the unions. I don't think I . . . there were always meetings . . . so we had no time to have children. I am sorry now."[11] Even after so many years, her discomfort at talking about her unusual choice was apparent. Despite difficulties, many first-generation immigrant women, Newman and Cohn among them, did not marry.

Then there were those whose marriages did not survive the urge to independence. Rose Pesotta, for instance, divorced two husbands, and anarchist Emma Goldman and novelist Anzia Yezierska divorced one before seeking satisfying lives outside marriage.

These women were not entirely beyond the pale, since American-Jewish culture urged women into marriage while its injunction to self-sufficiency encouraged a militant sense of independence. In this respect, Jewish women may have been luckier than most. They came from a class-conscious background of which competitive individualism and the desire to make it in America were only two facets. A well-developed ethic of social justice was equally important and played its part in producing perhaps the most politically aware of all immigrant groups. Socialist newspapers predominated in the Yiddish-speaking Lower East Side. Jews were well represented in the Socialist Party after 1901 and were among the best organized of semi-skilled immigrants.[12] On the Lower East Side, as in Europe, women absorbed much of their community's concern for social justice.[13] A popular lullabye provides a clue to the extent to which women experienced a prevailing class consciousness:

> Sleep my child sleep.
> I'll sing you a lullabye.
> When my little baby's grown
> He'll know the difference and why.
>
> When my little baby's grown
> You'll soon see which is which.
> Like the rest of us, you'll know
> The difference between poor and rich.
>
> The largest mansions, finest homes
> The poor man builds them on the hill.
> But do you know who'll live in them?
> Why of course the rich man will!
>
> The poor man lives in a cellar,
> The walls are wet with damp.
> He gets pain in his arms and legs
> And a rheumatic cramp.[14]

There is no way of knowing whether Cohn, Newman, or Pesotta knew that song, but it is likely that they sang the following tune:

> No sooner in my bed
> Than I must up again
> To drag my weary limbs
> Off to work again.
>
> To God will I cry
> With a great outcry!
> Why was I born
> To be a seamstress, why?
>
> Should I once come late—
> 'Tis a long way—
> They dock me straight off
> A full half-day!
>
> The machines are old
> The needles they break.
> My bleeding fingers—
> Oh, how they ache!
>
> I've nothing to eat
> I'm hungry all the day.
> They tell me, forget it
> When I ask for pay! [15]

Like the women who sang them, the songs traveled to America, steerage class. In the garment shops of the Lower East Side, they could sometimes be heard over the noise of the machines, reflecting always the conscious desire of working women not only to get out of the shops but to make life in them better.

Faced with the exploitative working conditions characteristic of the early twentieth century, many women turned naturally to unionism. Founded and nurtured by Jewish-socialists from New York's Lower East Side, the ILG offered an appropriate organizing agency, and early expressions of enthusiasm indicate something of its romantic appeal. "I think the union is like a mother and father to its children," one young woman declared in 1913. "I'd give my whole life for the union."[16] Half a century after she joined the union in 1908, an eighty-year-old woman wrote to David Dubinsky, the ILG's president: "And I still have my membership book of that year. And I will keep it with reverence until the end of my days."[17] Another recalled her experience on the picket line: "I felt as if I were in the holy fight when I ran after a scab."[18]

It could be said of the early 1900s that Jewish women courted the unions that should have been courting them. Rose Schneiderman solicited the signatures of twenty-five cap makers before the union would acknowledge them or provide aid.[19] Her friend, Pauline Newman, recalled that when she and her friends "organized a group, we immediately called the union . . . so that they would take the members in and naturally treat them as they would treat any member who joined the union. Our job was to attract women which men were not willing . . . to do."[20] But unions did not treat their male and female members even-handedly. During a cap-makers' strike, for example, married men got strike benefits amounting to $6.00 per week, but women, even those who supported widowed mothers and young siblings, got nothing.[21]

Women who had had to struggle to create and enter trade unions, who were baited, beaten, and arrested on picket lines, and who had already rejected traditional roles sought help from other women, identifying their problems as different from those of male workers. They indicated their militancy by participating in spontaneous strikes. Those working on women's clothing tended to strike without union support more than 1½ as many times as workers on men's clothing (largely male).[22] In the early years of organizing, attacks against women often elicited support from female co-workers. Part of the appeal exercised by Clara Lemlich, whose proposal to strike sparked the 1909 uprising of 20,000 in the dress and waist trade, came from the fact that she had been badly beaten by thugs a few months before. A woman who had participated in the Chicago garment strike of 1911 recalled that violent attacks against other female strikers had persuaded her not to return to work until the strike was won. As she and her fellow strikers were negotiating with their employer to end the walkout, they heard a terrific noise. "We all rushed to the windows, and there we [saw] the police beating the strikers — clubbing them on our account and when we saw that we went out."[23] A sense of female solidarity joined the oppressed together. A 1913 striker who claimed to be "in good" at her job nonetheless refused to work without a union "for the sake of those that didn't have it good."[24] Women strikers, when imprisoned, passively resisted efforts of jail officials to separate them.[25]

Yet solidarity among women was limited by ethnic and class antagonisms which persistently interfered with the best efforts of organizers and of which the organizers themselves were often guilty. Organizers repeatedly complained that their work was hampered by ethnic conflict among women. Jewish women, for instance, thought that they were superior unionists. They treated non-Jews in the garment shops suspiciously, complaining, for example, that Polish women listened to their speeches quietly and then reported them to the boss.[26] Italian women were thought to be unreliable allies, and fear that they would not join in a strike sometimes hindered other garment workers from walking out.[27] Language barriers were also divisive and, consequently, Italian and Jewish women met separately during the 1909 strike. Seeking to encourage Italian women to continue the strike but not having an Italian-speaking organizer, the ILG leadership fell back upon daily harangues in English until the Italians agreed to remain out of the shops.[28] Some of the same ethnic elitism appeared a decade later. Julia Poyntz, the ILG's first educational director, used the pages of *Justice*, its official journal, to argue in 1919 that "our Italian sisters who are still suffering from the age long seclusion of women in the home need a long and serious education to enable them to function intelligently as members of the working class in the shop and in the political field."[29]

"American" women, as the organizers persistently called them, were hardest of all for Jewish women to unionize. But it was a necessary assignment in order to prevent some shops from undercutting the wages of others and thus being able to charge lower prices for finished goods. Nonetheless, Jewish organizers found such unionization drives very distasteful. They saw "shickses" as, at best, indifferent to unionism and, more often, as strike breakers and scabs.[30] Any success at organizing "Americans" evoked unconcealed glee. Pauline Newman wrote to Rose Schneiderman from Massachusetts that they had "at last succeeded in organizing an English-speaking branch of the waist makers union. And my dear not with ten or eleven members — but with a good sturdy membership of forty. Now what will you say to that!"[31] Long after most Jewish women were comfortable within unions, Rose Pesotta complained, she was having a "hell of a job" with the Seattle workers she had been sent to organize. They were the "100% American white daughters of the sturdy pioneers. They are all members of bridge clubs, card clubs, lodges, etc. Class consciousness is as remote from their thoughts as any idea that smacks with radicalism."[32] Women from such an ethnic background could severely inhibit the success of an organization drive. Pesotta complained that she could not call a strike because the women would not picket: "No one will stand in front of the shop . . . as they will be ashamed. Not even the promise of getting regular strike benefits moved them."[33]

Isolated from the mainstream of the labor movement and divided from other working women who came from less class-conscious backgrounds, Jewish women gratefully accepted help from middle-class groups like the Women's Trade Union League (WTUL). But financial and moral support of the WTUL came at a price.[34] Jewish women had been nurtured in the cradle of socialism and, for them, alliances with other women were largely ways of achieving a more just society. Many middle-class members of the WTUL, in contrast, held that the political, social, and biological oppression of women was their major problem. They saw labor organization among women as a way of transcending class lines in the service of feminist interests.

Contemporary testimony and filtered memory agree that the WTUL provided enormously valuable organizing help. Yet the tensions were not easily suppressed. Rose Schneiderman, working for the WTUL in 1911, needed reassurance from a friend: "You need not chide yourself for not being able to be more active in the socialist party. You are doing a much needed and splendid work"[35] Nevertheless, it was always clear to those who undertook union work that WTUL women had only limited access to and limited understanding of the Jewish labor movement. "Remember Rose," wrote Newman, "that no matter how much you are with the Jewish people, you are still more with the people of the League." [36] And again, Newman comforted her friend: "They don't understand the difference between the Jewish girl and the gentile girl." [37]

Neither the trade union nor solidarity with middle-class WTUL members offered adequate support to the exceptional women who devoted themselves to organizing. How did they choose between the two? And at what cost? They worked in a lonely and isolated world, weighing the elements of their success against the conflict and tension of their lives. They were not typical of rank-and-file union women. Nor can their lives be seen as symbols of a more general struggle. The three female ILG organizers I have selected chose not to conform to traditional patterns. Rather they pursued what for women was an extraordinary lifestyle. Their particular struggles crystallize the tensions that other women faced and more easily resolved in the service of a familiar destiny. As their relationship to the union was filled with conflict, so their attitudes toward women reflected the way feminism was experienced by working women. Their lives illustrate a continuing uncertainty over the sources of their oppression.

Pauline Newman became the ILG's first female organizer in the aftermath of the Great Uprising of 1909. She had a stormy relationship with the union until she settled down in 1913 to work for the Joint Board of Sanitary Control, a combined trade union and manufacturers unit designed to establish standards for maintaining sanitary conditions in the shops. Fannia Cohn worked for the union from 1919 to the end of her life. For most of that time she was educational director although she also served as an executive secretary and briefly as a vice president. Rose Pesotta (some ten years younger than the other two) became a full-time organizer in 1933 and a vice president of the union in 1934. She remained active until 1944, when she returned to work in the shops.

Their lifestyles varied. Pauline Newman, warm, open, and impulsive, had a successful long-term relationship with a woman with whom she adopted a baby in 1923. Fannia Cohn lived alone, a sensitive, slightly irritable woman who was concerned with her ability to make and retain friends. Rose Pesotta married twice and then fell in love with two married men in succession. Cohn and Newman called themselves socialists. Pesotta was an anarchist. No easy generalization captures their positions on women or their relationships to the union. But all felt some conflict surrounding the two issues.

From 1909 to 1912, just before she went to work for the Joint Board, Newman vacillated between the ILG and the middle-class women of the WTUL. Frequently unhappy with a union that often treated her shabbily she nevertheless continued to work for them throughout her life. "I cannot leave them," she wrote in 1911, "as long as they don't want to accept my resignation." "Besides," she rationalized some months later, "They are beginning to realize . . . women can do more effective work than men, especially where girls are involved." [38] Yet later that year she angrily severed her connection with the ILG, for which she had been organizing in Cleveland. "They wanted me to work for *less* than the other organizers get, and while it was not a question of the few dol[lars] a week with me, I felt that I would lower myself before the others were I to go out on the price offered to me." Her anger increased as the letter continued to describe the women selected to replace her by John Dyche, the union's executive secretary: "Well they too are not bad looking, and one is rather liberal with her body. That is more than enough for Dyche." [39] Two months later she was still angry. "The International does not give a hang whether a local lives or dies." [40] And several weeks after that she wrote: "I for one would not advise you to work for any Jewish organization." [41] But within a few months she was back at work again for the ILG.

Newman had little choice. Though she disliked the union's attitude toward women, she had equal difficulty relating to the WTUL's middle-class members who were potential nonunion allies. Not that she disagreed with them on the women's issues: she was more than sympathetic. An ardent supporter of the ballot for women, she could not, she claimed later, recall any woman, except for Mother Jones, "in any of our organizations who was not in favor of getting the vote." Like her friends, she was convinced that the ballot would "add greatly to our effectiveness for lobbying or sponsoring labor legislation." [42] Moreover, she not only willingly accepted assistance from women who were not workers but actively solicited it. [43] She even quoted Christ to induce church women to help garment workers and visited women's clubs to gather support for striking corset operatives in Kalamazoo, Michigan, in 1912. When local officials and the mayor were unable to help resolve the strike, she "decided that the best thing to do would be to ask the ladies who wear corsets not to buy that particular brand." [44]

Yet the task of reconciling class and feminist interests exhausted Newman. "My work is horrible," she complained a few months before the Kalamazoo strike. "The keeping sweet all the time and pleading for aid from the 'dear ladies' and the ministers is simply sickening." [45] Her greatest praise went to the St. Louis, Missouri, WTUL: It was "a strictly working-class organization in spirit as well as in action." When she sent off an article praising the chapter's freedom from middle-class intervention to the WTUL journal, *Life and Labor,* Margaret Dreier Robbins, WTUL president and the journal's editor, suppressed it. [46] In a remarkable letter to Schneiderman written in 1911, Newman recorded her perceptions about the WTUL's effect on women workers. Mrs. Robbins "has made all the girls of the League think her way and as a consequence they do not use their own mind and do not act the way they feel but the way Mrs. R. wants them to." She frowned at the League's Saturday afternoon teas (which served "a glass [of] Russian Tea") and disapproved of giving the girls folk-dancing lessons. "It is of course very nice of her," conceded Newman, "but that is the instinct of charity rather than of unionism." [47]

Newman's disagreements with the WTUL extended to the bargaining table. She was more than willing to give way when she thought a well-spoken woman could influence a stubborn manufacturer, but she considered it bad strategy to raise issues of morality when they threatened to interfere with negotiations over wages and hours. To be sure, she stated, a factory owner's son and his superintendent had taken liberties with female employees. "There is not a factory today where the same immoral conditions [do] not exist . . . . This to my mind can be done away with by educating the girls instead of attacking the company." [48]

Caught between the union and the middle-class allies, Newman called for help, a pattern repeated by other women involved in the labor movement. Her letters to Schneiderman are filled with longing—"All evening I kept saying If only Rose were here"—and with loneliness—"No matter how good the people are to me, they do not know me as yet."[49] One can only guess at the emotional demands of her work. She repeatedly wrote of trying to "get away from the blues" and complained: "I am just thrown like a wave from one city to another. When will it end?"[50] Respite came at last in the form of the Joint Board of Sanitary Control. With the struggles to organize behind her, Newman could now devote her energies to improving working conditions in the sweat shops.

Feelings of displacement and the need for mutual support may have prompted the drive by women members of the ILG's Local 25 to create first an educational department and then a vacation retreat. At first reacting impatiently to this demand, male unionists responded, one woman activist recalled, with snickers: "What do the girls know — instead of a union they want to dance."[51] But the women persisted, insisting that the union would be better if the members danced with one another. The women proved to be right. By 1919 Unity House, as the vacation home was called, had moved to quarters capable of sleeping 900 people, and two years later Local 25 turned it over to a grateful International.

Unity House may have symbolized a growing solidarity among working-class Jewish women in the needle trades. In any event, the feminism of ILG members appears to have become a problem. Just at the peak of its success, *Justice*, the union's official journal, began to attack middle-class women. Could it have been that some union leaders feared that working women were seeking alliances with others of their sex and would eventually cease to identify their interests with those of working men? In what seem like a clear attempt to divide women of different classes, a *Justice* editorial warned in early 1919 that wage-earning women were not to be compared with "that type of woman, who to her shame be it said, is less a person than a thing."[52] Increasingly, *Justice's* writers insisted that working women could defend themselves without the help of middle-class allies. When female pickets faced attacks by gangsters, *Justice* insisted that the strikers themselves could handle the situation. It urged women to "take a little trip down to City Hall and get the vote that will put these fellows out of business."[53] Julia Poyntz, *Justice*'s writer on the women's affairs, demanded that middle-class women no longer interfere with their sisters: "The

interests of the women of the working classes are diametrically opposed to those of the middle classes." [54] A month later she attacked
a conference of the Women's International League for Peace and
Freedom, an organization of middle-class reformers, for virtually
excluding working women and their problems.[55] Although *Justice*
continued to solicit support for the WTUL and the ILG continued
to send women to the Bryn Mawr Summer School, the attacks did
not cease. For example, in a 1923 article, *Justice* protested the
absence of working women at a conference on women in industry:
"The ladies who employ domestics came to Washington to
speak about higher wages, shorter hours, and better working conditions for their help. The domestics, of course, or their representatives were not invited." [56]

Fannia Cohn climbed to a position of authority in the ILG at this
time. She was fully aware of women's issues. In 1919, in the
aftermath of a successful shirtwaist strike, she pleaded for
tolerance from male union members. Recalling the militancy of the
young female strikers, she wrote: "Our brother workers in the past
regarded with suspicion the masses of women who were entering
the trades. They did everything to halt the 'hostile army' whose
competition they feared." [57] Wasn't it time, she asked, to accept
fully the women strikers who had so often been jailed and beaten?
An ardent supporter of the Bryn Mawr Summer School and a regular contributor to the WTUL, Cohn had friendly relations with
many WTUL officers. [58] In 1926 she protested the absence of
women's names on a list of antiwar petition signatures, and later
she was to fire off a rapid telegram insisting that Anne Muste be included in a tribute offered to her husband.[59] Her experiences strike
familiar chords. She complained of the difficulty of holding views
independent of her male co-workers but noted that it was even
more painful when women put down their sisters' attempts to be independent. This behavior she attributed to childhood training and
a tradition which led women "to resent when some other woman
dares to be her own self — her own master."[60] She laughed with a
friend whose husband was called by his wife's surname ("let men
have the sensation of changing their lifelong name for a new one")
and supported Mary Beard's proposed world center to preserve a
record of women's achievements. [61]

Cohn's strong empathy for women's feelings was surely shaped in part by her painful experiences in the ILG. Theresa Wolfson, later to become a well-known economist and an expert on the problems of working women, glimpsed her suffering in 1923: "Never have I realized with such poignancy of feeling, what it means to be a woman among men in a fighting organization as last Monday when I heard your outcry and realized the stress under which you were working."[62] In a letter she at first hesitated to mail, Cohn shared some of her angry frustration with a woman who taught at Brookwood Labor College. She had urgently requested the college's faculty to make two studies of union women for her. The faculty had repeatedly postponed the request which prompted her comment: "I wonder whether they would treat in the same manner, a 'man' who would find himself in a similiar position . . . the labor movement is guilty of not realizing the importance of placing the interests of women on the same basis as of men and until they will accept this, I am afraid the movement will be much hampered in its progress."[63]

Despite the anguish caused by her male colleagues and her strong sympathy with women's causes, Cohn came down on the side of organized labor when a choice had to be made. She rejected a request to segregate men and women workers in evening classes: "I am a great believer that men and women working together in the labor movement or in the classroom have much to gain from each other."[64] In 1925 she appealed to William Green, the AFL's president, "not as an officer speaking for her organization [but as] a woman trade unionist" in protest against conferences called by ladies. "When the deplorable conditions of the unorganized working women are to be considered," she objected, "a conference is called by many ladies' organizations who have no connection with the labor movement and they are the ones to decide 'how to improve the conditions of the poor working woman.' "[65] At a later date she regretfully refused an invitation to attend a WTUL conference on working women, cautioning the delegates to "bear in mind that it is very difficult nowadays to even organize men and they should remember that in proportion there are not enough men organized in our country as yet."[66] On the question of protective legislation for women, Cohn only reluctantly sided with the middle-class reformers who favored it: "I did not think the problem of working women could be solved in any other way than the problem of working men and that is through trade union organization, but considering that very few women are as yet organized into trade unions, it would be folly to agitate against protective legislation."[67]

These contradictory positions were not taken without inner struggle. Cohn knew well the sacrifice necessary to stay in the labor movement — "the inner pain, worry and spiritual humiliation."[68] Her remedy, like Newman's, was close friendship. "You know that I . . . must be in constant touch with my friends," she wrote. "If I can't have personal contact then the medium of letters can be employed."[69] Elsewhere she declared, "To satisfy my own inner self, I must be surrounded by true friends . . . [who] never for a moment doubt my motives and always understand me thoroughly."[70] Cohn found refuge in the education department of the ILG where she could continue the battle and yet remain sheltered from the worst of the storm.

Rose Pesotta, however, took no shelter and asked no quarter. By 1933 when she began full-time organizing for the ILG, the depression had convinced many that women, married and unmarried, were in the work force to stay and the unions willingly committed both money and resources to organizing them.[71] Membership campaigns no longer focused on the East-Coast cities. In the garment centers of the Far West and in places like Buffalo and Montreal, Jews took second place to Mexican, Italian, and "American" women. But Pesotta was a Russian Jew who worked for a still Jewish union and, like her predecessors, she suffered the turmoil of being a woman in ambivalent territory. Sent by the ILG to Los Angeles in 1933, she went on from there to organize women in San Francisco, Seattle, Portland, Puerto Rico, Buffalo, and Montreal before becoming involved in the Akron sit-down strikes and war mobilization.

No one could question Pesotta's awareness of women's particular problems. Persuaded by the argument that there were no women on the union's General Executive Board, she accepted a much-dreaded nomination for vice president. "I feel as if I lost my independence," she confided to her diary.[72] She often berated the union leadership for its neglect of women: "Our union, due to the fact that it has a WOMAN leader is supposed to do everything, organizing, speechmaking, etc., etc." [73] She was not shy about requesting courtesies that men could obtain only with difficulty. Women who earned meager wages could not be expected to pay even modest union initiation fees, she maintained at one point, urging a hardship exception for female recruits. At another, she demanded that the ILG pay a Spanish woman, elected to attend the biennial convention, not only expenses but full compensation for lost income. [74] She knew the advantages of solidarity among women, making personal sacrifices to "win the support of the ladies who might some day be of great help to the girls." [75]

Repeatedly, however, Pesotta and her fellow West Coast organizers sacrificed feminist issues in the interests of generating an enthusiastic and loyal membership. To keep striking women happy, they agreed to double strike benefits before Easter Sunday "for the girls to buy something." [76] They welcomed the husbands of newly organized women to discussion meetings. [77] In 1933 Pesotta compromised her own feminism to the extent of surrendering the negotiating process to men and confining her own activities to organizing women. She feared that employees would simply refuse to take a woman seriously: "Our late President Schlesinger once told your humble servant to stop this kind of business and go home and get married. I hate to hear that from an employer." [78] Her perspectives were not always those of other women. While WTUL officials were praising the NRA codes, Pesotta condemned them. Organizing in Seattle and witness to how badly the codes were abused, she complained that "the women are satisfied that the N.R.A. gave them 35 hours and better wages [and so] why pay dues to a union that does nothing for the workers?" [79]

Pesotta carried the usual scars of the women organizer. "A flitting happy little whirlwind," her friends described her, but it was an image that did not fit: "Nobody knows how many cheerless, sleepless nights I have spent crying in my loneliness." [80] Unlike Newman and Cohn, she sought solace with men, but depriving herself of close women friends only exacerbated her isolation. She was tormented by the gossip of her female colleagues and struggled with her self-image. Occasionally, she confessed, "I feel so futile," or lamented: "Everybody has a private life. I have none."[81] In 1936 in order to avoid entanglement with a married man, she went into self-exile to Montreal. It was no use. From Montreal she wrote to her lover: "Why must I find happiness always slipping out of my hand . . . . I'm sinking now and who knows where I will land."[82] For ten years thereafter, Pesotta battled against police alongside her union colleagues. Then she returned to the comparative peace of the garment shop from which she had come.

By the middle thirties, with unionism apparently secure and the ILG's membership expanding rapidly, it looked as though women might at last begin to ask questions peculiar to them within the confines of the union. Fannia Cohn, for example, wrote a play in 1935 which raised critical issues. Intended for presentation at union meetings, it described a husband and his "intellectually superior" wife. Each of them worked, but the wife also had to devote her evenings to caring for their home. As a result, the husband rapidly developed more interests and became increasingly discontented with his wife. The wife, wrote Cohn, voiced the resentment and "the protest of a women worker, wife and mother against an economic condition that compels her to work days in the shop and evenings at home."[83] Rose Schneiderman phrased it differently and bitterly: "Chivalry is thrown away" when a girl enters the factory or store; "Women have to work and then are thrown on the dust heap the same as working men."[84] By 1935, enough women had been organized so that the ILG, no longer afraid of imminent disintegration and collapse, could lend an ear to the women's issues. Perhaps in consequences, the solidarity of women within unions diminished.

Those who had gone before walked an uneasy tightrope, slipping first to one side and then to the other. Tempted on some occasions by the money and support of middle-class women, at others by the militance of a changing labor-union leadership, alternately repelled by "ladies" and hurt by their union's male leadership, women who tried to organize their sisters were in a precarious position. They were not feminist in that they did not put the social and political rights of women before all else. They did draw strength and support from the solidarity of women both inside and outside unions. Their lives illustrate the critical importance of female bonding and of female friendship networks. Newman and Cohn, who had particularly strong relationships with women and who managed to find relatively passive roles within the union, maintained their relationship with the ILG far longer than Pesotta, who relied on men for support and who stayed in the front lines. All were class conscious, insisting that the class struggle was preeminent. When their class consciousness and their identification as women conflicted, they bowed to tradition, with its customary sex roles, and threw in their lot with the working class.

NOTES

1. In 1913, 56.56 percent of the workers in the industry were Jewish and 34.35 percent were Italian; 70 percent or more were women. See Hyman Berman, "Era of the Protocol: A Chapter in the History of the International Ladies Garment Workers Union, 1910-1916" (Ph.D. dissertation, Columbia University, 1956), pp. 22, 24. Jewish women were much more likely to be working inside a garment shop than were Italian women, who often preferred to take work home; 53.6 percent of all employed Jewish women were in the garment industry in 1900. Nathan Goldberg, *Occupational Patterns of American Jewry* (N.Y., 1947), p. 21. The relative proportion of women in the garment industry declined between 1900 and 1930. In addition to dresses and waists, women were heavily employed in kimonos, house dresses, underwear, children's clothing, and neckwear. Melvyn Dubofsky, *When Workers Organize: New York City in the Progressive Era* (Amherst, 1968), p. 73, has a good description of conditions in the garment industry.

2. The industry was characterized by the rapid turnover of its employees. In 1910 about 50 percent of the dress and waist makers were under 20 years old. The best estimate is that less than 10 percent of the women working on dresses and waists were married. See U.S. Senate, 61st Congress, 2nd Session, *Abstracts of the Report of the Immigration Commission*, Doc. #747, 1911, vol. II, p. 336; Berman, "Era of the Protocol," p. 23.

3. The proportion of women in the Jewish immigration movement between 1899 and 1910 was higher than in any other immigrant group except the Irish. See Samuel Joseph, *Jewish Immigration to the U.S.: 1881-1910* (N.Y., 1914), p. 179. This can be accounted for in part by the high proportion of family emigration and in part by the numbers of young women who came to America, without their parents, to work. Rose Pesotta, Rose Cohn, and Emma Goldman fall into this category.

4. Unpublished autobiography #92. Archives (YIVO); see also #160, p. 8. Etta Byer, *Transplanted People* (1905), p. 28.

5. Flora Weiss, Interview in Amerikaner Yiddishe Geschicte Bel-Pe, YIVO Archives, June 15, 1964, p. 4. See also Anzia Yezierska, *Bread Givers* (New York, 1925), p. 28.

6. Rose Pesotta, *Bread Upon the Waters* (New York, 1944), p. 4. The novels of Anzia Yezierska, who arrived in America from Russian Poland in 1901, beautifully express these aspirations. See *Bread Givers: All I Could Never Be* (New York, 1932); *Arrogant Beggar* (Garden City, New York, 1927); and her semi-fictional autobiography, *Red Ribbon on a White Horse* (New York, 1950).

7. Ruth Rubin, *A Treasury of Jewish Folksong* (New York, 1950), pp. 43, 97.

8. See, for example, Rose Schneiderman as quoted in "Finds Hard Job Unionizing Girls Whose Aim is to Wed," *New York Telegram and Sun,* June 18, 1924; Julia Stuart Poyntz, "Marriage and Motherhood," *Justice* (March 18, 1919), p. 5; Matilda Robbins, "My Story," unpublished manuscript, Matilda Robbins Collection, Wayne State University Archives of Labor History, p. 38. Tamara Hareven has concluded that French-Canadian women in Manchester, New Hampshire, did not expect to stop working in factories after marriage. See "Industrial Work and the Family Cycle," paper presented at the Conference on Class and Ethnicity in Women's History, SUNY at Binghamton, September 21, 1974. The mechanics of organizing women are illustrated in Alice Kessler-Harris, "Where Are the Organized Women Workers?" *Feminist Studies* III (Fall 1975), 92-110.

9. Although the same tensions existed for non-Jewish women, one does not always get the impression that they were quite so torn. May Kenney, for example, continued to be active after she married John O'Sullivan. The most prominent Jewish women who remained active after marriage married outside their ethnic group. Anna Strunsky Walling and Rose Pastor Stokes are two examples. In some ways Emma Goldman's life acted out the protest many women must have felt but expressed in more limited ways. See Blanche Wiesen Cook, "Emma Goldman and Crystal Eastman," unpublished paper delivered at the Organization of American Historians meeting, April 1973.

10. Rose Schneiderman, with Lucy Goldthwaite, *All for One* (New York, 1967), p. 50.

11. Interview with Pearl Halpern in Irving Howe Collection, YIVO (undated), p. 8.

12. U.S. Senate, Abstracts of the Report of the Immigration Commission, vol. 11, p. 317, indicates that in 1910 23.9 percent of Jewish men belonged to trade unions as opposed to 14 percent of Italian men.

13. See, for example, unpublished autobiography #160, YIVO, pp. 8 and 12.

14. Rubin, *A Treasury of Jewish Folksong*, p. 23.

15. Ibid., p. 97. These songs, with their hope of escape, should be compared with the hopeless and agonized verse of Morris Rosenfeld. See Rosenfeld, *The Teardrop Millionaire and Other Poems* (New York, 1955), pp. 14, 19.

16. "Manhattan's Young Factory Girls," *The World*, March 2, 1913.

17. Lillian Mallach to David Dubinsky, December 18, 1964, Glicksberg MSS, YIVO.

18. Weiss, Interview, YIVO, p. 11; on p. 20, the same woman recorded the influence that the legend of Mother Jones had had on her.

19. Schneiderman, *All for One*, p. 49. Officially, ILG policy was to organize who-

ever was in the shop, regardless of sex. It was easier in practice to discriminate against women since they were often employed in sex-segregated jobs.

20. Pauline Newman, Interview, Amerikaner Yiddishe Geshichte Bel-Pe, June 26, 1965, YIVO, p. 19.

21. Schneiderman, *All for One*, p. 61.

22. Issac Hourwich, *Immigration and Labor: The Economic Aspects of European Immigration to the United States* (New York, 1922), p. 373. These figures are for the period from 1880 to 1905.

23. *Life and Labor* (February 1911), p. 52.

24. "Manhattan's Young Factory Girls," *The New York World,* March 2, 1913.

25. Weiss, Interview, YIVO, p. 28.

26. Faigele Shapiro, Interview, Amerikaner Yiddishe Geshichte Bel-Pe, August 6, 1964, YIVO, p. 9.

27. Constant D. Leupp, "Shirtwaist Makers Strike," in Edna Bullock, ed., *Selected Articles on the Employment of Women* (Minneapolis, 1919), p. 126.

28. Louis Lorwin, *The Women's Garment Workers: A History of the International Ladies Garment Workers Union* (New York, 1924), p. 156.

29. Julia Stuart Poyntz, "What Do You Do with Leisure," *Justice,* February 22, 1919, p. 13.

30. Unpublished autobiography #160, YIVO, p. 13.

31. Pauline Newman to Rose Schneiderman, September 20, 1910. Rose Schneiderman Collection, Taniment Library, New York University, Box A94. Pauline Newman and Rose Schneiderman are hereinafter referred to as P.N. and R.S.

32. Rose Pesotta to David Dubinsky, February 6, 1935, Rose Pesotta Collection, New York Public Library, General Correspondence. See also Rose Pesotta to Eva Ehrlich, February 8, 1935. Rose Pesotta is hereinafter referred to as R.P.

33. R.P. to David Dubinsky, February 23, 1935.

34. See Weiss, Interview, YIVO, p. 32, for one acknowledgment of WTUL aid. For the WTUL's side of the story, see Nancy Schrom Dye, "Creating a Feminist Alliance: Sisterhood and Class Conflict in the New York Women's Trade Union League, 1903-1914," paper presented at the Conference on Class and Ethnicity in Women's History, SUNY at Binghamton, September 22, 1974; and Robin Miller Jacoby, "The Women's Trade Union League and American Feminism," paper presented at the Second Berkshire Conference on the History of Women, Radcliffe, October 27, 1974.

35. "Joe" to R.S., November 8, 1911, R.S. Coll., A94.

36. P.N. to R.S., April 17, 1911, R.S. Coll. A94.

37. P.N. to R.S., February 9, 1912, R.S. Coll. A94.

38. P.N. to R.S., April 17, 1911 and P.N. to R.S., August 9, 1911, R.S. Coll., A94.

39. P.N. to R.S., November 14, 1911, R.S. Coll., A94. Three months later, the ILG fired the new organizers and Pauline exulted, "I tell you, Rose, it feels fine when you can say to a secretary of the International to 'go to hell with your job together' and after have the same man beg you to work for them again!" P.N. to R.S., February 22, 1912. R.S. Coll., A94.

40. P.N. to R.S., January 17, 1912, R.S. Coll., A94.

41. P.N. to R.S., February 9, 1912, R.S. Coll. A94.

42. Newman, Interview, YIVO, pp. 21, 22. See also P.N. to R.S., May 17, 1911, R.S. Coll., A94, in which Newman expresses sadness at not being able to attend a conference to discuss the "woman problem": "You must tell me about it in your next letter."

43. P.N. to R.S., April 11, 1910, R.S. Coll., A94.

44. Newman, Interview, YIVO, p. 2.

45. P.N. to R.S., March 5, 1912, R.S. Coll., A94.

46. P.N. to R.S., November 7, 1911, R.S. Coll., A94. Newman had already had a similar experience with the *Ladies Garment Worker* (*Justice's* predecessor), which mutilated an article on the League she had written for them.

47. P.N. to R.S., December 1, 1911, R.S. Coll., A94.

48. P.N. to R.S., July 11, 1912, R.S. Coll., A94.

49. P.N. to R.S., October 19, 1910 and April 11, 1910, R.S. Coll., A94.

50. P.N. to R.S., October 29, 1911 and November 7, 1911, R.S. Coll., A94.

51. Shapiro, Interview, YIVO, p. 17.

52. "On Lightheaded Women," *Justice*, March 8, 1919.

53. Julia Poyntz, "The Unity Corner," *Justice*, March 29, 1919, p. 3.

54. "The Problem of Life for the Working Girl," *Justice*, February 1, 1919, p. 3.

55. *Justice*, March 15, 1919, p. 5.

56. B. Maiman, "Conference on Women in Industry," *Justice,* January 19, 1923, p. 4.

57. Fannia Cohn, "With the Strikers," *Justice*, February 22, 1919.

58. Fannia Cohn to R.S., January 24, 1929, Fannia Cohn Papers, New York Public Library, Box 4; see also E. Christman to Fannia Cohn, October 2, 1915, Fannia Cohn Papers, Box 1. Fannie Cohn is hereinafter referred to as F.C.

59. James Shotwell to F.C., December 31, 1926, F.C. Papers, Box 1; F.C. to James Maurer, March 6, 1931, F.C. Papers, Box 5.

60. F.C. to Helen Norton, February 9, 1932, F.C., Box 5. The rest of the letter reads in part: "It hurts me also to know that while 'men' frequently come to each others' assistance in an emergency, 'women' frequently remain indifferent when one of their own sex is confronted with a similar emergency. Of course, a woman is expected to assist a man in his accomplishments, but she (the woman) is forced in her aspirations — in social and economic field — to struggle along. She is compelled to depend upon her own resources, whether this be material, moral or intellectual."

61. F.C. to Dorothea Heinrich, February 3, 1937, F.C. Papers, Box 5; F.C. to Mary Beard, January 23, 1940, F.C. Papers, Box 5.

62. Theresa Wolfson to F.C., November 19, 1923, F.C. Papers, Box 1.

63. F.C. to Helen Norton, February 9, 1932, F.C. Papers, Box 5.

64. F.C. to Evelyn Preston, September 21, 1923, F.C. Papers, Box 4.

65. F.C. to Wm. Green, March 6, 1925, F.C. Papers, Box 4.

66. F.C. to R.S., October 5, 1926, F.C. Papers, Box 4.

67. F.C. to Dr. Marion Phillips, September 13, 1927, F.C. Papers, Box 4.

68. F.C. to Theresa Wolfson, May 15, 1922, F.C. Papers, Box. 4.

69. F.C. to Evelyn Preston, September 9, 1922, F.C. Papers, Box 4; see also F.C.

to E.P., February 19, 1924, F.C. Papers, Box 4.

70. F.C. to Theresa Wolfson, May 15, 1922. F.C. Papers, Box 4.

71. Fannia Cohn, "A New Era Opens for Labor Education," *Justice*, October 1, 1933, p. 9. The article may be more hopeful than realistic. Cohn said in part: "the women strikers, many of whom were married and their younger sisters, too, increasingly realized that no longer do they want a strong union as a temporary protection for themselves but as a permanent safeguard for their present and future families." There is no question, however, that the industry's workers were increasingly drawn from married women and older women.

72. R.P., diary, June 9, 1934, R.P. Coll., In her autobiography, *Bread Upon the Waters*, p. 101, Pesotta wrote that "the voice of a solitary woman on the General Executive Board would be a voice lost in the wilderness."

73. R.P. to Rae Brandstein, April 9, 1934, R.P. Coll.

74. R.P. to David Dubinsky, April 26, 1934, R.P. Coll.

75. R.P. to David Dubinsky, March 3, 1934, R.P. Coll. Pesotta on this occasion stayed in a YMCA because it was "respectable."

76. R.P. to Jennia Matyas, April 16, 1935, R.P. Coll.

77. R.P. to Paul Berg, February 15, 1934, R.P. Coll.

78. R.P. to David Dubinsky, September 30, 1933, R.P. Coll. Pesotta's snippy attitude comes through in the rest of that letter. "Now, my dear President, you will have to come across with the help we need namely; financial, moral and the representative for a week or two. After we'll pull this through you will come to visit these whores and I am confident that you will see with your own eyes that enthusiasm is not such a bad thing after all."

79. Rose Schneiderman called the codes "the Magna Charta of the working woman" and characterized them as "the most thrilling thing that has happened in my lifetime." *N.Y. Evening Journal*, October 24, 1933 (clipping in R.S. Coll., A97); R.P. to David Dubinsky, February 1, 1935, R.P. Coll.

80. R.P., diary, November 3, 1931, R.P. Coll.

81. R.P., diary, February 24, 1934, March 12, 1934, August 9, 1934, R.P. Coll.

82. R.P. to Powers Hapgood, February 21, 1937, R.P. Coll.

83. F.C. to Jess Ogden, June 25, 1935, F.C. Papers, Box 5. A second play described how two sisters, both of whom worked, nevertheless waited on their brother at home because they had to atone for earning less than he did.

84. Quoted in a clipping entitled, "Says Chivalry Stops at Door of Workshop," from an unidentified newspaper, 1912. R.S. Coll., A97.

IMPERFECT UNIONS: CLASS AND GENDER IN CRIPPLE CREEK, 1894-1904

8

by Elizabeth Jameson

Western mining towns were class-conscious and masculine, and Cripple Creek, Colorado, was no exception. From 1894 to 1904 the Cripple Creek district with its twelve towns, was a stronghold of radical labor. Centered around nine locals of the militant Western Federation of Miners (WFM), thirty-six unions organized everyone from waitresses and laundry workers to bartenders and newsboys.[1] Through successful organization, workers achieved a large measure of control over job conditions and over the social, political, and economic life of the towns. This effective degree of labor control meant that a secure homelife was at least partially accessible to working-class families and helped to insure that middle-class concepts of appropriate sex roles were not challenged in Cripple Creek.

The industrial structure of gold mining supported both passionate class allegiances and genteel definitions of manhood and womanhood, but it made class concerns of primary importance. Cripple Creek replicated the rapid industrial transformation which produced the WFM and its radical outlook.[2] Nowhere was industrial change more dramatic than in western metal mining. In less than twenty years small-scale placer mining (panning ore from streams or gravel beds) was replaced by lode, or quartz, mining (deep shaft operations which removed rock from which the ore had not been separated and which was later milled and refined). The profitable development of such mining required railroads, advanced technology, large refining facilities, a specialized work force, and considerable capital.

This process occurred with particular rapidity in Cripple Creek, one of the later mining bonanzas. The district lay atop an unusual volcanic formation which produced few outcroppings of ore, so gold was not discovered there until 1890. Robert Womack, who found it, sold his claim for $500 and died penniless: he could not have afforded to develop his property had he kept it. There was little room for the old prospector in Cripple Creek. By 1900, 90 percent of the mines in the district were owned or controlled by Colorado Springs capitalists or by eastern or foreign corporations.[3]

Corporate mining drastically altered the relationship of miners to their labor and transformed social relationships in mining communities. Older traditional views of work and ownership heightened their awareness of loss. In the old mining districts, ownership of a claim required work and occupation in good faith.[4] A miner kept virtually all that he produced. The product of his labor was precious metal. More than any other commodity, gold was tangible wealth. Under the wage system, however, the gold was not kept by the men who mined it but given in the form of profits to absentee owners who neither worked nor lived in mining towns.

Mining was dangerous work, and miners' wives, unlike owners or resident managers, shared the hazards which endangered the workers' health and wages. Women were well aware that, without the unions, corporate power could jeopardize family security. The first strike, in 1894, like most of the others of that time, was defensive, called to oppose mine owners' attempts to cut wages and lengthen the work day. It was the only mining strike of the time in which state power was used to protect civil peace rather than mine owners' property. Populist Governor Davis Waite was the exception in a long line of Colorado executives who sent the militia to help break unions. He helped to negotiate the agreement which guaranteed a $3 minimum daily wage, an eight-hour day, and the right to union membership for district miners. That agreement lasted until the Cripple Creek strike of 1903-1904, when the power of employers, the state, and the military crushed the miners' unions.[5] The WFM was the keystone for Cripple Creek workers: it protected other, nonmining district labor from 1894 to 1904. But the support of such workers could not prevent its defeat, and the defeat of the miners' locals marked the end of all organized labor in the district.

The Western Federation of Miners (so named from 1893 to 1916, but from 1916 to 1967 the International Union of Mine, Mill and Smelter Workers) has long been considered one of the nation's most radical unions for its endorsements of socialism and its responses to corporate control of mining. It did not favor regulation of trusts or a return to individual enterprise but instead supported an end to private ownership of basic industry and of the wage and profit system. It advocated workers' control of production and the establishment of a socialist cooperative commonwealth. Its slogan from the beginning was "Labor Produces All Wealth — Wealth Belongs to the Producer Thereof."

Believing that the AFL divided workers and created a labor aristocracy, the WFM opposed its conservative craft unionism and virtually exclusive concentration on skilled workers. Rather, the miners favored industrial unionism: the organization of all workers in each industry into one big union, regardless of skill, in order to contest corporate industrial power. The WFM regarded the AFL's belief in the identity of the interests of capital and labor as class collaboration; it instead supported the Western Labor Union (1898-1902), the American Labor Union (1902-1905), and the Industrial Workers of the World (1905-) as alternatives.[6]

These principles animated the Cripple Creek labor community from 1894 to 1904. The mutual aid and class understanding shared by the men and women of Cripple Creek were fairly typical of associations throughout the mining West. While feminism was not of central concern, a variety of radical and reform sentiments flourished in the district, from populism and the single tax to self-help through cooperatives. Socialism, both utopian and scientific, had many adherents. Workers dissatisfied with the emerging corporate order believed that they could build a new society "within the shell of the old." The nature of that society was debated as they moved from advocacy of free silver to socialism and proposed a variety of reforms, often in combination with a class analysis which denied the effectiveness of piecemeal measures.[7]

Given its high degree of class awareness, Cripple Creek provides a particularly significant insight into the overlapping claims of class and gender in America. Women shared the class concepts and the social support of the labor community, but organized labor rarely addressed the private world of the family or the specific situations of women in mining towns. Labor's failure to integrate conceptions of class and sex roles not only weakened class action but left women subordinate, isolated, and often alienated.

Both labor organization and family roles were based on the work structure of gold mining, the only major industry in the district. The towns were largely working-class and the work force was largely male. By 1900 some 8,000 men — roughly a fourth of the district's total population — were engaged in mining labor, and other wage work consisted of support services either for the mines or for the miners and their families.[8] The population was similarly male-dominated. While females outnumbered males under age twenty-one, the adult population was predominantly male. The sex ratio was closest in the town of Cripple Creek, the commerical center, where more jobs for women existed. There were proportionately more men in Victor, the "city of mines," and in smaller towns like Anaconda, Altman, and Goldfield, which were residential centers for miners and their families.[9]

Virtually all adult women were economically dependent upon male breadwinners. With a male-dominated work force and an excess of men of marriageable age, paid work for women was limited. Women were involved chiefly in service occupations as cooks, waitresses, retail clerks, dance-hall workers, and prostitutes. Many were proprietors of small boarding- and roominghouses, restaurants, and groceries. Schoolteachers formed the largest group of women professionals. Still, an unusual number of professional women practiced in the district: at least four physicians, one osteopath, one dentist, and twenty-five nurses in 1902. Married women, however, rarely worked outside the home. They might take in laundry, cook, clean, or mananage boardinghouses, but they could not teach or engage in public business. As one resident recently recalled, "Women just didn't get jobs, women belonged in the home."[10]

There were three groups of women in Cripple Creek who could reasonably be considered working-class: women wage workers, prostitutes and dance-hall women, and the women of male workers' families, who were by far the largest group. Most women had ascribed class status: they were working-class because their husbands, fathers, or brothers worked for wages. Their security depended on the men's incomes, health, and generosity, and on the regularity of work in the mines. Even women wage laborers who earned their class position were still subordinate to male unionists. While it was possible for a single woman or a widow to support herself, all district workers relied on the economic control of the miners' locals. The leverage of these locals was powerful since merchants depended on the patronage of miners and their families.

The roles and expectations of working-class women were based on two interlocked ideologies: the ideas of class which were formed as mining came under the control of corporate capital in the late nineteenth century, and the concepts of womanhood and manhood produced by the earlier shift from household manufacture to factory production which began around 1820. The class experience was paramount. After all, relationships between women and men did not appear to jeopardize workers' communities and control. Capitalist employers were a much more obvious and tangible threat.

Working-class women shared the class philosophies of male workers and espoused them with eloquence. In 1902 a Cripple Creek stenographer informed Colorado's Bureau of Labor Statistics that there was no essential difference between chattel and wage slavery:

> Chattel slaves labor for their masters, are poor, dependent upon the whims of owners for food, clothing and shelter and are kept in mental darkness. Free laborers (God save the world) toil for their employers, are poor, dependent upon the caprice of monopolists for wages with which to procure food, clothing, shelter . . . . One system of exploitation is simple and direct in its execution, the other is complex and roundabout.[11]

Similarly, a Cripple Creek housemaid declared that the point had been reached "where there is a clear, well-defined class interest which separates the laboring class from the their employers . . . . The working class must become class conscious and enter politics through the Socialist movement." She wanted to end the wage system and establish an industrial government

not to manipulate politics and parcel out patronage, but to take charge of and direct and control
production and distribution. The actual workers in
each industry will control that industry, waste will
be eliminated, earnings will be vastly increased,
and the hours of labor will be shortened to less
than half what they are at present. Almost all the
work now is performed by people who are working
for wages. They would surely work better if they
were getting all that they earned, instead of a small
part of it . . . . [R]eform measures may help a little, but not until we get the co-operative commonwealth will the question be settled so that it will
stay settled. [12]

However powerful such responses to capitalism were, they did
not directly address the experience of most women. The daughter
of a Cripple Creek prospector recognized the harshness of her
mother's life — "the bare, ugly camp, so alien to her nature; the
wide gap between her dream of a home and the drab reality of the
house on Golden Avenue; her never-ending loneliness." She
promised herself "never to marry a man of the mines." [13]

There is a vast distance in feeling and outlook between the
cramped loneliness of the prospector's wife and the working
women's class outlook and faith in political action. That distance
reflects an important contradiction for working-class women, who
were expected to accept an analysis of industrial conditions which
was based on class and definitions of "natural" sexual attributes
which transcended class lines.

If the world of work was divided into laborers and employers,
the world of women was divided into good women and bad. Men
were defined by their relationship to production, women by their
relationship to men and morality. Like class awareness, concepts of
sex roles were rooted in economic change. As production moved
from households to factories, married women became less important as manufacturers of commodities, and a new definition of
their sexual sphere developed which reflected women's loss of central economic roles and restricted them to a special social function.

In this context, what Barbara Welter has called the "Cult of True Womanhood" developed between 1820 and 1860: the ideal woman was pious, pure, submissive, and domestic. Women were to preserve the national morality through their influence within the family household. [14] They were expected to provide a stabilizing moral center while men were trained to be aggressive, acquisitive, and competitive.

Both roles were defined as "natural," common to every man and woman regardless of class. All men were expected to work to provide for themselves and their families. All women were to be private, decorative, and supportive of men engaged in purposive economic activity. All homes were intended to be comfortable and comforting retreats from the competition of the marketplace.

Neither True Manhood nor True Womanhood was a fully human role and fully attainable. True men, while defined as productive and sexual persons, were not encouraged to be emotional, and their functions as parents were largely restricted to conception and financial support. While True Women were emotional and nurturing, they were not encouraged to think of themselves as economically productive or socially powerful, and their sexuality was understood chiefly as a necessary means to motherhood. Both roles required the repression of human capacities, and neither was completely attainable. Concepts of manhood and womanhood had been formulated in an age of laissez-faire individualism which judged deviation from accepted sexual spheres as an indication of individual failure. Yet these roles could be achieved only by those few who succeeded in a competitive world: urban entrepreneurs, manufacturers, professionals, and their wives.

Cripple Creek workers considered the achievement of genteel sex roles an important measure of collective success, thereby endorsing the traditional view of True Women and the prevailing sexual ideology, although this idealized role of women, which had first appeared in an earlier factory age, took on more complex and social meanings for workers in the age of corporate mining. Role separation would not have been so definite if low wages had forced married women into the work-place. Thus, union control over wages and working conditions helped to maintain the wide distance between home and work. Compounding this irony, the miners realized that union organization was necessary to gain genteel homes. The traditional view of the sexual spheres, therefore, remained essentially unchallenged in Cripple Creek because the unions were strong enough to guarantee wages sufficient for a man to support a family.

Consequently, although men and women challenged industrial capitalism, neither questioned traditional relations with the other. Men judged themselves by their abilities to support families. Women were presumed to be morally superior and economically dependent, and their place in the home was not questioned. They were told that class allegiance derived from responsibility to husband and household, and that their own potency lay in being class-conscious housewives and mothers. The strongest demonstration of class loyalty was to "find a man who's a union man." In a WFM song, "Scab, Scab, Scab," a suitor was rejected for his opposition to unionism.

> And when I popped the question she said "You make me sad,
> Do you know I can marry a union man? Do you think I'd look at a scab?
> My father is a W.F.M., my brother is the same,
> My mother joined the Auxiliary — I guess I'll not take your name."[15]

After marriage, the worlds of husbands and wives were often separate. Women were home-centered; men's lives revolved around work and work associations. Those work relationships could be very close. Many men considered themselves "partners," a term implying cooperation in work, close friendship, and frequently shared living arrangements.[16] After work, men often spent their time downtown in bars, gambling rooms, or at union and lodge meetings.[17]

The district union newspaper, the *Cripple Creek Daily Press*, reflected the masculine dominance of the mining camp. The frequent prize fights were front-page news, and union and lodge smokers received full coverage. Lydia Pinkham never advertised in its columns, but a wide variety of "male complaint" remedies were touted, indicating preoccupation with sexuality and inadequacy. Cupidene, Nervita Pills, and Vitaline vied with local doctors who specialized in sexual problems. Dr. Schultz's cure included a "very new system of inhalation of compound vapors," and the Doctors Sims and Sims, "expert medical electricians," delicately claimed to work wonders with "first class electrical equipment." Mormon Bishops' Pills, "in use over 50 years by the leaders of the Mormon Church and their followers," promised to cure "lost manhood, impotency, lost power, night losses, spermatorrhoea, insomnia, pain in back, evil desires, seminal emissions, lame back, nervous debility, headache, unfitness to marry, loss of semen, varicocele, or constipation . . . quickness of discharge, and nervous twitching of eyelids."[18]

"Real men" were not only concerned with strength and sexuality; they also worked hard and supported their families. the high wages gained by unions made that support possible, and manhood was tied less to rugged individualism than to militant unionism. Workers believed that a "man who is not alive to his interests enough to join a union of his craft is unworthy to be the husband of a good woman or the father of innocent children."[19] Scabs were derided for their "lack of manhood"; to be an active unionist was to be a "man — not a makeshift."[20] Manhood was understood in terms of traditional masculine qualities as well as in relation to class membership and loyalty, just as women were defined in traditional terms and their class membership was indirect. Their status derived from their men's relationship to the means of production, and their class involvement was dependent on male organization.

Western labor assumed, with some accuracy, that it treated women in an enlightened manner. Many demands of the middle-class women's movement had been achieved. Women had the vote in Colorado and were considerably more active in district politics than in the unions. They held public office and participated regularly in party politics.[21] It was not unusual for women to vote in the old mining districts, and they were granted the vote in school elections when Colorado achieved statehood in 1876. In 1893, during a Populist insurgency, women achieved the full franchise since, with the limited franchise, "the heavens have not fallen and the efficiency of the public schools has been greatly improved.[22]

District labor prided itself on these achievements, defined them as valuable working-class tools, and considered them sufficient to women's needs. As with the suffrage movement nationally, womanly virtue became a justification for granting women electoral equality. But it was assumed that, with the franchise, women's concerns had been met and that only class issues remained. Indeed, women's public and social influence was given class meaning. Both the ballots and the purchasing power of working-class women, the miners believed, were weapons to be used in behalf of organized labor.

In Cripple Creek, prevailing national concepts of sex roles, home, and family were incorporated into labor's critique of industrial capitalism. Miners opposed capitalism partly because it forced women to work and destroyed the home; one measure of the unions' strength was their ability to protect women and children from wage labor. The *Daily Press* insisted that a man should receive wages "sufficient to keep his wife and children out of competition with himself, and give them the same opportunities for improvement and intellectual and moral training and comfortable living as are enjoyed by those who do not labor. No other condition of society is just." [23] Tying respectable family life to unions, Cripple Creek gold miners contrasted the homes they had won through organization with those in areas with no unions:

> A comparison of the interior of the home of the average industrious miner of the Cripple Creek district and a comparison of its contents with that of a coal miner in the eastern states . . . would be a revelation to that class of people who look upon a man who delves in the earth and who gets black and dirty when on shift as an inferior sort of animal ignorant and brutal, drinking up his wages and beating his wife and living in dirt and squalor. Instead of those conditions the opposite are the rule. Their homes are neatly furnished, carpets on the floors, kitchen furnished with all the conveniences a good housewife is so proud to own . . . . The father, when off shift, is neatly

dressed, and with his papers and books becomes
intelligent and well posted. The mother, though
often hard worked, finds time to put on a neat,
clean dress in the evening. The children attend
school, and are comfortably clothed and well
fed. [24]

Union control made Cripple Creek a considerably more pleasant
place than most mining camps. It was a stark contrast to coal towns
where workers lived in company houses, traded at company stores,
sent their children to company schools, and were paid in company
scrip. Cripple Creek was a single-industry area devoted to gold
mining, but it was not a company town. Workers owned or rented
their own homes, were paid in cash, traded with private merchants,
and elected school officials and most other office holders. For
women, such benefits meant greater material and social security,
greater emotional support, and a more meaningful interpretation
of an often ugly reality than was available to most of their class.

The unions did much more to relieve the dislocations of industrialization for working-class people. Enormous human loss accompanied corporate mining in the forms of sickness, injury, and
death; these were daily facts of mining life.[25] Industrial hazards
affected not only miners but their families as well. Women, whose
security depended upon their men, were all too aware of the human
costs of mining, costs for which mining corporations took scant responsibility. "Now, I happen to know that the Hull City Placer
mine is in a most dangerous condition . . . . My husband worked
there; he is an old time miner and a good one, too. When he explained the dangerous position he was daily placed in I insisted on
him drawing his time, which he did.[26] Not all women were so lucky
or so adamant, and deaths and accidents occurred each day from
falling rock, improper timbering, dynamite explosions and missed
shots, or faulty machinery. When electric hoists were first introduced, for instance, mine managers did not know how to ground
them, and a number of miners were electrocuted.

One of the first tasks of union locals was to provide relief in cases
of sickness and death. Major expenditures went to care for widows
and children, sick benefits, and for funerals and shipping bodies

for burial elsewhere. In 1903 WFM locals cared for the victims of at least 193 accidents and conducted the funerals of 35 members. The Altman local alone paid $2,235 in sick benefits in 1898-1899. Further security was provided by life insurance offered through the unions.[27]

Emotional support was as important as material assistance. The concern of other workers mattered deeply. When Henry King, a prominent member of the Victor Miners' Union, died in a mining accident, it was his wife's "express desire that a union man make whatever remarks are deemed necessary or appropriate." The service was held in the union hall, and the eulogy was delivered by a district labor leader. When Mrs. King went to Denver to bury her husband, she was accompanied by members of lodges to which she belonged, a woman friend from the Ladies' Auxiliary, and a representative of the *Daily Press*.[28] This level of support was typical. The *Daily Press* contained frequent notices for unionists to attend funerals and numerous announcements of fund raisings for the families of departed members. Nothing could totally ameliorate such losses or the consequent economic uncertainty but the unions did a great deal to relieve suffering, to provide friendship and support, and to give class meaning to life—and death—in the district.

Such support meant at least as much to workers' wives as to the men. The women were more alone at home than were their husbands on the job. Union functions and friends gave some relief from loneliness and isolation. Women suffered indirectly when the men's incomes were insecure and when unions could not effectively counter the power of mine owners. The pain which derived from economic and emotional ties to working-class men could partly be ameliorated by class ideologies which provided social explanations for the plight of working-class families. Sharing the community and vision of organized labor, women's auxiliaries expressed their own blend of love and militance. The Victor Women's Auxiliary reflected these sentiments on the occasion of the death of a woman whose husband had been imprisoned during the 1903-1904 strike.

> Women's Auxiliary No. 2 of Victor has parted with a beloved sister. For labor's cause she has suffered. The crown of thorns pressed against her

> brow, the "cross" laid on organized labor in this
> district rested heavily on her shoulders, and the
> patience with which she endured her burden, the
> loyalty she displayed to our cause, has endeared
> her to organized labor throughout the Cripple
> Creek district, and her death has cast a deeper
> gloom, a deeper sorrow over our hearts than words
> can express. To her bereaved husband this auxiliary
> extends its sympathy and sorrow.[29]

Mutual assistance was given larger meaning by recognition of
shared loss, anger, and oppression, all of which lent coherence to
working-class experience and provided a social, rather than an individual, meaning. Human caring and social relief were both central
to Cripple Creek's working-class community, but they could not
achieve ultimate class aims. Reforms and social services might help
to insure class survival locally until workers were sufficiently well
organized nationally to achieve a cooperative commonwealth. But
a socialist state could not be attained through local organization
alone, and if larger goals were to be reached, education and organization had to be considered social priorities. Both were successfully
pursued in Cripple Creek and both involved women.

With the possible exception of Butte, also a WFM stronghold,
the Cripple Creek district was probably the most organized area in
the country. By 1902 a clear majority—some estimates run as high
as 70 percent—of the district's workers belonged to a union.[30] The
educational and social events that they sponsored enhanced daily life
for laboring people, provided enjoyment, and advanced political
and economic education. The unions operated free public libraries
in Victor and Cripple Creek and for four years published the *Cripple Creek Daily Press*, established to counter the capitalist press
and to provide a forum for union news and class education. The
largest daily in Teller County, its masthead read "The Only Daily
Newspaper Owned By Organized Workingmen." [31]

While education was necessary to working-class organization, it
was also fairly happily merged with sociability. The union halls
were centers for social and political activities which included
unionists' families and involved them in class politics and ed-

ucation.[32] Social life helped to provide for labor's survival: locals and auxiliaries sponsored events to raise money to support strikes and to meet legal costs. These functions aided workers in other localities. During the 1903-1904 strike, for instance, the Women's Auxiliary raised relief funds by presenting a play and holding a leap year ball, with tickets "furnished free of charge to sisters whose husbands were out on strike."[33]

The unions' effectiveness depended on the influence of workers in the local exchange economy. In an area where almost all consumers were laborers, consumer boycotts went far to enforce union demands. By successfully advertising and boycotting establishments which refused to meet the demands of the smaller unions, organized labor forced merchants to grant six o'clock closing to retail clerks, prevented laundries from shipping clothes out of the district to nonunion shops, made boardinghouses and restaurants hire union help, and eliminated nonunion products from saloons, groceries, and other retail houses — in short, it enforced demands for union recognition, wages, and hours for all district workers.[34]

These tactics depended upon the women. Since purchasing power was a vital union weapon, women were courted for their control of household budgets and told that they belonged to unions through their husbands. One woman declared: "My husband is a member of a labor union. Am I not his better half? The good husband brings his union wages to his wife. That is as it should be. But if the wife spends the union wages for non-union goods, she is undoing the work of the labor unions."[35] The District Trades Assembly decided to form a Women's Auxiliary to organize feminine support for union-label drives. "The results of researches made by the home industry committee have convinced the assembly that so long as the wives and home keepers of union men remained in a measure indifferent to the sources from which the necessities of life were supplied, just so long would their efforts in behalf of the blue label be but partially successful."[36]

Boycotts worked only for trades which produced items for home consumption; they were ineffective for heavy industry, especially for gold mining. (Imagine the slogan: "Support your class — demand union-label gold.") Miners had to rely upon successful strikes, informal organizing drives, and social pressure both at work and in the towns. These tactics were sufficient until 1904. For ten years women benefited from union control and confronted contradictions between class and sex roles from within an organized and established labor community. Understandably, with their security and home life dependent on male organization, women placed class loyalty above their own specific needs.

Women whose primary loyalty was to their class were isolated from exclusively women's organizations. The local women's clubs were largely the province of the wives of merchants and professionals. More preoccupied with women's rights and civic projects than with class, they sometimes came into conflict with organized labor. For example, when the Victor Women's Club planned to petition Andrew Carnegie for funds for a town library, the unions objected. Labor preferred to build its own reading rooms and regarded "Carnegie's money as 'blood money,' coined from the sweat and blood of our fellow workmen, and therefore consider[ed] such a proposition an insult to organized labor and refuse[d] to patronize any library or reading room established in whole or in part with Carnegie's money.''[37] The conflict between the Victor Women's Club and the Trades Assembly was understood as a class issue. Gender was not of importance, partly because the ideology of the sexual spheres was well established before the development of a class ideology.

Unions seemed more crucial than feminism because conditions in hard-rock mining exerted the greatest influence on the lives of all the people of the district, because class awareness came from a much more immediate experience than concepts of womanhood, and because workers by no means accepted the inevitability of their class position. Production had been removed from homes long before miners were separated from the means of production. Cripple Creek workers had either been present during the creation of a wage-labor class in mining — a relatively recent development — or knew people who had lived through that transformation. Conversely, they had not lived through the earlier definition of manhood and womanhood when concepts of True Womanhood had first emerged. Sex roles, therefore, appeared natural, unchanging, and biologically determined, while class relationships had an obviously historical, changing — and changeable — character.

While consciousness of another conceptual definition which satisfactorily fused class and gender would not have guaranteed labor's triumph in its battles with mine owners, the failure to achieve such a definition created crucial rifts in working-class programs. Believing that a middle-class feminist movement was sufficient and that its aims had been achieved locally, Cripple Creek miners projected class goals that were confused by allegiances to genteel sex roles. Labor's analysis of industrial capitalism was not complete, since it neglected the relationship of the household to the total economy as well as the social and economic value of housework. Visions of an equal and humane socialist society did not include projections of equality between men and women or challenge economic dependence within the family. It was assumed that if workers did achieve a cooperative commonwealth, socialism would guarantee a secure family unit, with a working husband and a wife who would not be forced to work outside the home but could devote herself to being a supportive wife and mother. Accepting genteel sex roles as both natural and desirable, labor failed to consider the relationship between class inequalities and inequalities within working-class households. Unresolved tensions at the job increased tensions and demonstrations of men's supremacy in the home, both of which were heightened by women's dependence on the alienated labor of men. The uneasy coexistence of strong loyalties to class *and* to middle-class family roles created rifts among women and within the working class. Consequently possibilities for achieving either class or feminist goals were diminished.

The national sexual ideology was appropriate at best only to a dominant class of wealthy manufacturing families; it created double binds and internal strain for workers. There was an abrasive, if unarticulated and uncomprehended, conflict between the sexual understanding of the ruling national culture and the class understanding of Cripple Creek workers, whose internalization of that contradiction limited class actions. The concept of genteel womanhood produced an incomplete analysis of the meaning of class and created particular stresses for all three groups of working-class women: women wage workers, prostitutes and dance hall women, and miners' wives.

Women workers received an inconsistent blend of support as workers and chivalrous patronage as women. It was assumed that women held jobs only if forced to do so by the absence of a male breadwinner or an inadequate income. The common fear prevailed that women took men's jobs and depressed wages. The more women worked, the more men would "be out of a job through the ingenuity of capitalism to economize on the profit reaping system."[38] District unions organized female labor to avoid that threat, but male workers shared the belief that women worked only temporarily and only to support themselves, not families.

Equality in the workplace would have been problematic had it ever been confronted. It never really was. Nor did it have to be. After all, there were no women miners. Most Cripple Creek women, moreover, were married and at home, and others hoped to be. Unionists believed their treatment of women was progressive, and so it was for that time. The Typographical Union was proud that it was "the first organization of men to recognize the rights of women to equal work."[39] Not all district workers agreed, however, and many considered women incompetent to work outside the home. R. E. Croskey, a Socialist, secretary of the District Trades Assembly, and president of the Western Labor Union's Hotel and Restaurant Employees Union, believed that no woman could cook in a restaurant or hotel because when "you put a woman at a range with three half springs to keep broiling with a long fork and a bowl of consomme coming up at the other end, she gets flustered."[40] Deviation from accepted work spheres was sexually as well as economically threatening. Deeper masculine fears surfaced when the Denver Women's Club requested that a woman police officer be hired. The *Daily Press* was opposed, claiming that hiring a woman for the job would "result in the effeminacy of the human race." Worse yet, wives would "confer with the young lady next door who is working the night shift on the force, and those aged and sacred excuses for coming home at 2 in the morning will not hold as much water as a sieve."[41]

Several hundred Cripple Creek women belonged to unions, especially to the Retail Clerks, Laundry Workers, Hotel and Restaurant Employees, and the Typographical locals. Clerks and typographers, who most often had equal work and wages, benefited particularly from union membership. But women's and men's work were generally distinct, and even women unionists often received lower wages than men. The 1900 census of manufactures, which probably underrepresents women wage workers, lists fifty women working in the district for an average $368.09 annually and 735 men whose average annual wage was $838.68 in nonmining manufacturing. [42] The wage scale enforced by the Cripple Creek Laundry Workers Union was generally lower than the $3 minimum daily wage for miners, and the lowest wages were for "female" jobs. The scale for a sixty-hour week ranged from a minimum of $15 for drivers to $8.50 for towel supply girls and $7.50 for mangle girls. Laundry wages were slightly better in Victor where the weekly scale ranged from $9 for mangle girls to "not less than $18" for fifty-four hours for men who worked inside. [43] The Victor Trades Assembly, after protracted debates, failed to act on a resolution which would have made "the wages of women who work where they have to board themselves not less than $10 per week, and the time for labor not more than 54 hours, which was amended to 48." [44]

Women's wages in Cripple Creek were somewhat higher than the national average, but their work was often irregular. Ten waitresses hired temporarily to serve a convention overflow crowd staged a walkout in 1902 because they received the standard $14 a week and board instead of the $3 a day and board usually paid temporary help. When the grievance committee of the Hotel and Restaurant Employes Union could not resolve the issue the union struck. One woman explained the strikers' position: "We wait a week for a month for two days' employment and get four dollars for it. Extra work is during a rush. It is hard and wearying work because there are so many people to wait upon, and a waitress earns every cent she gets. My brother earns four dollars a day at the mines, and comes home fresh and ready for a frolic, but I am so tired and weary that I must go to bed if I would be in any shape to work the next day." [45]

Even in traditionally female occupations, women were seldom a majority of the work force, and all the unions were male strongholds. The "thirty-eight beautiful women all members" of the Cooks and Waiters Union who graced a Labor Day float belonged to a local which had a total membership of some two hundred. [46] Few women achieved union leadership. Several served as secretaries of the Clerks' locals, but more were found on arrangements committees for socials and in other more "feminine" roles. Nellie Kedzie, one of the few prominent women unionists, represented the Cripple Creek Federal Labor Union at the State Federation of Labor convention in 1900. She "spoke well for early closing [shorter hours]" and "seemed at home, too." But her influence in the masculine convention atmosphere was such a novelty to male unionists that one facetious reporter could only associate Kedzie's forcefulness with the fact that she had survived when "she had once been run over by a street car in Denver." [47]

If the attitude of district labor was ambivalent toward working women, at least its judgment on their class and moral status was unambiguous: they were workers and they were good women. Class and morality interacted with greater complication for working men's wives and for "bad" women. Prostitutes performed wage labor, but a prostitute's class status depended on her race and on the class of her clientele. Myers Avenue, Cripple Creek's wide-open red-light district, reflected class in its geography. At one end of the street were the fancy parlor houses frequented by mine owners and other wealthy men. Next were the smaller houses, then the one-woman "cribs" of white, Oriental, Mexican, and black women (in that order) who were patronized chiefly by miners and other laborers. [48]

Unionists' reverence for "good women" stood in stark contrast to the "row" and to living and working conditions there. In 1901 and 1902 the *Daily Press* covered at least fifteen suicide attempts among prostitutes and dance-hall women, seven successful, and most attributed by the male reporters to desertion by pimps or lovers. There was some sympathy for the "soiled doves." To be sure, they could not be approved but they could nonetheless be seen as victims of exploitation, forced into their vocations by a capitalist economy. "Under our present social and industrial system the breeding and propagation of the female prostitute class is as inevitable and unavoidable as the appearance of the maggot in the putrid carcass that lays in the July sun." [49]

Dance halls compromised men and women, but it was hard to condemn the women who worked there, especially since, despite professed veneration of True Women, many male workers obviously tolerated a fair amount of feminine "falseness." Labor reserved its greatest venom for employers. "The inmates of such places . . . deserve pity rather than censure. They are victims of conditions which should not exist in any country. But for the men who live from the product of these women's shame, we have no words adequate to express our contempt." [50]

A partially developed economic analysis of prostitution notwithstanding, allegiance to genteel morality was sufficiently strong that organizing dance-hall workers, much less prostitutes, was never seriously considered. But in 1902, true to the union spirit of the community, dance-hall women called a strike to oppose a 10 percent reduction in their share of liquor sales and established a Dance Hall Girl's Protective Association. The strike succeeded, but the union was apparently short-lived and the women never applied for membership in the Trades Assembly. [51]

For union men, it was enormously important to protect "good women" from the taint of the tenderloin. It was impossible to eliminate gambling and prostitution, but numerous campaigns were waged to regulate them. While men could move between the "half world" and the home world, a woman could rarely regain her virtue, and it was a source of male pride that union wages saved "families from the soup house and the brothel." [52] But the definition of union wives as "good women" failed to distinguish them from middle- and upper-class women, including the few women mine owners. The boardinghouse keepers and restaurant owners whom organized labor boycotted for anti-union hiring practices were True Women, too.

Women accepted the notion that they should be supportive and furnish a refuge from the workplace. If a working man provided a comfortable home, he expected wifely support. He wanted to come home to a "rosy wife" who could "sing at the wash tub," one woman wrote, and find "nothing under the sun that makes her as merry as housecleaning." She should save money and be agreeable since "the working man has all the vicissitudes he wants when he goes to his work." But she recognized that women's supportive roles derived from economic dependence and suggested that a happy marriage required that a woman take "to the altar a sum of money to give her some share of independence for life." [53] The supportive role was difficult; housework absorbed most waking hours and life was often tense and uncertain. Women were rarely economically independent and the reliance of the whole family on a male breadwinner did much to reinforce an ideology of natural and separate sexual spheres.

Women were assumed to be preoccupied with home, morality, children, and femininity. One page of the Sunday editions of the *Daily Press* was devoted to news of the various unions and to columns on labor philosophy. It also contained fashion items. Next to a story about a waitresses' strike or an article entitled "For the Abolishment of the Wage System" appeared fashion photos captioned, for instance, "A Moire Blouse Jacket," "The 'Zenana' Coat," and "Smart Paris Costumes." Working-class women were encouraged to be pretty and popular, to strive for male approval. They were advised to "look always young and charming, be as happy as you can. Dress as well as your means will allow, dress becomingly and dress modestly; give every attention to your underclothing."[54] While men were lauded for their civic and work activities, the *Daily Press* ran popularity contests for women — the most popular teacher, the most popular married lady, the most popular clerk in the district. Jennie Wolf, "the popular and attractive saleslady at Pierce Cigar Store," won a theater box; the *Daily Press* had no doubt that she would "be a charming hostess and sustain her position with grace and dignity."[55]

Labor demanded respect for feminine gentility. Even union politics could not absolve the man who swore in the presence of a lady.

> Residents of Victor Avenue in the vicinity of Sixth Street are incensed over the speech of one Jim Olvie in that locality yesterday noon . . . . Yesterday Mrs. Ed. Vinton, wife of a letter carrier, remarked that the president (McKinley) was growing better. Olvie is alleged to have expressed his regret with much profanity and some obscenity in the presence of ladies and particularly to Mrs. Walenberg. The latter is the wife of P. Walenberg, a member of the executive board of the miners' union, and is a lady of respectability and refinement. Olvie, she states, refered to the president as a s— of a b— and hoped he would die.[56]

Chivalrous amenities were appreciated — even demanded — by women as well as men, but they did not always produce contented households.[57] Fifty-six divorces were reported in the *Daily Press* from July 1899 through December 1901. Many couples lived apart and wives left the district for months at a time. Separations were generally explained in acceptably genteel terms: vacations were for the benefit of the wife's health, and couples lived in different cities for the health of the family or for the sake of the children's education.[58] The exercise of these options also suggests that some workers' homes were not fully satisfying. It may also help to explain why traditional family roles received so much public allegiance and why women were so strongly encouraged to support class goals without challenging the limitations imposed on them by their traditional role.

The supposition that women were either good or bad and the further assumption that working-class women were good and therefore preoccupied with home, family, and civic morality shaped men's understanding of women's social power and had an important effect on labor politics. Suffrage brought women some recognition, but that recognition was often simply a matter of political expediency. The WFM decided to organize women's auxiliaries in 1902 partly because it was moving to a policy of political action and it was "estimated that by organizing the women just about 200,000 votes will be added to the political strength of the organization."[59] Cripple Creek unionists had recognized women's political importance earlier and had announced that "the question of trusts, imperialism, free silver and other political issues are of no consequence or importance whatever compared to the emancipation of women."[60] There was, however, more opportunism than conviction in this assertion since it was intended to encourage women to oppose an anti-union politician who had also opposed suffrage. District labor's attention to women's issues, consequently, was often simply recognition of their political power. Nonetheless, it was progressive to encourage women's participation in politics for whatever reason. Clara Stiverson, the daughter of a Victor saloon owner, remembers: "My dad told my mother, 'You do not vote or I'll leave home. 'Cause I will not be embarrassed by having you go and vote.' "[61]

It was assumed that women were less partisan than men and that special appeals were necessary to win their votes. Appeals were therefore based on neither feminist nor class goals but on the supposed moral and domestic concerns of working-class women. In 1900 Cripple Creek women were asked to support Democrats because Republicans squandered education funds and because, invoking the usual stereotypes, women were "more intimate with the home and school life of the children than the husband." [62]

Appeals to womanly virtue created political hostility toward prostitutes, probably the largest group of women wage earners in the district. This attitude diminished the possibility of political success for organized labor, as an important local election in 1899 illustrates. In that year, the unions formed the Co-operative Party and joined with the Populists to run a labor slate for county offices. Assuming that union strength guaranteed male support and that the women's vote must be won, organized labor made the suppression of gambling and prostitution its only real campaign issue. The "good civic housekeeping" argument of the national suffrage movement was adopted, and women were asked to prove their right to vote by opposing local vice. "The ladies have an opportunity to show that the right of suffrage has not been thrown away upon them — the opportunity to throw their influence for purity in politics." [63] Voters were reminded that "every gambler, every keeper of a bawdy house, every man in the Cripple Creek district who makes a living by violating the law, is working and fighting for either the democratic or republican candidates for county offices." [64] But purity was no vote grabber. The Co-operatives came in an abysmal third to the Democrats and the Republican-Silver Republican coalition, and for the next few years organized labor supported the Democrats. [65]

Neither union power nor the ideas of class developed by organized labor sufficiently explain the tactics adopted in the 1899 election campaign. A highly organized and class-conscious labor community projected political goals and tactics, not from class understandings, but from genteel concepts of home, family, and sex. Perhaps working-class women were not primarily concerned with prostitution; perhaps working-class men considered it necessary to their public image and self-image to oppose prostitution, but did not really desire its elimination; perhaps everyone knew that no political party could end prostitution. An internally consistent definition of class might have led to demands for legalized prostitution, but adherence to genteel morality meant that taking such a position was both inconceivable and politically unwise. Nor were working-class women encouraged to formulate their own political demands which might, for instance, have involved issues such as the extension of sewer lines to working-class neighborhoods. It was clear, however, that class concerns were more likely to insure political success than were issues of social morality. When labor candidates concentrated on such measures as support of a state eight-hour law and raising mine owners' taxes, they won in Cripple Creek. Nor was the 1899 defeat a simple matter of old party allegiances. In 1903 organized labor elected the secretary of the District Trades Assembly to the office of county tax assessor on an independent ticket.[66]

Part of the difficulty was that few goals remained in Cripple Creek which were susceptible to local political solutions. Like an eight-hour day and a living wage, a secure home and woman suffrage were important gains. But those achievements did not result in a cooperative commonwealth, and they could protect neither labor nor women when union control was threatened in 1903. Socialism could not be won locally, and workers were prevented from extending union benefits even to the nearby smelter workers of Colorado City, who refined Cripple Creek ores and for whom, in 1903, Cripple Creek miners risked all that they had achieved.

Certainly, local concerns were not at issue in the 1903 strike.[67] True to the WFM's commitment to the industrial unionism, the strike was called to support the smelter workers, who toiled longer hours for less pay than the miners and who were blacklisted when they attempted to form their own locals. The WFM struck Cripple Creek mines that shipped ore to smelters which had fired union laborers, hoping that this economic pressure would force the smelters to reemploy unionists.

Both miners and mine owners were fully class-conscious and both sides thought that they dealt from strength. The unions were well-organized, had ample treasuries, and controlled most public offices. But the Mine Owners' Association had important allies, including Governor James Peabody. A Canon City banker, Peabody had helped to set up the local Citizens' Alliance, an association of anti-union business people and professionals. Cripple Creek merchants organized the district Citizens' Alliance and cut off credit to strikers. The WFM quickly established four cooperative stores to distribute strike relief.

The strike was initially uneventful, but in September 1903 local business petitioned Peabody for troops. With scant investigation, without talking to labor, and over the objections of local officials who denied any danger to civil order, Peabody sent in the militia. Military salaries were guaranteed by a mine owners' loan to the state. Led by Adjutant General Sherman Bell, who was superintendent for large Cripple Creek mining companies and who promised to "do up this damned anarchistic federation," the soldiers did little to preserve peace. They arrested unionists wholesale and held them without charge. On the legal pretext that limited martial law had been declared in the district, the military defied *habeas corpus* orders. Soldiers invaded the Teller County courthouse, surrounded it with gatling guns, and trained a cannon on it. Peabody declared full martial law in early December after someone had pulled spikes from train tracks and after an explosion in the Vindicator mine had killed two men. Strikers were held for both acts, although the mine was under military guard and there was strong evidence that an employers' detective had pulled the spikes but had warned the engineer to prevent a train wreck.

In March 1904 employers instituted a work-permit system and denied employment to union men. The end came for the miners on June 6 when a train depot was blown up, killing fourteen scabs. Labor insisted that the explosion was a mine owners' plot to justify destruction of the unions, but the charge was not investigated. Local officials were deposed by mine owners and the Citizens' Alliance, who took over the legal apparatus of the county. (They gave the sheriff a choice of resigning or being hanged.) The mob then destroyed union halls and stores, rounded up prominent unionists, and deported them to Kansas and New Mexico. The deportees who tried to come back were beaten, redeported, and threatened with death if they returned. The employers' slogan was, "They Can't Come Back."

With the strike broken, all unions were suppressed, union

miners were blacklisted, and merchants refused to employ any union help. All retail clerks were forced to surrender their union cards and all locals were required to withdraw from the District Trades Assembly. Washerwomen who had sympathized with strikers were prohibited from working in the district, although some apparently eked out a precarious living.[68] Unions were never again permitted in the Cripple Creek district, and the class aid and communalism that they had supported could continue only at considerable risk of discovery by the mine owners or the militia.

During and after the strike, women performed valuable service to the unions and to one another. Notions of feminine weakness and gentility were used as class weapons in publicizing the excessive force used against labor. When the Women's Auxiliary was invaded by soldiers, when women and children were beaten by mine owners' gunmen, and when women were separated from their husbands, the employers and the state were attacked for violating womanhood and destroying the home.[69] Women, however, could sometimes do things which men could not, and they were also praised for their strength and bravery during the strike. They crossed military lines without being imprisoned or shot; they and their children taunted scabs and soldiers and otherwise harassed them. The militia tried to deter the women but did not jail them.

> Mrs. James Prenty and Mrs. Blixer, both prominent in the women's auxiliary . . . were in custody, though not under arrest, for about an hour today. They were charged with having indulged in insolent criticism and denunciation of the military. They were allowed to sit on the stairs leading to the bullpen for a while and were then taken before Provost Marshal McClelland, who gave them a lecture on the necessity of using caution in their public speech.[70]

After the deportations, organization and relief work fell to the women. They raised bail bonds, provided food for the incarcerated miners, and distributed strike relief. Margaret Hooten and Estella Nichols, both Women's Auxiliary members, were arrested and told to stop the relief effort; after that the work went on in secret.[71]

Even before the brutal aftermath, the strike produced a heroine. Financial difficulties forced the *Daily Press* to fold, and the only other prolabor paper in the district, the *Victor Record*, agreed to publish WFM statements. In an attempt to silence the *Record*, the militia jailed its work force. Emma Langdon, a union linotypist, crawled in a back window, worked all night, and brought out the paper with the headline, "Somewhat Disfigured But Still In The Ring." For her action she became the first woman elected an honorary member of the WFM and was hailed as a "Colorado heroine."[72]

Women joined the battle as allies and were among the casualties. They shared an outlook which explained their experience in class terms, and they still had the material and social support of the WFM and other unions.[73] But class support could not stop the destruction of unionism or its human toll.

Women watched helplessly as their husbands were deported and endured separation and poverty when the men were not allowed to return. Harriet Minister, the wife of a deported union man, told a newspaper reporter: "They sent my man away, and he will not come back, if he takes my advice, until things are quite different from what they are now. I make my living taking in washing. It is better than begging. One who has six mouths to feed has to work pretty hard."[74]

For some it was even worse. Emil Johnson, a deported member of the Altman miners' union, turned on the gas in his Denver roominghouse and killed himself. The Denver papers reported that Johnson was driven to suicide by concern for his family. "Johnson's wife and children, at Altman, had been refused provisions because of an order issued by General Bell. When Johnson heard of this he was driven almost to the verge of madness to think his innocent family should be made to suffer so much on account of his insisting on his rights. He brooded over this, at times laboring under the hallucination that his family was starving . . . . The suicide was the result."[75]

Fred Minister and Emil Johnson were both WFM members. But in the polarized strike situation there was no neutral ground, and some nonunionists suffered as well. The small middle class was forced to take sides, and union sympathizers were punished along with the striking miners. W.H. Morgan, an assayer who supported the strikers, was among the first to be deported from the district. Frightened that he would be arrested and taken back to the military bullpen and despondent about his family's welfare in his absence, Morgan also committed suicide. Several letters from his wife were found on his body.

> Willie was beaten badly by one of the soldiers last night because he would not tell where you were hiding . . . . Two or three of the neighboring women have been to see their husbands but have not been allowed to see them. Mrs. W. says her man was not even allowed to change his underwear, and he called to her that most of the men were bothered with vermin . . . .

> I saw General Bell tonight to let me get some groceries and he said he hoped Denver would soon be put under martial law so he could search for you. He said he would fix it so no union man could vote at the next election. He talked awful to me . . . . Please stay in hiding and do not let this horrible man and his soldiers get hold of you, for they will never let you get away. I hope to God this terrible thing will soon be settled in some way, so you can return to your home again. I do not see why innocent men should be made to suffer. You say you are discouraged. Brace up and write soon to
>
> GAY [76]

The Morgans, the Johnsons, and the Ministers were not alone in their anguish. However conflicted the lives of working-class women, those conflicts were less painful than their suffering as the unions were destroyed.

When class action became imperative, women left their homes and violated prescribed roles. The "good women" of Cripple Creek were good resisters. Emma Langdon, who believed that "women's natural sphere should be in the home and not in public life," nonetheless acted as a worker in the strike. "They *are brothers* . . . . We are both subjected to the same conditions. He is on strike today. I may be tomorrow. We both stand for the same cause — unionism." [77]

Langdon later wrote a history of the strike. Like many union women, she performed that work in addition to her household duties. "I have compiled the work, set the type, read the proofs, and made the pictures from which many of the illustrations are made, folded the pages and while getting out the work have taken care of my work as usual, doing my own sewing, baking, washing and ironing and other work that falls to the lot of women . . . . I have worked at my trade sufficient to pay the greater part of the expenses of halftones and press work. I attended the trials of my union brothers and fulfilled my duties as secretary to orders and membership on committees." [78] Stacking the roles of woman, worker, and class activist, Langdon became an organizer for the WFM and for the Socialist Party.

For Emma Langdon, as for the now anonymous stenographers, housekeepers, and miners' wives, class identity was real and important. (That important sense of community was denied to those married to old-fashioned prospectors who fiercely resisted labor unions.) Unions made a significant difference for many Cripple Creek women: they provided social and material aid, a community of class understanding, and a haven — a place to go to escape from household isolation. As significant as these benefits were, they were insufficient to meet all the needs of women or of organized labor.

Industrial change not only produced class militance but also separated production from the home and made wage work the province of men. To protect their homes and their women, unionists diluted their social programs and political action. It is not surprising that women and households did not become an integral part of the understanding of what class means; such a definition has begun to be formulated only recently as the economic role of the household has become more narrowly restricted to consumption and as married women have moved in greater numbers into the paid work force. So long as family and productive roles were kept separate, men could be seen primarily as workers and women primarily as homemakers. It is only since the spheres have become less separate that their relationship has begun to receive serious analysis.

Nor is it surprising that the working-class women of Cripple Creek desired a stable home life and did not clamor to enter the drudgerous work world. They gave primary allegiance to their class rather than to their sex because class organization, indirectly at least, achieved a great deal for them. But it could not overcome the loneliness of the privatized household or protect that household when corporate power crushed the unions.

Cripple Creek workers who developed collective means to confront the power of corporate capitalism accepted definitions of the sexual spheres which undermined class action. True Womanhood belonged with *laissez-faire* capitalism if it belonged at all. This acceptance of an ideology that made women economically dependent on their husbands and men economically responsible for their families meant that it was more difficult for men to escape work that was alienating. If women were dependent on the wages of men, men were equally dependent on unpleasant jobs; they could not easily risk unemployment by individually challenging working conditions. The individualism implicit in the concept of manhood not only impeded collective action but also meant that men could feel only a sense of isolating personal failure if they did not successfully provide for their families. Cripple Creek workers combatted individualism by providing social explanations and solutions for the economic position of working-class men. But successful unionism paradoxically insured that the sex roles of an individualistic age were not challenged.

The contradiction between class and gender existed partly because the class battle had not been won; the home still served to absorb some of the tensions of the workplace. But idealization of the home endangered the class cause and left women with only escapist alternatives. If they did not accept their status as miners' wives, women could only go "on vacation" leave town or sue for divorce.

That women did not challenge their genteel roles is understandable. A comfortable home was not a real possibility for many working-class women, and, women's lives would have been more difficult and uncertain without the local unions. Nor is it easy to project — or to want to project — a situation in which women might have demanded the opportunity to enter the paid work force and risk their lives underground along with the men. Economic dependence was the root of sexual inequality within the working class, and it is difficult to imagine an alternative in a nineteenth-century mining town. But it is significant that the ability to provide for one's family was such an important measure of male success that the sexual ideologies on which it was based were idealized rather than questioned.

If labor's understanding of industrial capitalism had been extended to encompass division of labor within the family and to embrace an historical rather than a "natural" understanding of sex roles, then women might have participated more meaningfully in the formulation of class goals and policies. Had women been encouraged to formulate demands on the basis of their own needs, an understanding which related inequalities of class and gender might have begun to be achieved. [79]

But these things did not happen, and one reason that feminist demands were not met in Cripple Creek is that women did not raise them. The most significant feminist achievement in the district, suffrage, was inadequate when employers could depose elected officials. The absence of feminism in Cripple Creek was only partly the failure of the national women's movement, which in the 1890s paid inadequate attention to the needs of working-class women. The most important cause was the tranferral of unequal work relationships from the mines to family households.

While corporate capitalism made class needs more immediate and crucial than feminist goals, the two were inseparable. Unequal attention to either class or feminism created internal contradictions in both. Restricting its goals narrowly to suffrage, the national feminist movement sacrificed immigrant, black, and working-class women and achieved only a partial victory. Class cut across sex lines and sex cut across class lines; feminist and class goals had to be pursued together or both would succeed only partially.

An understanding of class that was not strained by sexual inequality would not have guaranteed the end of women's isolation in the home in Cripple Creek. Like wage labor, the household had an economic base which could be changed only through collective action. But a perfect union of class and gender would have meant that labor confronted capitalist power untorn by internal contradictions. As it was, working women remained subordinate within the unions, prostitutes were politically attacked, and married women could enter the union hall only after the dinner dishes were done and children tucked in. In Cripple Creek, class and gender, like Emma Langdon's list of tasks, were stacked together but never successfully merged.

NOTES

1. Colorado Bureau of Labor Statistics, *Eighth Biennial Report of the Bureau of Labor Statistics of the State of Colorado, 1901-1902* (Denver, 1902), pp. 66-82. Separate locals also existed for barbers; bricklayers and masons; musicians; printers; painters and paper hangers; retail clerks; sheet metal, tin, iron, and cornice workers; tailors; typographers; newspaper writers; stage employees; electrical trainmen; miners; stationary engineers; and mill workers. Two federal labor unions and two junior federal labor unions included all other workers.

2. There is some debate over the nature and derivation of western mining radicalism. I essentially agree with Dubofsky that militance was rooted in industrialization and accompanying changes in work and social relations. See Melvyn Dubofsky, "The Origins of Western Working Class Radicalism, 1890-1905," *Labor History* (Summer 1966): 131-154. For other interpretations and further accounts see: John E. Brinley, Jr., "The Western Federation of Miners" (Ph.D. dissertation, University of Utah, 1972); Vernon H. Jenson, *Heritage of Conflict: Labor Relations in the Nonferrous Metals Industry Up to 1930* (Ithaca, New York, 1950); and Ch. 7, "Syndicalist Socialism and the Western Federation of Miners," in John H.M. Laslett, *Labor and the Left* (New York, 1970), pp. 241-286. In light of arguments that radicalism sprang from the isolation of mining towns or was imported by immigrants, it should be noted that Cripple Creek was a major urban area, with three railroads and two interurban lines which made it readily accessible to Colorado Springs and Denver; that its population was largely native-born and immigrants were mostly Canadian or Northern and Western European, and naturalized; and that more isolated mining towns with different ethnic compositions were also involved in strikes during 1903 and 1904. U.S. Census Office, *Twelfth Census of the United States, 1900, Population*, vol. 2, Part 2, pp. 740-741, 973.

3. Marshall Sprague, *Money Mountain* (1953; reprint, New York, 1971), p. 87; Catherine Rinker, "The History of Cripple Creek, Colorado, 1891-1917" (M.A. Thesis, University of Colorado, 1934), pp. 62-63.

4. Charles Howard Shinn, *Mining Camps: A Study in American Frontier Government* (1884; reprint, New York, 1965), 280-283.

5. For accounts of the 1894 strike, see: Jenson, *Heritage of Conflict*, pp. 38-53;

Benjamin M. Rastall, *The Labor History of the Cripple Creek District* (Madison, 1908); and Emma Langdon, *The Cripple Creek Strike* (1903-1905; reprint, New York, 1969), pp. 34-44.

6. The WFM withdrew from the IWW shortly after its formation and joined the AFL in 1911. This shift, however, did not signify a repudiation of either socialism or industrial unionism; nor did the WFM retract its critique of dominant AFL policy. Rather, Federation affiliation reflected a tactical decision to try to "bore from within" the AFL to advance socialism among workers and at the same time try to secure stable financial support for the WFM.

7. For samples of unionists' political opinions, see Colorado Bureau of Labor Statistics, *Seventh Biennial Report of the Bureau of Labor Statistics of the State of Colorado, 1899-1900* (Denver, 1900), pp. 102-119, and *Official Proceedings of the Tenth Annual Convention, Western Federaton of Miners* (Denver, 1902), pp. 106-107.

8. *The Report of the State Bureau of Mines, Colorado, for the Years 1903-1904* (Denver, 1905), pp. 20-21, gives these figures for district miners: 1896: 3,575; 1897: 5,386; 1898: 5,764; 1899: 7,925; 1900: 7,920; 1901: 6,484; 1902: 5,940; 1903: 5,200; and 1904: 5,667. Cripple Creek "boosters" claimed a population of 50,000 at the turn of the century, but the 1900 census for Teller County enumerated ony 29,002. Robert Guilford Taylor, *Cripple Creek* (Bloomington, 1966), p. 205, contains probably the most accurate population estimates for the area. Taylor places the 1900 population at 32,000.

9. In 1900 there were 12,144 men to 9,968 women over twenty-one in the district, and earlier the sex ratio was even more unbalanced. U.S. Census Office, *Twelfth Census of the United States, 1900, Population,* vol. 2, part 2, pp. 177, 212-213.

10. Interview with Mrs. Clara Stiverson, age 81, a resident of the district from 1899 to 1925, conducted July 29, 1975, in Golden, Colorado. Figures for women's occupations were obtained from the *Cripple Creek-Victor Mining Directory* (Cripple Creek, 1895), and *Cripple Creek District Directory, 1902-1903* (n.p., 1902). The 1895 *Directory* lists 353 women, of whom 117 (33%) have no listed occupation; the 1902 *Directory* lists 1,521—703 (46%) with no occupation. From those who listed occupations, the following figures were computed. Dressmaker or seamstress: 11% (1895 and 1902); rooming, boardinghouse, or restaurant proprietor: 29% (1895), 21% (1902); proprietor of other establishments: 6% (1895), 3% (1902); clerk: 8% (1895), 12% (1902); milliner: 5% (1895), 1% (1902); stenographer: 3% (1895 and 1902); cook: 3% (1895 and 1902); laundress or laundry worker: 12% (1895), 9% (1902); waitress: 8% (1895), 7% (1902); housekeeper, maid or domestic: 7% (1902); school teacher: 6% (1902); telephone or telegraph operator: 4% (1902); other: 15% (1895), 12% (1902). The 1902 figures do not add up to 100% due to rounding. The actual numbers are certainly underestimates; there were both boardinghouse keepers and professionals who advertised in the local press but were not listed in the 1902 *Directory*. Prostitutes, of course, are not listed. However, comparisons with newspapers and other sources suggest that the proportions approximate women's occupational participation and accurately reflect jobs available for women.

11. Colorado Bureau of Labor Statistics, *Eighth Biennial Report*, p. 47.

12. *Ibid.*, pp. 55-56.

13. Mable Barbee Lee, *Cripple Creek Days* (Garden City, New York, 1958), pp. 69, 169.

14. Barbara Welter, "The Cult of True Womanhood: 1820-1860," *American Quarterly* (Summer 1966): 151-174.

15. *Miners' Magazine* (January 7, 1904), p. 15.

16. This term was widespread in local newspapers and appeared with some frequency to denote a household relationship in the 1900 Manuscript Census for Teller County.

17. In 1895 the district had 53 saloons; by 1902 there were 106. *Cripple Creek District Directory*, 1895, pp. 448-450; and 1902-1903, pp. 607-610.

18. *Cripple Creek Daily Press*, passim.

19. *Ibid.*, "Labor Notes," June 22, 1902.

20. "Business Interests Demand Strong Unions," *Cripple Creek Daily Press*, (August 14, 1901). See also "Cripple Creek News Notes," *Colorado Springs Gazette*, (September 15, 1901).

21. Lists of delegates to party conventions from the city to the congressional levels from 1900 to 1903 indicate that roughly one-fifth of all delegates were women; the figures range from none at one Republican gathering to one-third at some Democratic conventions. Women were most often elected city clerks or treasurers; almost always the county school superintendant was female. Delegate lists were printed in the *Cripple Creek Daily Press*.

22. Governor Davis Waite, quoted in Charles Hartzell, *History of Colorado During the Turbulent Reign of "Davis the First"* (Denver, 1894), p. 14. See also Billie Barnes Jensen, "The Woman Suffrage Movement in Colorado" (M.A. Thesis, University of Colorado, 1959). The Cripple Creek district ratified women suffrage in 1893 by a vote of 548 to 254; Altman, then the labor stronghold, favored suffrage 92 to 27. "Official Vote of El Paso County," *Colorado Springs Weekly Gazette*, (November 16, 1893), p. 5.

23. "Labor Notes," *Cripple Creek Daily Press*, (October 5, 1902).

24. "Business Prosperity Depends on Labor," *Cripple Creek Daily Press*, (April 23, 1901).

25. *The Report of the State Bureau of Mines, Colorado, for the Years 1903-1904*, p. 25, gives the following state figures for hard-rock mining accidents: 1896: 103 fatal, 107 nonfatal; 1897: 110 fatal, 169 nonfatal; 1898: 108 fatal, 184 nonfatal; 1899: 103 fatal, 481 nonfatal; 1900: 107 fatal, 526 nonfatal; 1901: 121 fatal, 633 nonfatal; 1902: 82 fatal, 561 nonfatal; 1903: 67 fatal, 494 nonfatal; 1904: 101 fatal, 539 nonfatal. Reports of accidents in the *Cripple Creek Daily Press* indicate that a significant number were not reported. While these were seemingly minor, a bruised hand from falling rock meant the loss of several days' work.

26. *Cripple Creek Daily Press*, (November 9, 1902).

27. *Official Proceedings of the Eleventh Annual Convention of the Western Federation of Miners* (Denver, 1903), pp. 86-88. "Good Work," *Cripple Creek Daily Press*, (December 13, 1899).

28. "Our Fallen Chief," *Cripple Creek Daily Press*, (March 10, 1903), and "Solemn Ceremony at Henry King Funeral," *Cripple Creek Daily Press*, (March 11, 1903).

29. *Miners' Magazine* (September 17, 1903), p. 7.

30. *Eighth Annual Report of the Bureau of Labor Statistics,* Colorado, 1901-1902, p. 88. James T. Smith, Deputy Labor Commissioner, supplied the estimate of 70 percent; WFM membership figures suggest that this may be an inflated figure. In 1903, when the district's population was some 30,000, the District Trades and Labor Assembly reported 5,300 members. Since this was after the 1903-1904 strike had begun and many union miners had left the district, a 50 to 65 percent estimate is probably reasonable. See "The Situation in Colorado," *Miners' Magazine* (December 24, 1903), p. 8.

31. *The Cripple Creek Daily Press*, which published during the period from 1899 to 1903, was purchased by thirty-four of the district's then thirty-five unions. Beside national, state,and local news, it covered union activities and reported gossip and daily social life for all the towns. It furnishes a wealth of material for understanding Cripple Creek working-class culture and reflects in its news coverage, advertising, and editorials the juxtaposition of conflicting ideas of class and gender. While I have footnoted several examples for my conclusions in this article, there are literally hundreds of items in the *Daily Press* which document important beliefs and associations. A nearly complete run of the *Daily Press* is available at the Western Historical Collections, University of Colorado, Boulder, Colorado, and a microfilm copy is available at the Wisconsin State Historical Society, Madison, Wisconsin.

32. See, for example, these articles in the *Cripple Creek Daily Press*: "Greatest Labor Day Celebration That Was Ever Held in Cripple Creek," (September 3, 1901); "Engineers' Union—Musicale and Entertainment," (October 27, 1901); and "Cooks and Waiters Entertain," (February 2, 1903); See also "Open Meeting at Victor," *Miners' Magazine* (April 4, 1904), pp. 11-12.

33. *Miners' Magazine* (April 14, 1904): "Dramatic Performance by Ladies of Victor Ladies Auxiliary No. 2," p. 11, and "The Woman's Auxiliary," pp. 12-13.

34. See, for example, the following articles in the *Cripple Creek Daily Press*: "Waiters Win Out," (December 12, 1899); "Dry Goods Stores Close at 6," (December 30, 1899); "Must Do Work at Home," (May 13, 1902); and "Trades Assembly Demands Union Made Cigars," (November 11, 1902). A typical unfair notice read: "The following eat and boarding houses have been declared unfair by Cooks' and Waiters' Union No. 24, and the Trades Assembly of Cripple Creek . . . . It is charged that the ladies do not treat their employees right" (August 12, 1900).

35. "How Women Can Help," *Cripple Creek Daily Press*, (December 21, 1902).

36. "Address to the Toilers," *Cripple Creek Daily Press*, (March 16, 1902). See, also in the *Daily Press*, "Labor Notes," (June 8, 1902 and March 29, 1903); and "Women's Work in Label Agitation," (June 29, 1902).

37. "Union Men Do Not Wish Library From Andrew Carnegie," *Cripple Creek Daily Press*, (April 8, 1902).

38. *Ibid.,* "Labor Notes," (December 21, 1902).

39. *Ibid.*, (April 20, 1902).

40. *Ibid.*, "Hotel and Restaurant Employees in Session," (May 31, 1901).

41. *Ibid.*, "Women for Policemen," (December 25, 1901).

42. U.S. Census Office, *Twelfth Census of the United States, 1900, Manufactures,* Part 2, vol. 8, *Manufactures*, p. 67.

43. "Oppose Barela Amendment," (August 5, 1902), and "Shipping Laundries Declared to Be Unfair," (August 19, 1902), both in *Cripple Creek Daily Press.*

44. *Ibid.*, "Assembly Discusses A.F. of L.," (November 18, 1902).

45. *Ibid.*, "Waitresses Walked Out of National," (August 5, 1902).

46. *Ibid.*, "Greatest Labor Day Celebration That Was Ever Held in Cripple Creek," (September 3, 1901).

47. *Ibid.*, "Convention Notes," (June 17, 1900).

48. Leland Feitz, *Myers Avenue — A Quick History of Cripple Creek's Red-Light District* (Denver, 1967), p. 18.

49. "Regulate It," *Cripple Creek Daily Press*, (August 24, 1899).

50. *Ibid.*, "Abate the Nuisance," (February 4, 1903).

51. *Ibid.*, "A Strike in Dance Hall," (April 23, 1902); "Labor Notes," (April 27, 1902).

52. *Miners' Magazine* (February 4, 1904), p. 5.

53. Augusta Prescott, "The Kind of a Woman a Workingman Should Marry," *Cripple Creek Daily Press*, (February 15, 1903).

54. "Women and the Home," *Cripple Creek Daily Press*, (January 30, 1901).

55. *Ibid.*, "Miss Jennie Wolf Winner Daily Press Voting Contest," (November 9, 1901).

56. *Ibid.*, (September 12, 1901).

57. See Anna Kirk, "Anna Kirk's Experience on a Car," *Cripple Creek Daily Press,* (November 10, 1901).

58. See "News of the District," *Cripple Creek Daily Press*, passim. Examples are: "Mrs. Warren Wise of Denver is here on a visit to her husband. He is a pumpman on the Legal Tender" ("Goldfield," April 25, 1901); and "Mrs. Jerry Kelly, wife of the local secretary of the Miners' Union, has returned with her children from Canon City, where she went to seek improved health" ("Victor Brevities," March 24, 1901).

59. "Miners Will Have Women's Auxiliary," *Cripple Creek Daily Press*, (June 3, 1902).

60. *Ibid.*, "Bonynge and Women Suffrage," (October 13, 1900).

61. Interview with Mrs. Clara Stiverson, July 29, 1975.

62. "What Will Women Do?" *Cripple Creek Daily Press*, (March 21, 1900).

63. *Ibid.*, "To the Ladies," (October 8, 1899).

64. *Ibid.*, (October 21, 1899).

65. *Ibid.*, "The Official Count," (November 6, 1899).

66. See, for instance, "Candidates for the Legislature," *Cripple Creek Daily Press*, (November 2, 1901); and Langdon, *The Cripple Creek Strike,* pp. 160-161.

67. The only full-length treatment of the 1903-1904 strike is Rastall, *The Labor History of the Cripple Creek District*. Accounts may be found in Melvyn Dubofsky,

We Shall Be All (New York; Quadrangle, 1969), pp. 49-55, and Jenson, *Heritage of Conflict*, pp. 118-159. Leslie Doyle Spell and Hazel M. Spell, *Forgotten Men of Cripple Creek* (Denver: Big Mountain Press, 1959), pp. 128-144, contains an eyewitness account of the Citizens' Alliance attack on the Victor Union Hall. See also Langdon, *The Cripple Creek Strike*, for a contemporary history.

68. "The Situation in Colorado," *Miners' Magazine* (June 16, 1904), p. 10; (June 23, 1904), p. 11; (June 30, 1904), p. 10.

69. See for example, "The Situation in Colorado," *Miners' Magazine* (January 28, 1904), pp. 8-12; (July 7, 1904), pp. 8-11; (July 14, 1904), pp. 8-11; and Langdon, *The Cripple Creek Strike*, pp. 224-225.

70. "The Situation in Colorado," *Miners' Magazine* (June 16, 1904), p. 9.

71. *Ibid.,* (June 23, 1904), pp. 11-12.

72. Ida Crouch-Hazlett, "A Colorado Heroine," *Miners' Magazine* (March 30, 1904), pp. 11-12.

73. See, for example, in *Miners' Magazine*: "The Colorado Labor Convention" (January 21, 1904), pp. 3-5; Mrs. M.R. Stephenson, "A Woman Surveys the Field" (May 26, 1904), p. 11; and Mrs. Annie Ballard, "Some Pertinent Questions" (July 7, 1904), p. 11. For relief reports, see *Official Proceedings of the Twelfth Annual Convention, Western Federation of Miners* (Denver, 1904), pp. 89-107, and *Official Proceedings of the Thirteenth Annual Convention* (Denver, 1905), pp. 160-186. 160-186.

74. "The Situation in Colorado," *Miners' Magazine*, (November 3, 1904), p. 7.

75. Langdon, *The Cripple Creek Strike*, pp. 357-358.

76. "The Situation in Colorado," *Miners' Magazine* (July 14, 1904), p. 9. Morgan worked primarily as an assayer but was also president and general manager of the Grouse Mountain Gold Mining Company, which was probably one of the many small mining companies that leased their properties or had small-scale operations in the district. He was a strong union sympathizer and probably depended on assaying for his livelihood. In one of her letters, Gay Morgan said that she would try to send her husband some money. "We have only $31 left. You took $10 when you left and we have used the rest."

77. Langdon, *The Cripple Creek Strike*, pp. 244, 410.

78. *Ibid.*, p. 249.

79. For an example of a situation in which this did occur, see the film "Salt of the Earth," which is based on a strike of the International Union of Mine, Mill and Smelter Workers in Bayard, New Mexico. There the women began by asking that the union include in its demands running water and nonwood stoves for the company housing that was furnished to chicano miners. Ultimately, the women took over picket duty when a court injunction prevented the union from picketing, and they demanded an equal voice in union decisions.

Research for this article was sponsored by the American Association of University Women, through the Sara McAnulty Nevins-Myra Bigelow Wilson and the Martha Hoag Clifford Endowed Fellowships. Some of the ideas developed in conversations with Marilyn Young, Ann Markusen, and Robert Conrow. I am grateful to Milton Cantor for thoughtful editing and to Carol Pearson and Robert Sklar for their helpful comments. Above all, I want to thank John Graham, whose critical and supportive help more than demonstrated the value of shared work.

THE WOMEN'S TRADE UNION LEAGUE AND AMERICAN FEMINISM

9

by Robin Miller Jacoby

The Women's Trade Union League (WTUL) provides an illuminating historical case study of the response of a certain group of women in the early twentieth century to the issues of feminism and class consciousness. As a mixed-class organization of women concerned about the problems of women workers during a period of an active male-dominated labor movement and a middle-class-dominated feminist movement, the WTUL was in an interesting position structurally. It was not concerned with theoretical issues of feminism and class identity, but it did explicitly and consistently define itself as the women's branch of the labor movement and the industrial branch of the women's movement.

The WTUL was founded in 1903 by a coalition of women trade unionists, settlement-house residents, and social reformers, and it remained in existence as a national organization with local branches in various cities in the East and Midwest until 1950, although its influence and activities declined significantly after the mid-1920s. The WTUL's membership consisted of women workers and "allies" — leisure-class women sympathetic to the general principles of the labor movement and to the special problems of women workers. Its goals, which were carried out with varying degrees of success, were to improve the situation of women workers through organizing them into trade unions, lobbying for legislation to control hours and work conditions, and educating women

Source: Reprinted by permission of Feminist Studies, Inc., Feminist Studies, 417 Riverside Drive, New York, NY 10025. This article first appeared in *Feminist Studies*, vol. 3, no. 1/2 (1975): 126-140. Copyright, Feminist Studies, Inc.

workers, union men, and leisure-class women. Such educational activities were designed to make those groups aware of the special problems of women workers and the value of organization and legislation on their behalf.

A comprehensive study of the League must take into account the various facets intrinsic to its dual identity as a women's labor organization.[1] Four different aspects require study for a thorough analysis of feminism in relation to the WTUL. First, there is the nature and content of the members' views regarding the actual and potential roles of women. Second, also involving an internal analysis, is the extent to which the feminist ideal of sisterhood was achieved across class lines. The third aspect is the extent to which feminist concerns were emphasized in the WTUL's relationship to the male labor movement, and fourth, there is the nature of the League's relationship to feminist issues and organizations in this period.[2] This article, however, will deal only with the last — the WTUL in its self-defined role as the industrial branch of the women's movement — by examining the League's relationship to some of the issues and groups that comprised the American feminist movement in the two decades after 1900.[3]

The impact of industrialization on women underlies the history of the WTUL and of the feminist movement of the nineteenth and early twentieth centuries. The process of industrialization served to define class differences between women more sharply.[4] As production moved outside the home, the distinction between middle-class and working women became more pronounced. For women who entered the industrial labor force, the patterns that characterized their situation in the first half of the nineteenth century had not significantly altered by the early twentieth century. They were predominantly young, single, clustered in the lowest-paying and least-skilled jobs, and unorganized. Cultural attitudes regarding women underlay and reinforced this constellation of economic conditions, and the combination of cultural and economic factors resulted in significant differences between the situation of men and women in the industrial labor force.

For women of the middle and upper classes, on the other hand, by increasing levels of wealth and by removing so many productive functions from the home, industrialization brought the possibility of a life of relative leisure. Intrinsically related to the economic changes of the antebellum decades is the codification of what has become known as the cult of true womanhood — the ideology that women belonged demurely and submissively in the home and that their primary function was to be the moral guardians of society through their maternal and wifely roles.[5] The development of the feminist movement and the working conditions faced by women workers are evidence that, by the late nineteenth century, industrialization had created an oppressive leisure life for many middle- and upper-class women and an oppressive work life for most women in the industrial labor force. WTUL membership and goals thus directly reflect the complex relationship between industrialization and the cult of true womanhood. In addition, the existence and activities of the WTUL were part of the feminist attack on economic and cultural patterns which prescribed extremely restricted roles for women in the work force and in the home. Throughout the nineteenth century, increasing awareness of the problematic consequences of industrialization led to a proliferation of reform organizations towards the end of the century. Those middle-class women drawn to the WTUL shared the mentality of the progressive movement in many ways: most had been involved in other reform activities which had developed their awareness of the problems of women workers. Working-class women were interested in the League because it was the only organization in existence whose priority was reforming the working conditions of women and because it was also the only one committed in principle to including women workers in this task.

Even though WTUL members were not particularly interested in theoretical approaches to feminism and class consciousness, these concepts provide a useful and important analytic framework for discussion. Feminism and class consciousness are complex notions in themselves, and scholars have paid very little attention to the relationship between them.[6] As I see it, feminism simultaneously complements and conflicts with the ideology that claims primacy for class identity. It is complementary in that it implies equal rights and opportunities for women within sexually mixed, class-based settings, such as labor unions; it is conflicting in that it also implies that gender identification based on physical and social differences creates a solidarity that transcends class divisions. Moreover, feminism and class consciousness are both ideologies that have utopian as well as historical dimensions. That is, the ultimate vision of a sexually equal and classless society is expressed and struggled for in different ways in different periods, and all people involved in movements to improve the lives of women and workers do not necessarily share the same ultimate vision. If this general framework is applied to the specific case of the WTUL and American feminism, it will be seen that for middle-class feminists outside the WTUL, class identity outweighed their rhetorical commitment to the ideal of cross-class female solidarity.

In the context of the period under discussion, feminism was an ideology that centered on two contradictory premises: one was that women should have the same political, legal, educational, and economic rights as men; the other was that women were physically, psychologically, and intellectually different from men because of their unique reproductive and maternal roles. Feminist thought held that the combination of these two situations — women as oppressed members of society and women as potential or actual mothers — created a bond of sisterhood between all women that transcended class, racial, and national differences.

These concepts shaped the WTUL from the outset and provided the rationale for its mixed-class membership. Members recognized that the inequality of rights and opportunities that women faced in society were mirrored in the context of the industrial labor force. Without fully analyzing the implication of the situation, they also realized that a fundamental cause of the condition of women workers was their expectation, shared by their employers and male co-workers, that they were only temporary members of the labor force. In other words, most women in the industrial labor force regarded themselves as women first and as workers second. They expected to marry and become full-time housewives, and their identification with the personal, domestic sphere of life was one of several factors that impeded the development of women's unions and long-term commitment to the labor movement. (The success of the British WTUL in organizing women workers suggests that the structure and attitudes of the American Federation of Labor, as contrasted with the Trades Union Congress, may have been the most decisive factor in the problems of getting American women organized and sustaining their membership and participation in the labor movement.) The relationship of women workers to the labor movement involves a complex set of factors, which are more fully discussed elsewhere. The point of raising the issue here is to indicate one of the reasons women workers were drawn into the feminist movement at this time; namely, that as women they felt alienated from the labor movement and felt that the feminist movement, especially the suffrage campaign, might be effective in helping them to improve their working conditions.

The struggle for suffrage was only one aspect of feminism, but it was the dominant thrust in 1903 when the WTUL was established. The National American Woman Suffrage Association, which had been formed in 1890, was its organizational vehicle. Differences among the first generation of suffragists over whether the Fourteenth Amendment should be supported if it did not extend the franchise to women as well as to newly freed black men led to the establishment of two rival suffrage organizations in 1869, the National Woman Suffrage Association, which Eleanor Flexner has characterized as "aggressive and unorthodox," and the more socially and politically decorous American Woman Suffrage Association.[7] By the late 1880s changes in America's social climate, changes in the attitudes of the leaders of the National Woman Suffrage Association, and the emergence of a new generation of suffrage leaders who were, "not, for the most part, distinguished by the breadth of their social views" led to the realization that significant differences no longer divided the two organizations. The result was their merger into the National American Woman Suffrage Association (NAWSA).[8] Its social composition is disclosed in a composite biographical profile of leading suffragists: of twenty-six major figures, all were middle or upper class, nearly all were WASPS, and nearly all were considerably better educated than the average American woman of this period.[9]

When the suffrage movement began in the 1850s, its primary argument was that women should have the vote on the grounds of basic justice and equality; by 1890, however, the movement's rhetoric had shifted to emphasize arguments of expediency.[10] Sharing and capitalizing on prevailing racist and nativist prejudices, women's suffrage advocates began to claim that being excluded from a political right extended to black, immigrant, and working-class men was an insult to native-born, middle-class white women and a danger to the nation at large. One example of this conviction is the following resolution, which was adopted unanimously at the 1893 NAWSA convention:

> We call attention to the significant facts that in every State there are more women who can read and write than the whole number of illiterate male voters; more American women who can read and write than all foreign voters; so that the enfranchisement of such women would settle the vexed question of rule by illiteracy, whether of the home-grown or foreign-born production. [11]

Belle Kearney, a southern suffragist, added a note of explicit racism to her address in the 1903 NAWSA convention. Reiterating the statistical argument of the proportion of white, native-born women to the rest of the population, she told the convention delegates: "The enfranchisement of women would insure immediate and durable white supremacy . . . . The South is slow to grasp the great fact that the enfranchisement of women would settle the race question in politics." [12]

While these attitudes never totally disappeared from the suffrage movement, by the early twentieth century more sympathetic views began to be expressed toward working-class people and immigrants, and suffrage groups attempted to reach out to those segments of the population. (The same was not true regarding blacks; in order not to antagonize southern congressmen and suffrage supporters, black women were consistently discouraged from participating in the suffrage movement.) This shift was partly due to the realization of the suffragists that whether they liked it or not, such groups of men did have the vote and it made more sense to have them as allies than as enemies of the women's cause. As Florence Kelley, head of the National Consumer's League (an organization dedicated to improving working conditions of women and children through the use of the boycott) told the 1906 NAWSA convention:

> I have rarely heard a ringing suffrage speech which did not refer to the "ignorant and degraded" men, or the "ignorant immigrants" as our masters. This is habitually spoken with more or less bitterness. But this is what the workingmen are used to hear applied to themselves by their enemies in times of strike.
>
> Rather we should recognize that, while for the moment they have power which we need, they have the same interest in the rising generation of citizens, so largely the children of working people.[13]

Another factor responsible for shaping this perspective was the influence of social feminists such as Jane Addams and Florence Kelley, but even more significant was the influence of Margaret Dreier Robins, the wealthy president of the WTUL, and other middle- and working-class WTUL members. These women acted as liaisons between the women's movement and the working class, and their speeches, writings, and commitment to suffrage stressed the problems of women workers and their special need for the vote.

The 1910 invitation to Agnes Nestor, a glove worker from an Irish immigrant family and an active member of the Chicago WTUL, to join the Suffrage Special, a train headed for Springfield for a special suffrage session of the Illinois legislature, was one example of this broadened outlook on the part of the suffragists. The train stopped at various communities along the way, permitting the suffragists to proselytize local groups, and Nestor was asked to be the main speaker in the industrial town of Joliet.

This tendency to broaden the issues and the constituency of the suffrage movement was even more clearly expressed in the constitution of the Illnois State Woman Suffrage Party, which was formed in 1911. According to Mary Gray Peck, a close associate of Carrie Chapman Catt (NAWSA president):

> The beginning of the Woman Suffrage Party of Illinois differs from that of any of the preceding organs. So, naturally and unobtrusively, a new intention in the struggle for suffrage was officially enunciated. It is true that from the first the N.Y.

> Party backed several measures looking to the bet-
> terment of women's working conditions, and in
> the second convention formally endorsed them.
> But the Illinois Party was the first to link suffrage
> with women's industrial betterment in the key-
> stone of its constitution. The older suffragists were
> a unit in fighting shy of "entangling alliances."
> The new generation boldly assume suffrage as a
> means to an end, valuable only as related to that
> end in the mind of every suffragist.[14]

Her view of the importance of this action was shared by the Political Equality Union of Chicago, an association of wage-earning
women, which immediately endorsed the Illinois Woman Suffrage
Party and applauded it for having the broadest platform of any
major suffrage organization.[15]

In 1912 Rose Schneiderman, a Russian-Jewish immigrant who
had worked as a cap maker and then as an organizer for the New
York WTUL, was hired by NAWSA as a temporary suffrage
organizer in the Ohio campaign. Recognizing that her political
views were not representative of most suffrage workers and not
wanting to take the job under false pretenses, she was straightfor-
ward in her interview with Anna Howard Shaw, proclaiming herself "a socialist and a trade unionist who looked upon the ballot as
a tool in the hands of working women with which, through legislation, they could correct the terrible conditions existing in industry."[16] Delighted that she was given the job, since it came at a lull
in her labor organizing work among New York's women underwear
makers, Schneiderman told her audiences that she did not expect a
revolution when women got the ballot. It was nonetheless imperative that women be enfranchised because they needed protection
through laws, and so long as they were without the vote, lawmakers
had no reason to pay serious attention to them.[17] Although other
suffrage speakers predicted more fundamental social changes as a
result of women's being given the vote, Schneiderman's view on the
legislative needs of women, especially working women, was shared
by many middle-class suffragists.

In response to a letter from Schneiderman describing her work in

Ohio, Pauline Newman, her close friend and sister WTUL member, wrote:

> I knew that you would make good on the road. For the "cultured" ladies may be very sincere in their desire for the balot, I don't doubt their sincerety, but because their views are narrow, and their knowledge of social conditions limited, they cannot do as well as some of us can. And as I come in contact with these women day after day, they are beginning to see the necessity of having a working girl tour a State rather than some professor.[18]

As this letter suggests, suffragists were increasingly aware that while they might support Schneiderman's arguments, she communicated more effectively the special need of working women to be enfranchised.

As far as Margaret Dreier Robins was concerned, the Ohio campaign was an example of NAWSA's doing too little, too late regarding the labor vote. It also indicated the necessity to expand the number of WTUL locals. Shortly after the Ohio vote, Robins wrote to Leonora O'Reilly, who had a long history of labor-movement activity on behalf of women and was one of the most active working-class suffragists in the WTUL:

> The big break in Ohio in the suffrage fight was the fact that there was no converted working women's movement for suffrage. The few women unionists in the state had no way of expressing themselves collectively for the ballot, and had no way of protesting collectively against the action of the Cincinnati and Dayton Federations of Labor, which refused to endorse women's suffrage. It is such situations which make me realize how really important our League's Union Federations may be, and I was really distressed at the voicelessness of our working sisters in Ohio.[19]

Two years later, thinking back to that Ohio campaign in another letter to Leonora O'Reilly, Robins mused: "You know one of the biggest reasons for the defeat of suffrage in Ohio was the inability of the suffragists to reach the mass of the working men. Röschen, our Röschen, was practically the only trade unionist they had."[20]

By 1915 the views of Ohio suffragists had been broadened to the extent that the Ohio Woman Suffrage Association formally declared its belief in the economic independence of women. It further affirmed "the right of all wage-earning women to organize for the purpose of protecting their industrial interests."[21] The statement deplored "the fact that the wage earning women of Ohio are not organized to the same degree as the wage earning men" and expressed the support of the Woman Suffrage Association for "any movement looking towards such organization."[22] Finally, it demanded "equal pay for equal work regardless of sex" and "the right of women to work in all trades and at all professions limited by no bound but that of their own capacity."[23]

By 1919 there was considerable interest in the situation of women workers. Clara Hyde, Carrie Chapman Catt's personal secretary, wrote to another prominent suffragist regarding the 1919 NAWSA convention: "The convention was a tremendous success . . . . The Industrial program under Mrs. Raymond Robins was the most satisfactory number of the whole convention, and to my mind the most popular."[24] The presentations in this section of the convention program "roused a spontaneous demand for the printing in pamphlet form of their speeches. They are the only ones in the convention to whom this happened — which shows quite clearly how popular interest is centering on industrial and economic questions."[25]

Some of this interest represented a genuine broadening of views of middle-class suffragists, but there is evidence that it also stemmed from pragmatic considerations on the part of NAWSA leaders. Florence Kelley's speech to the 1906 NAWSA convention, which pointed to the need to conciliate working-class men partly because of their political power, is one indication of the dual basis of this shift. One suffragist privately admitted that the 1917 offer of a NAWSA vice presidency to Margaret Dreier Robins was in fact "a bait for the labor vote."[26] (Robins declined, claiming her time was fully occupied with WTUL work.) An indication of how much this shift was based on tactical considerations rather than genuine changes in social attitudes is revealed by Carrie Chapman Catt. Disclosing some of her feelings about workers and immigrants, she confessed:

> I am a *good* democrat in theory but my faith weakens when it meets bad air, dirt . . . and horrid smells. I rather enjoy onions for instance when the odor pervades a clean home and is diluted with good air. To my nostrils it becomes a real aristocratic perfume, but when it is a democratic odor diluted with perfumes of beer and uncleanliness, the blood of my royal ancestors boils in protest. Of course I do not know positively that I have any royal ancestors, but if I had not why this shrinking from my fellow beings because of smells? [27]

Fully aware of the class bias of the suffrage movement, the WTUL nonetheless gave its whole-hearted support to the principle of women's suffrage and actively worked for it both on its own and in coalition with NAWSA groups. Its suffrage activities directed at women workers and trade-union men consistently stressed that women's suffrage was relevant to WTUL struggles for better working and living conditions. When dealing with NAWSA members and groups, the WTUL emphasized the special problems of women workers and their particular need for the vote; in addition, it urged that NAWSA organizations and publications broaden the scope and content of their activities and rhetoric to incorporate the views and participation of women workers.

The WTUL's leaders and members seem to have been committed to the principle of women's suffrage from the beginning. Their first publications included news of the suffrage movement, and their first national convention, in 1907, included "full citizenship for women" as a plank in their six-point platform. (The others were "equal pay for equal work, the organization of all workers into trade unions, the eight hour day, a minimum wage scale, and all the principles embodied in the economic program of the American

Federation of Labor."[28] By 1908 a Suffrage Department had been established, and agitation for suffrage was a significant aspect of WTUL activities until 1920. Although the suffrage movement had existed for half a century prior to the establishment of the WTUL, it was not until the early twentieth century that any kind of sustained interaction developed between working-class women and middle-class suffragists. Nor were there ever significant numbers of working-class activists in the suffrage movement, but those who did belong tended to come from the WTUL, and for good reason. The League provided one of the few structures in which women's suffrage could be discussed in the context of the needs and problems of women workers.

Some of the instances mentioned above indicate the basic thrust of WTUL arguments for suffrage. Members consistently advanced the view that while all women deserved the vote on the basis of simple justice, women workers especially needed it because enfranchisement would enable them to exert some degree of control over their miserable working conditions. They never saw suffrage as a total solution to the problems of working women, but they did feel that legislation was a crucial vehicle for ameliorating working conditions and that without it, women workers were severly hampered in their attempts to obtain state or federal measures. Rose Schneiderman's speech at a 1912 mass meeting in Cooper Union, organized by the New York Wage Earners' Suffrage League, is typical of this viewpoint. Replying to a recent public statement by an antisuffrage New York legislator, she told the assembled crowd:

> I did some lobbying work last year for the 54-hour bill, and I can tell you how courteous our Senators and Assemblymen are when a disenfranchised citizen tries to convince them of the necessity of shorter hours for working women . . . .
>
> During the hearing at Albany our learned Senators listened to the opposition very carefully . . . . But when the Committee, who spoke for the working women came to plead for the bill, there was only one Senator left in the room — he was the chairman — he couldn't very well get out . . . .

> Mind you, we were pleading for a shorter work
> week for working women. We had evidence to
> show that physical exhaustion of women will lead
> to the deterioration of the human species. What
> did ˙these men care. We were voteless working
> women — no matter what we felt or thought we
> could not come back at them.[29]

The WTUL linked itself to NAWSA in many ways: from 1909 on
the two organizations exchanged delegates to their national conventions; the WTUL encouraged and organized the participation of
working women in NAWSA rallies and parades; and *Life and
Labor*, the WTUL's monthly journal, gave considerable publicity
to NAWSA activities. But the WTUL also realized that working
within NAWSA groups was not always easy or comfortable for
working women. To meet this difficulty, the WTUL encouraged
the formation of independent wage-earner suffrage leagues as a
way of actively involving workers in the suffrage movement.

The first such league was formed in San Francisco in 1908 or
1909, and its establishment was the direct result of class conflict between working-class and middle-class suffragists in that city. The
San Francisco delegate to the 1909 WTUL convention reported that
the mixed-class suffrage organization in that city had fallen apart
because the middle-class women had refused to support a strike of
street-car conductors. They had regarded the strike as ill-timed and
as a personal inconvenience and, in discussions with the working-
class suffragists, had displayed no sympathy for or understanding
of the labor cause. On the basis of this incident, working-class
women decided that they could no longer work in the same group
with the middle-class women and withdrew to form their own suffrage organization.[30]

Another example of this kind of class tension was expressed in a
letter from Maggie Hinchey, a laundry worker, to Leonora
O'Reilly. While attending a NAWSA conference in New York City,
Hinchey wrote:

> I feel as if I have butted in where I was not wanted.
> Miss Hay gave me a badge was very nice to me but

you know they had a school teacher represent the
Industrial workers if you ever herd her it was like
trying to fill a barrell with water that had not bottom not a word of labor spoken at this convention
so far . . . I am not goying to wait for sunday
meeting I am goying home satturday.[31]

Like the San Francisco women, Hinchey was not lost to the suffrage cause, despite this experience, but shifted her activities to the
Industrial Section of the New York Suffrage Party, which had been
organized and led by WTUL members.

The New York Wage Earners' Suffrage League was founded in
1911 by Leonora O'Reilly, who became its president. Clara Lemlich, who was known for her role in precipitating the 1909 shirtwaist strike, became its vice president. The membership was confined to wage-earning women "to preserve harmony of purpose
and propaganda and admit of greatest possible freedom of discussion at meetings."[32] O'Reilly was a very committed feminist, and
she felt that the WTUL had a crucial role to play in broadening the
base and scope of the women's movement. Writing to Margaret
Dreier Robins in 1912, she declared, "from my point of view, we
have to build a woman's movement in this land on a Labor
Foundation and ours are the only people who have had any training
for this work."[33] Justifying her determinaton that the New York
Wage Earners' Suffrage League be totally controlled by working
women, O'Reilly told Robins, "really and truly the other women
with the best intentions in the world rub the fur the wrong way,
they really don't speak our language and so they use the w.w.
[working women] and then throw them over."[34] Another passage
in the same letter indicates how effective the activities of such
working-class suffrage groups could be in winning support for
women's suffrage among the working class. The Wage Earners'
Suffrage League, she told Robins, had put an enormous amount of
work into producing a vaudeville show for a working-class
audience. She described how pleased she was to hear a murmur run
through the theater when the curtain fell, which she thought indicated the collective sentiment of "Gee I never thought of Votes
for Women as meaning anything like that before."[35]

In addition to trying to organize women workers into wage-earner suffrage leagues, the WTUL put considerable energy into working with trade-union men to gain their active support for the suffrage cause. Its national conventions passed resolutions directed at organized labor in states where suffrage referenda were pending, and members of local leagues presented their case before union locals and state labor federation conventions. New York's WTUL members comprised the Industrial Section of the State Suffrage Party, and their activities included writing letters to labor papers, visiting union meetings across the state, and making street speeches in industrial areas. Maggie Hinchey was one of the most effective workers in this arena. According to a *New York Times* account, she had her male audiences alternately shaking with laughter and moved to tears.[36] The Industrial Section also prepared a series of sixteen letters, addressed to trade-union men, explaining why wage-earning women and working-class housewives wanted and needed the vote.[37] According to Mary Dreier, chairperson of the Industrial Section, over two million copies were distributed throughout the state. Voting returns, she also noted, indicated that labor areas played a key role in the 1917 suffrage victory in New York State.[38]

This examination of the relationship between the WTUL and the suffrage movement has revealed two general tendencies. First, there was a broadening of the rhetoric and constituency of the suffrage movement in the last fifteen years of its existence, and I would contend that that achievement was directly due to the WTUL's work and influence. However, while the suffrage movement involved both middle-class and working-class women striving for a common goal, the evidence of social and political tensions, generated primarily by the class biases of the middle-class suffragists, indicates that it was at best a tenuous alliance. Thus, despite the increased commitment to suffrage on the part of working-class women in the early twentieth century, it cannot be said that the last phase of the woman suffrage movement represented a genuine achievement of sisterhood on a cross-class basis.

In addition to its work for suffrage, the WTUL directed a considerable amount of energy into public-relations work with other women's groups, mostly middle-class organizations. The work was done through letters, speeches, and the exchange of convention delegates. Its aim was to educate middle-class women and to gain their support and sympathy for the general and specific struggles of working women. However, it discovered that sensitivity and commitment to working-class women was even harder to achieve when the cover of a common goal (e.g., suffrage) was not present.

In 1904 one of the first activities of the Chicago WTUL was to take up the cause of a group of striking corset workers in Aurora, Illinois. After talking with those involved, the Chicago WTUL sent out letters to every Illinois women's club, telling them of the conditions under which these women worked, explaining their strike demands, and asking the clubwomen to boycott products of the Kabo Corset Company until the walkout was settled. Its appeal for a boycott prompted the company attorney to threaten suit, an action which Anna Nichols, a clubwoman and "ally" member of the Chicago WTUL, brought to the attention of an Illinois State Federation of Women's Clubs convention. Her efforts generated so much publicity that the company dropped its threat of litigation. WTUL records do not indicate whether the boycott was effective, but there was enough interest in and sympathy for its work that the convention of the Illinois State Federation of Women's Clubs of the following year voted to amend its constitution and allow organizations like the WTUL to affiliate. However, as Agnes Nestor noted in her autobiography, not all the clubwomen supported this move, and one was overheard saying: "Isn't it dreadful! I suppose next year we'll have those corset workers here as members!"[39]

Another early activity of the Boston and New York City WTULs was to send out circulars to women's clubs in Massachusetts and New York listing members and sympathizers who were prepared to speak to women's clubs on various topics related to women in industry. Some of the speakers and topics were: Margaret Dreier, "The Objects of the Women's Trade Union League"; Leonora O'Reilly, "The Song of the Shirt"; Virginia Dock, "The Settlement and the Working Woman"; Rose Schneiderman, "Why We Believe in Trade Unions"; Mary Kenney O'Sullivan, "Women in Trade Unions"; and Mabel Gillespie, "Club Women and Trade Union Women."[40] But some of the working-class members who accepted invitations to speak before women's clubs encountered elitist reactions to their appearances before such groups.

At the urging of Mary McDowell, a settlement resident, WTUL ally, and chairperson of the Industrial Program Committee for the 1905 convention of the Illinois State Federation of Women's Clubs, the State Federation invited Agnes Nestor to address convention delegates. Nestor wrote in her autobiography that "it was a bold step" for the clubwomen to consent to having a woman worker speak to them on trade unionism and that she was anxious to present her case effectively. Wanting to look her best in their company, she had a lovely silk blouse made for the occasion and described herself as looking as "gay as a butterfly." After the event, she was pleased to have her speech described as "stirring and informative," but terribly disappointed by a newspaper reference to her "dark and shabby appearance." [41]

There is a sequel to the blouse story. Rheta Childe Dorr, a League ally and an active member of the General Federation of Women's Clubs, arranged for Nestor to speak before the Federation's 1906 national convention. Nestor described her experiences as a glove worker and a trade unionist and urged support for working women in their fight for eight-hour-day legislation. After her talk, a clubwoman came up to Nestor, felt the material of her blouse — the same blouse she had worn to the Illinois meeting the year before — and said "You're not a real working girl. Look at the good blouse you are wearing!" [42] Nestor, amused by the incident, wrote, "At least this time I had the satisfaction that the blouse was recognized for what it was." [43] Incidents such as these reveal how stereotyped conceptions of women workers influenced the response of the media and of middle-class women to WTUL attempts to gain support for the cause of women workers.

Probably the best-known instance of the WTUL's generating a positive reaction from leisured women concerns the supportive activities of what Rose Schneideman called the "Mink Brigade" during the 1909-1910 strike of New York's women garment workers. [44] Prominent women, such as Mrs. O.H.P. Belmont and Mrs. Henry Morgenthau, staged fund-raising benefits and served as observers of police treatment of those on the picket lines. Their involvement generated extensive publicity for the walkout. But, as Theresa Malkiel, one of the strikers and a Socialist, pointed out, the financial contributions of these women, while significantly helpful, were not as great as they could have been. In reference to the well-known Hippodrome rally sponsored by Mrs. Belmont, Malkiel wrote in her diary:

> The most of our girls had to walk both ways in order to save their car fare. Many came without dinner, but the collection baskets had more pennies than anything else in them — it was our girls themselves who helped to make it up, and yet there were so many rich women present. And I'm sure the speakers made it plain to them how badly the money was needed, then how comes it was that out of the $300 collected there should be $70 in pennies? [45]

As part of the fund-raising effort during the walkout, women strikers traveled throughout New York and New England, soliciting support from local women's groups. They raised a considerable amount of money but did not receive uniform support. Margaret Dreier Robins recalled one such instance in a letter describing the WTUL-YWCA relationship:

> One of our very fine young working women, a leader of one of the strikes in New York City, an English-American girl, was not permitted to stay overnight in the YWCA House in a small town in New York state because her name was so well known and the Matron said they would not accommodate any strikers. It was ten o'clock at night when this girl came in good faith to the YWCA for a night's lodging. This and some similar experiences naturally embittered the Trade Union girls against the YWCA. [46]

Life and Labor acknowledged the significant help of the Woman Suffrage Party of Illinois during the 1911 Chicago garment workers' strike when it contributed over $700 to the strike fund. [47]

But the experience with suffragists who supported the Cleveland garment strike that same year was not so positive. Pauline Newman and Margaret Dreier Robins had arranged a mass meeting to publicize and explain the walkout, and among the speakers were two prominent suffragists, both relatively wealthy women. They made stirring speeches in support of the striking workers but then billed the WTUL for a total of $40 for their services, and showed no further interest in the strike after their one appearance. [48] Thus, WTUL attempts to develop awareness of the problems of women workers among middle-class women and to gain their support for specific strikes met with only limited success. The extent of generosity, sensitivity, and sustained commitment that the WTUL was able to elicit from middle-class feminists was consistently disappointing to its members, who believed in the feminist ideal of cross-class sisterhood.

Although material on the relationships of the WTUL to the feminist movement tends to be impressionistic rather than quantitative, the incidents and activities discussed were representative of its role as the industrial branch of the women's movement. The WTUL identified itself with the women's movement for two major reasons. First, many of its leisure-class members had social and cultural ties to organizations (such as NAWSA and the General Federation of Women's Clubs) that comprised the women's movement, and such ties greatly facilitated contacts between it and these middle-class organizations. Second, since the labor movement tended to be only superficially interested in the plight of women workers, the WTUL put increasing emphasis on legislative lobbying as a means of improving working conditions for women. The shift in emphasis from organizing women into trade unions to legislative and educational activities was a further reason for members to work for suffrage and seek support from leisure-class women, for it brought the WTUL closer to the goals and tactics of the women's movement. However, a study of the WTUL and American feminism in the years 1903 to 1920 reveals that while middle-class women were increasingly interested in an alliance with the WTUL over issues of common concern, they were not very active, sensitive, or supportive in joining women workers — as represented by the WTUL — in their struggles for better working conditions. Ironically, it was these middle-class women whose conscious and un-conscious sense of class precluded the possibility of cross-class feminist solidarity. As a result, the WTUL did considerably more for the women's movement than the women's movement did for it and the cause of women workers.

NOTES

1. For a more comprehensive account of the WTUL, see Nancy Schrom Dye, "The Women's Trade Union League of New York, 1903-1920" (Ph.D. dissertation, Department of History, University of Wisconsin, 1974). I also have a study in progress, "A Case Study of Feminism and Class Consciousness: The British and American Women's Trade Union Leagues, 1890-1925" (Ph.D. dissertation, Department of History, Harvard University).

2. For discussion of some of these issues in relation to the New York WTUL, see Dye, "The Women's Trade Union League," and Dye, "Creating a Feminist Alliance: Sisterhood and Class Conflict in the New York Women's Trade Union League," *Feminist Studies* 2, no. 2-3 (1975): 24-38.

3. 1920 is an arbitrary cut-off date; it does not represent the end of the organized women's movement or of the WTUL. During the 1920s, the WTUL was primarily involved in legislative work, and it put considerable energy into mobilizing other women's groups to fight against the equal-rights amendment advocated by the National Woman's party. The WTUL was against the amendment because it felt that it would cancel gains made in the legislative areas that improved working conditions for women. It attacked the Woman's party for being selfish and elitist in not realizing or caring that the legislation that it advocated would hurt many more women than it helped.

4. Gerda Lerner, "The Lady and the Mill Girl: Changes in the Status of Women in the Age of Jackson," *Mid-Continent American Studies Journal* 10 (Spring 1969): 5-15.

5. See Barbara Welter, "The Cult of True Womanhood: 1820-1860," *American Quarterly* 18 (Summer 1966): 151-174.

6. The classic nineteenth-century works on this subject are August Bebel, *Woman Under Socialism*, trans. Daniel DeLeon (New York, 1971), and Frederick Engels, *The Origin of the Family, Private Property, and the State* (London, 1940). The most important contemporary discussions are Juliet Mitchell, *Woman's Estate* (London, 1971), and Sheila Rowbotham, *Women, Resistance and Revolution: A History of Women and Revolution in the Modern World* (New York, 1972).

7. See Eleanor Flexner, *Century of Struggle* (New York, 1972), pp. 141-155, for further discussion of this split in the early suffrage movement.

8. Ibid., p. 219; see pp. 215-225 for a more comprehensive account of the reunification.

9. Aileen Kraditor, *The Ideas of the Woman Suffrage Movement, 1890-1920* (New York, 1971).

10. Ibid., and Aileen Kraditor, ed., *Up from the Pedestal: Selected Writings in the History of American Feminism* (Chicago, 1968).

11. Kraditor, *Up from the Pedestal,* p. 260.

12. Ibid., p. 264.

13. Kraditor, *Ideas*, p. 115.

14. This comment was made in a note by Mary Gray Peck on the back of a letter to her from Myra Straun Hartstrom, Feb. 7, 1911, NAWSA Papers, Box 24, file "Mary Gray Peck," Library of Congress.

15 "Votes for Women," *Life and Labor* 2 (February 1911): 62.

16. Rose Schneiderman, with Lucy Goldthwaite, *All for One* (New York, 1967), p. 121.

17. Ibid., pp. 121-122.

18. Pauline Newman to Rose Schneiderman, July 26, 1912, Schneiderman Papers, Tamiment Library, New York University.

19. Margaret Dreier Robins to Leonora O'Reilly, Sept. 14, 1912, O'Reilly Papers, Box 6, folder 51, Schlesinger Library.

20. Robins to O'Reilly, July 19, 1914, O'Reilly Papers, Box 6, folder 55.

21. "Votes for Women," *Life and Labor* 5 (May 1915): 94.

22. Ibid.

23. Ibid.

24. Clara Hyde to Mary Gray peck, April 13, 1919, NAWSA Papers, Box 24, folder "Mary Gray Peck."

25. Ibid.

26. Hyde to Peck, Sept. 26, 1917, NAWSA Papers, Box 24, folder "Mary Gray Peck."

27. Carrie Chapman Catt to "Frances and Pan," Oct. 15, 1910, Catt Papers, Box 7, folder "Mary Gray Peck 1909-1910," Library of Congress.

28. See "The Woman's Department," the WTUL's section in the *Union Labor Advocate*, 1904-1910, and notes from the 1907 WTUL convention in NWTUL Papers, Box 1, vol. 1, Library of Congress.

29. Wage Earners' Suffrage League, New York, "Senators vs. Working Women: Miss Rose Schneiderman Replies to New York Senator," O'Reilly Papers, Box 6, folder 51.

30. National American Women's Trade Union League, "Proceedings of the 1909 Convention," pp. 26-27, NWTUL Papers, Library of Congress.

31. Margaret Hinchey to Leonora O'Reilly, 1913?, O'Reilly Papers, Box 6, folder 52.

32. "The Woman Voter," *Life and Labor* 2 (November 1912): 344.

33. O'Reilly to Robins, Sept. 23, 1912, Robins Papers, University of Florida.

34. Ibid.

35. Ibid.

36. *New York Times*, May 5, 1915.

37. A set of these letters is in the Schneiderman Papers.

38. Mary E. Dreier, "Building the Suffrage Victory," *Life and Labor* 7 (December 1917): 186.

39. Agnes Nestor, *Woman's Labor Leader: An Autobiography* (Rockford, Illinois, 1954), p. 66. See Nestor, *Woman's Labor Leader,* p. 65; "Minutes of the First National Executive Board Meeting," March 20, 1904, NWTUL Papers, Box 25, folder "NWTUL Historical Data," Library of Congress; and Alice Henry, *Women and the Labor Movement* (New York, 1923), p. 119, for accounts of this incident.

40. "Club Programs of 1905-1906," NWTUL Papers, Box 1, vol. 1, Library of Congress.

41. See Nestor, *Woman's Labor Leader*, pp. 66-68, for a more complete account of this incident.

42. Ibid., p. 74.

43. Ibid.

44. Schneiderman, *All for One*, p. 8.

45. Theresa Malkiel, *The Diary of a Shirtwaist Striker* (New York, 1910), pp. 40-41.

46. Carbon copy of a letter from Margaret Dreier Robins to Mr. Roberts, April 3, 1925, Robins Papers.

47. "Votes for Women," *Life and Labor* 1 (February 1911): 62.

48. Pauline Newman to Margaret Dreier Robins, Aug. 5, 1911, Robins Papers.

CREATING A FEMINIST ALLIANCE: SISTERHOOD AND CLASS CONFLICT IN THE NEW YORK WOMEN'S TRADE UNION LEAGUE, 1903-1914

10

by Nancy Schrom Dye

A "small band of enthusiasts who believed that the nonindustrial person could be of service to her industrial sister in helping her find her way through the chaos of industry" formed the Women's Trade Union League (WTUL) of New York late in 1903.[1] The organization's members — a unique coalition of women workers and wealthy women disenchanted with conventional philanthropic and social reform activities — dedicated themselves to improving the working conditions of female laborers and their status in the labor movement.

The women who formed the core of New York WTUL membership were both trade unionists and feminists. As unionists, they worked to integrate women into the mainstream of the labor movement. As feminists, they tried to make the early twenthieth-century women's movement relevant to working women's concerns. To these ends, the WTUL attempted to serve as a link between women workers and the labor movement as well as a focal point for unorganized women interested in unionism. It agitated among unorganized women workers in an effort to educate them to the importance of unionization. In addition, it made concrete efforts to change the negative attitudes of male trade unionists toward women. The WTUL offered assistance to municipal labor organizations and often aided local unions during strikes. League members also worked as union organizers and helped to establish several dozen unions composed predominantly of unskilled and semi-skilled women workers in New York City. Most notably, the New York WTUL played an important role in building the shirtwaist makers' union (International Ladies Garment Workers Union Local 25) and the white-goods workers union (International

Source: Reprinted by permission of Feminist Studies, Inc., Feminist Studies, 417 Riverside Drive, New York, NY 10025. This article first appeared in *Feminist Studies*, vol. 2, no. 2/3 (1975): 24-38. Copyright, Feminist Studies, Inc.

Ladies Garment Workers Union Local 62). In a later period of its history, particularly during the 1910s and 1920s, the New York WTUL abandoned its single-minded emphasis on union organizing in order to concentrate most of its efforts on the campaigns for woman suffrage and for women's protective labor legislation.

Women of a variety of backgrounds joined the WTUL. Many members were young working women who learned of the WTUL through their unions or through WTUL publicity campaigns. Other members were wealthy women. Often college-educated, the "allies," as upper-class members were called, usually had had experience in charity organizations, social reform societies, or social settlements. The New York City Consumers' League, the working girls' clubs, and the Workingwomen's Society were among the groups dedicated to improving the position of women in the labor force. Such organizations as the Municipal League and the Young Women's Christian Association occasionally conducted investigations of women's working and living conditions. Residents of the city's settlement houses frequently took an interest in working women and in the rapidly growing trade-union movment.

The WTUL, however, differed from these organizations in two essential respects. First, it stressed the importance of actual union organizing efforts rather than such customary reform activities as social investigations. Many women joined precisely because they were discouraged by the slow approach of social reform organizations or by the elitism of traditional charity work. As Gertrude Barnum, a leading upper-class member in the WTUL's early years, explained:

> I myself have graduated from the Settlement into the trade union. As I became more familiar with the conditions around me, I began to feel that while the Settlement was undoubtedly doing a great deal to make the lives of working people less grim and hard, the work was not fundamental. It introduced into their lives books and flowers and music, and it gave them a place to meet and see their friends or leave their babies when they went

out to work, but it did not raise their wages or shorten their hours. It began to dawn on me, therefore, that it would be more practical to turn our energies toward raising wages and shortening hours. [3]

Second, the WTUL stressed the importance of cross-class co-operation between upper-class and working-class women, and it was the only early twentieth-century women's organization that attempted to build such an egalitarian, cross-class alliance into its organizational structure. Membership was open to any woman who professed her allegiance to the American Federation of Labor and who indicated her willingness to work to unionize New York's women workers. Members stressed that allies as well as workers could be dedicated trade unionists and effective labor organizers.

Examining the day-to-day relationships that WTUL members established among themselves and studying the alignments on policy issues make it possible to observe the dynamics of cross-class cooperation and conflict. Two questions are of particular importance: how successful was the WTUL in establishing an egalitarian, cross-class alliance and what were the sources of conflict within it that undermined the alliance?

The WTUL's success depended upon maintaining harmony and a sense of purpose within its coalition of workers and allies. Its founders did not expect the coalition's stability to be a problem. The first WTUL members — most of whom were settlement residents and social reformers — apparently anticipated few difficulties in relating to one another: women could, they believed, surmount social and ethnic differences and unite on the basis of their common femininity. In this respect, the WTUL was typical of the early twentieth-century women's movement. A conviction that women could relate to one another across class lines in the spirit of sisterhood and an emphasis on the special qualities that women shared linked many members to the larger feminist movement. That women were different, emotionally and culturally, from men was one of the major ideological strains in American feminism around 1900. Unlike mid-nineteenth-century feminists who had inveighed against the notion of a separate sphere for women and who had argued that both sexes shared a common humanity, early twentieth-century feminists, suffragists, and social reformers stressed the importance of sex differences. As WTUL member Rheta Childe Dorr expressed this philosophy:

> Women now form a new social group, separate, and to a degree homogeneous. Already they have evolved a group opinion and a group ideal . . . . Society will soon be compelled to make a serious survey of the opinions and the ideal of women. As far as these have found collective expressions, it is evident that they differ very radically from the accepted opinions and ideals of men . . . . It is inevitable that this should be so.[4]

WTUL members, like other feminists in the early twentieth century, were often vague when they tried to define women's sisterhood. They usually used the term to convey the idea that social class was less important than gender for understanding a woman's status. The primary social dichotomy was a sex distinction rooted in differences between women and men, not a distinction between classes. Women, some members argued, shared distinct emotional qualities: they were more gentle and moral than men, more sensitive and responsive to human needs. Members also argued that women, regardless of class, could empathize with one another because they belonged to an oppressed social group.[5] This belief in sisterhood provided the ideological impetus for the WTUL's formation and helps explain its appeal for many women.

In certain basic respects, members found that their ideal of sisterhood could be realized. As an organization in which both upper-class and working-class women played important roles and in which working-class and upper-class women could gain knowledge and confidence from one another, the WTUL remained viable for several decades. It is possible to document many examples of close personal and working relationships within it that transcended class lines.

In many other respects, however, WTUL members discovered

that it was considerably easier to make verbal assertions of sister-hood than it was to put the ideal into practice. In contrast to the WTUL's public affirmation of sorority, its internal affairs were rarely harmonious. Beyond a basic commitment to unionizing women workers and to the American Federation of Labor, there was little upon which its members could agree. Far from behaving in sisterly fashion in their day-to-day affairs, members were often at odds with one another over objectives and policies: Who should be allowed to join the organization? How much money and energy should be committed to labor organization, to educational activi-ties, to suffrage agitation? Should the WTUL support protective legislation for women? Personal animosity and rancor accom-panied debates over these questions and over priorities. Leading members frequently submitted resignations or threatened to resign. They wrote angry letters denouncing one another or defending themselves against attacks. In short, WTUL women were a con-tentious lot. "If we have failed in what might be our greatest use-fulness to the workers," Leonora O'Reilly, a leading working-class member, concluded wearily in 1914, "it is just in proportion as we have exhausted the energy of our friends and ourselves . . . in per-iodical tiffs and skermishes [*sic*]."[6]

What accounted for the high level of animosity within the New York WTUL? It is tempting to single out class conflict as a blanket explanation for its factionalism, policy disputes, and difficult per-sonal relationships. Without doubt, class conflict was a reality and a factor which undercut members' attempts to create an egalitarian alliance. Allies and workers came to the organization with different conceptions of social class, different attitudes toward work and, of course, radically different social, educational, and cultural backgrounds. The ideal of sisterhood notwithstanding, difficulties and misunderstandings between women from different social back-grounds were inevitable. Yet class conflict in and of itself is not an adequate explanation for the controversies that regularly shook the organization. Indeed, personal relationships among members sometimes tended to mitigate serious class conflict. More impor-tant, there were no simple class alignments on WTUL issues. Clear-ly, factors in addition to class conflict were involved.

The women who made up the organization were never able to reconcile their dedication to women as an oppressed minority within the work force and their commitment to the labor movement as a whole. Belief in sisterhood, they discovered, was not always compatible with a belief in the importance of class solidarity. In other words, members were unable to develop a satisfactory solution to the problem of women's dual exploitation: were women workers oppressed because they were workers or because they were female? In effect, many controversies which troubled the organization were in large part a reflection of its struggle as well as ideological ramifications for many members.[7]

Although differences in members' social backgrounds did not fully account for the conflicts within the League, they were an important contributing factor. In the WTUL's first years, from late 1903 through 1906, the so-called allies joined much more readily than working women. During those years, when there were rarely more than fifty members, upper-class women dominated numerically. Although the first president was a working women — Margaret Daly, a United Ladies Garment Workers Union organizer — she remained in the WTUL for only a short time. She was succeeded by Margaret Dreier, an ally. With the exception of Daly, all of the WTUL's officers and a small majority of the executive board members were allies. References can be found to young working women who joined between 1903 and 1907, but their role in the organization was shadowy, and few remained members for more than a year or took a vocal role in the organization's activities.[8]

To stem the tide of young college graduates and settlement residents who flocked to the WTUL in its first years, Gertrude Barnum, an ally herself, suggested that a quota system be imposed to limit the number of upper-class members and that prospective allies be required to endorse the principle of the closed shop as a measure of their commitment to the labor movement. The WTUL did not implement either of these policies. Its constitution contained a major safeguard against upper-class domination, namely, a clause which stipulated that working women were to hold the majority of executive board positions. In addition, positions of leadership on organizing committees were sometimes reserved for working women. Such safeguards, however, could not alter the trend of those first years when the allies dominated numerically. Although no one questioned the desirability of large numbers of working-class adherents, the first members had difficulty recruiting them.

By 1907, the WTUL had established itself and had begun to come to the attention of young working women through its organizing efforts and its support of labor activities. More workers joined the organization. In 1907 three of its five officers were working women, as was a clear majority of the executive board. After the 1909 general shirtwaist strike, in which the WTUL played a central role, workers joined in greater numbers than at any time previously. The year after the strike, eight of the ten executive board members were working women. For the rest of the period under review, the active membership totaled several hundred, and working women and allies were numerically balanced.[9]

Numerical equality, however, could not solve the more serious problem of upper-class cultural domination, an ever-present dilemma. Most upper-class members were seemingly unconscious of the genteel atmosphere that permeated the WTUL, despite its unpretentious headquarters in dingy Lower East Side flats. Allies apparently saw nothing incongruous about juxtaposing "interpretive dance recitals" with shop meetings or inviting women to stop by for an afternoon of "drinking tea and discussing unionism." For working women, however, the WTUL had an aristocratic air about it. For example, Rose Schneiderman, a young Jewish cap maker who had grown up on the Lower East Side, recalled her amazement when she attended her first WTUL meeting and watched the participants dance the Virginia reel. Like many workers, she had to overcome initial reluctance to join an organization with so many wealthy, college-educated women. On a personal level, WTUL gentility undermined the self-confidence of working-class women and made them feel awkward; on an ideological level, the organization's aristocratic character was foreign and often suspect. "Contact with the Lady does harm in the long run," Leonora O'Reilly declared at one point. "It gives the wrong standard."[10]

Ideally, allies were to repress any trace of the attitude of the "Lady with something to give to her sisters."[11] They were to allow working-class members to take the initiative in labor affairs. In short, they were to learn about trade unionism, labor organizing, and working conditions from the women who had first-hand ex-

perience in such matters. Despite the emphasis on egalitarian relationships between working-class and upper-class members, however, allies often took the lead in day-to-day affairs, in part because
of their educational and financial advantages. Then, too, allies
were, on the average, ten years older than working-class members,
and their age may also have given them additional confidence and
authority.[12]

The patronizing attitudes of certain allies toward working-class
members were evident in the WTUL's educational work. Upper-
class members occasionally assumed the self-appointed task of dis-
covering and developing natural leaders among New York City
working women. As historian Mary Beard confided to another
member, "It has been my dream to develop young women to be a
help in the awakening of their class.[13] One young organizer recorded in her monthly work report that her scheduled activities
included writing lessons: "Miss Scott felt that I ought to practice
my writing as I would have to do a great deal of it in the future. I
put in several days at nothing else but writing. I had two lessons
with Mr. Charles Beard."[14] Instead of working-class members
teaching allies how to relate to women workers and to be effective
organizers, the opposite was sometimes the case.

Such attitudes did not go ignored or uncriticized. Leonora
O'Reilly, a working woman with long experience as a garment-
trades organizer and labor speaker and one of the original members
of the WTUL, was particularly vocal in expressing her dislike of
college women who came to the labor movement with lofty ideals
of feminism and solidarity but who knew nothing of the realities of
labor organizing or of working for a living. She was determined
that working-class members should not be intimidated by the
academic and financial advantages of upper-class women. Specifically, she carried on a running campaign against Laura Elliot, an
older ally who joined the WTUL in 1910. Elliot offered members
courses in singing, elocution, and art history; she organized a
chorus and took groups of young women workers to museums and
concerts. Most members apparently regarded her as eccentric but
harmless, and paid her little mind. O'Reilly, however, found
Elliot's ideas pernicious enough to attack. She accused her of condescending attempts to save working women by filling them with

useless and pretentious notions of culture. Elliot was hurt and confused by such criticism, but insisted that she had a contribution to make to the WTUL.

> You cannot push me out and you cannot make me afraid of any working girl sisters or render me self-conscious before them, I refuse to be afraid to take them to the Metropolitan Museum and teach them and help them . . . . I feel no fear in putting my side of the proposition up to any working girl. I'm not afraid that she will misunderstand or resent what I say. She needs my present help just as the whole race needs her uprising.[15]

Workers sometimes asserted that allies, despite good intentions, did not know how to appeal to working women: their experiences and background were simply too different. Pauline Newman, a young Jewish immigrant who joined the WTUL during the 1909 shirtwaist strike, summarized her impressions of upper-class limitations in both the WTUL and the suffrage campaign with her remark: "the 'cultured' ladies may be very sincere. . . . I don't doubt their sincereity [*sic*] but because their views are narrow and their knowledge of social conditions limited, they cannot do as well as some of us can."[16]

Workers' frustration with the well-intentioned but sometimes inept efforts of their affluent colleagues was understandable. The allies, as the executive board admitted at one point, could be "trying."[17] They were sometimes responsible for decisions which exasperated working women. For example, officers scheduled a conference on Yom Kippur, despite the protests of Jewish members. In the WTUL's book of English lessons, *New World Lessons for Old World People*, references to Jewish working girls going to church slipped by uncorrected. Of the allies, only one is known to have studied Yiddish, and some held stereotyped conceptions of immigrant women. Jewish women were often described as "dark-eyed," "studious," and "revolutionary" in WTUL literature, and Italians were usually "docile," "fun-loving," "submissive," and "superstitious."[18]

Overt class and ethnic conflict in the WTUL reached its peak
during a 1914 presidential contest between Rose Schneiderman and
Melinda Scott. At the time of the election, Schneiderman was the
WTUL's East Side, or Jewish, organizer. Scott, a skilled hat trim-
mer and president of an independent union in her trade, served as
the WTUL's organizer of American-born women in the neckwear
and dressmaking industries. Although both candidates were
workers, they represented widely divergent approaches to the problems of organizing women. Schneiderman had always emphasized
the importance of reaching immigrant women. Scott was pessimis-
tic about organizing the newcomers and advocated a policy of concentrating on native-born workers. Thus, the election involved attitudes and policies toward immigrants. Nevertheless, support for
the two candidates divided along class lines; allies backed Scott
while working women voted for Schneiderman. [19] When Scott won
by four votes, Pauline Newman related the details to Schneiderman.

> Your vote, with the exception of three or four was
> a real trade Union vote. On the other hand, the
> vote for Linda was purely a vote of the social
> workers. People who have not been near the
> League for four or five years, came to vote . . . .
> but they could not get the girls from the Union to
> vote against you . . . . So you see, that nothing
> was left undone by them to line up a vote for Linda
> on the ground that you were a socialist, a Jewes
> [*sic*] and one interested in suffrage. [20]

Different conceptions of class caused part of the difficulty underlying clashes between allies and workers, — with the importance
of these differences usually far more obvious to the latter. Upper-
class members were not as acutely aware of class antagonism
within the WTUL and often played down the importance of social
background. Many were confused by the emphasis that workers
placed on class differences. As Laura Elliot wrote to Leonora
O'Reilly: "Before I was unconscious about this class and that class
and this stupid difference and that stupid difference. Girls were just

girls to me, and now you people are putting all sorts of ideas in my head and making me timid and self-conscious."[21]

Social class was flexible, not immutable, many allies believed. With great effort, an individual could transcend her social background. To be sure, when allies talked of such efforts, they were referring to young women from wealthy families who became self-sufficient and who could relate to workers without self-consciousness. Helen Marot, an ally who came from a comfortable, affluent Philadelphia family, regarded herself as a worker because she worked as the League's secretary and supported herself on her earnings. In similar fashion, Violet Pike, a young woman who had joined shortly after graduating from Vassar in 1907, was included among the working women on the executive board because she performed some clerical duties and had joined the Bookkeepers, Stenographers, and Accountants' union.[22] Maud Younger, a wealthy ally, was listed on the WTUL's masthead as a representative of the Waitresses' Union because she conducted an investigation of waitresses' working conditions and attended meetings of the union. In a sense, these women were workers, and they were proud of being self-supporting and resisted being categorized in the class of their fathers.

Allies and workers also came to the League with different conceptions of work. Upper-class members frequently had romanticized views of poverty and often regarded self-sufficiency as a kind of luxury. Work meant liberation from the confines of proper femininity. This attitude contributed to the allies' naivete concerning the role of labor in the lives of female wage-earners. Because they idealized work and equated it with economic and emotional self-sufficiency, many allies never seemed to recognize that most women were not independent laborers but part of a family economic unit in which work did not connote financial independence.[23] "Thank God working girls have a chance to be themselves because they earn their own wage and nobody owns them," one typical WTUL article began. "I am pretty sure you are somebody, because you are self-supporting."[24]

There can be no doubt that the New York WTUL was characterized by personal, cultural, and political strife. But Pauline Newman's 1914 depiction of an organization sharply divided between

"social workers" and "trade unionists" was overdrawn and simp-
listic. Although it is easy to document class conflict, it is also possible to document experiences that mitigated serious, sustained
clashes between upper-class and working-class women. There were
cohesive factors as well as divisive tendencies that operated within
the WTUL and enabled the organization to function.

Personal relationships between members constituted one factor
that undercut the class conflict inherent in the organization. Sisterhood sometimes became a tangible reality in friendships. Mary
Dreier, the WTUL's president from 1907 through 1914, and
Leonora O'Reilly, for example, maintained a warm personal relationship for many years, and it survived numerous political and cultural differences between the two women. "You say you wonder
whether I would always trust you," Dreier wrote to O'Reilly after
some disagreement over policy:

> There doesn't even seem to be such a word as trust
> necessary between thee and me . . . . I might not
> always understand, as you might not always un-
> derstand my activities — but as to doubting your
> integrity of soul, or the assurance on which trust is
> built seems as impossible to me as walking on a
> sunbeam into the heart of the sun for any of us hu-
> mans — a strange and beautiful mixture of person-
> al and impersonal is my relationship to you and I
> love you. [25]

Such relationships were not uncommon among WTUL women.
Some, like that of Dreier and O'Reilly, cut across class lines. Other
close friendships were established between women of the same
social background.

It is not surprising that such relationships were common. For
many, the WTUL was a full-time commitment, a way of life. Then,
too, that the emotional ties shared by some of the members should
be among the closest in their lives is not surprising in light of the
social conventions that governed personal relationships in the
pre-Freudian culture around 1900. Emotional attachments between
individuals of the same sex were not viewed with the sort of sus-

picion that would characterize a later period. Intense relationships involving open expressions of tenderness and affection were accepted as natural. [26]

Furthermore, the longer a working woman remained a member, the more she had in common with an upper-class ally. Both groups of women were atypical in early twentieth-century American society: the majority were single at ages when most women were married: they prided themselves on being independent and self-supporting: and they lived in a gynecentric environment in which other women were their closest companions, their working colleagues, and their sources of emotional support. Only an extremely mechanistic definition of social class could neglect the many important life experiences which these women shared.

Finally, class conflict is not an adequate explanation for the disagreements within the organization for the simple reason that a member's social background did not dictate her stand on WTUL policies. On every important issue, alignments were unclear. Suffrage, traditionally regarded as a middle-class issue, was an important priority for many working-class members. Rose Schneiderman and Pauline Newman were the first members to devote themselves full-time to the suffrage campaign. Ally Helen Marot, on the other hand, resisted the WTUL's growing emphasis on the importance of the vote. Protective labor legislation, an issue that was enormously important in the WTUL's history during the 1910s and 1920s, was a more controversial issue than woman suffrage, but on that issue as well there were no clear class alignments. Allies and workers could be found on both sides of the question. In short, one cannot argue that only upper-class members endorsed such reform issues as protective legislation while only workers advocated labor policies such as direct organizing. There is no evidence to support the view that working women saw the WTUL as a labor union and that allies viewed it as a social-reform organization. Rather, it is clear that factors in addition to class conflict shaped the controversies which embroiled members. [27]

Regardless of class background, its members viewed the WTUL as both a labor and a women's organization. Therein lay the second and perhaps more pervasive source of discord. Members had difficulty reconciling their commitment to organized labor with their commitment to the women's movement. They could not agree on a solution to the problem of the dual exploitation of women workers or find a way to reconcile their belief in sisterhood with their belief in the importance of working-class solidarity. Commitment to the cause of protective legislation or suffrage, or advocacy of separate unions for women workers, left them open to the charge of dividing the working class. But neglect of women's issues might prompt the accusation that women's special problems in the work force were being ignored. This dilemma was real, and neither the WTUL nor its individual members fully resolved the question.

Some members felt strongly that commitment to the labor movement should override feminist leanings. In their analysis, the problems of women workers were bound up inextricably with the problems of working men. Class, not gender, was the main concern. True, they said, women suffered discrimination in the labor movement, but such opposition was not insurmountable.

Other members found their primary orientation in the women's movement. Or, as happened more frequently, women first attempted to cooperate with organized labor but ultimately despaired of changing the attitudes of male unionists. They then moved away from the labor movement and turned to suffrage and protective legislation as reforms that would ameliorate the conditions of women workers.

Helen Marot, WTUL secretary and an organizer, epitomized the first, or "woman as worker," position. Although she had never been an industrial worker, she unwaveringly believed that the WTUL should be committed to organized labor as a whole and not to women as a separate group. Female workers, she emphasized, should be regarded as inseparable from male workers: to think otherwise was to impede class solidarity and to denigrate women's capabilities. Throughout her career in the WTUL and in her book, *American Labor Unions*, Marot vigorously opposed any policy that smacked of caste consciousness. She emphasized that women were difficult to organize because they were unskilled, not because they were female. She was vehement in her opposition to the minimum wage for women only, despite the fact that the measure eventually won the approval of many working-class members. "If women need state protection on the ground that they do not or-

ganize as men do," she told the New York State Factory Investigating Commission, "then also do the mass of unskilled, unorganized men who do not appreciate or take advantage of organization
. . . . The reasons for trade unionists to oppose State interference in wage rates apply to women workers as they do to men."[28]

Harriot Stanton Blatch, a well-known suffragist, represented the other strain of the WTUL. Unlike Marot, her interest in women workers derived from her involvement in the women's movement, not from a concern with industrial problems. Unions for women were only one aspect of a multifaceted campaign for women's rights, not an end in themselves. For Blatch, every class-related issue was secondary to the vote. In part, expedient considerations motivated her participation in the WTUL: she realized that the support of working women was vital for the ultimate success of the suffrage movement, and the WTUL offered a way to reach them. On another level, however, Blatch was convinced that political equality was a prerequisite for any other improvement in women's status. Only when women could vote would they command the respect of the labor movement. And only with suffrage would women develop the confidence to fight for industrial equality. "I have . . . [been] working with the Women's Trade Union League and attending meetings of the women's local the E. Side," Blatch wrote American Federation of Labor president Samuel Gompers in 1905. "Those young women need stirring up, need independence, and some fight instilled into them . . . . I am understanding of all that the vote would mean to them — [it] would help in the trade union work as nothing else could."[29]

Marot and Blatch were sure of their objectives and their ideological orientation. But the issue of women's dual status was not so clear-cut for most of the members. For working-class members, the problems posed by the WTUL's dual commitment to its constituents as women and as workers were particularly vexing. To them, the matter was not only a theoretical and political issue, but frequently a personal dilemma as well. On the one hand, workers identified with their class background. They came to the WTUL with experience in organizing activities and committed to trade unionism. On the other hand, they, like allies, were also feminists. Although workers were less likely than allies to come to the WTUL with an interest in the women's movement and probably became acquainted with the ideas of organized feminism and with the goals of the women's movement through their relationships with allies, most became dedicated feminists. More important, by comparing their experiences in the WTUL with their role in trade unions, they often came to a realization that the WTUL offered more opportunities for women to fill autonomous, responsible positions than male-dominated unions did.

Leonora O'Reilly's career in the WTUL provides a good example of working-women's difficulties. Her commitment to the WTUL was always ambivalent. She was faced with what she regarded as a conflict between her class background and her work in a women's organization. This was aggravated by her conviction that any serious attempt to organize working women had to be a feminist as well as a labor effort. An outspoken feminist herself and a dedicated suffragist, she recognized the need for an organization such as the WTUL to devote special attention to women. She knew from her own experience as a United Ladies Garment Workers Union organizer that women could count on little assistance from male unions. For all that, O'Reilly never came to terms with her ambivalence. She vacillated between urging the WTUL to refrain from interfering in union affairs and stressing that it should implement its policies in an autonomous fashion. [30] Sometimes she exalted the ability of women to fend for themselves in the work force, independent of men. "I want to say to my sisters," she once declared to a WTUL convention, "for mercy's sake, let's be glad if the men don't help us!" [31] From her days in the Workingwomen's Society in the 1890s, O'Reilly had stressed the importance of sisterhood. On a number of occasions she spoke of "women's real togetherness." "Personally," she wrote, "I suffer torture dividing the woman's movement into the Industrial Group and all the other groups. Women real women anywhere and everywhere are what we must nourish and cherish." [32] Yet at other times, she denounced the WTUL as an elitist organization that had no real concern for working-class people. "The League ought to die," she reportedly said at one point, "the sooner, the better." [33] Her two resignations, in 1905 and 1914, indicated her continual difficulty in resolving the conflict. In both instances, she emphasized that working women would have to organize themselves. [34]

Rose Schneiderman and Pauline Newman exhibited similar confusion and ambivalence about their role as working women in the WTUL. On the one hand, they identified with the East-Side immigrant working-class community in which they had grown up. On the other, they regarded themselves as feminists devoted to women's issues. Like O'Reilly, they frequently experienced enough conflict to consider resigning. [35]

Both women were torn between working in the WTUL and devoting themselves to the East Side Jewish labor movement. Yet to work as an organizer for a Jewish union or for the International Ladies Garment Workers Union, as both women discovered, was often an isolated and lonely experience. If the WTUL was not sufficiently interested in the progress of the working class and did not sufficiently appreciate efforts and ability to reach immigrant women, the Jewish labor organizations ignored the special problems of women altogether and discriminated against the small number of women organizers. Newman, after several years of unhappy and unrewarding work as an ILG organizer, concluded that WTUL work was more desirable than she had thought originally: "remember Rose that no matter how much you are with the Jewish people, you are still more with the people of the League and that is a relieff [*sic*]." [36] Clearly, working women could compare the WTUL favorably with trade unions: it offered women organizers considerably more autonomy and responsibility than unions did, and, what was more, it provided the company of women who shared interests and experiences.

Still, both Schneiderman and Newman continually had difficulty reconciling the women's movement and the labor movement. On occasion, both women denounced the superficial efforts of upper-class philanthropists and reformers to improve industrial conditions. Yet they were the first WTUL members to work as full-time suffrage agitators. Later in the WTUL's history, both were vocal supporters of women's protective legislation, especially of minimum-wage statutes and maternity insurance, despite the fact that the labor movement frowned upon the principle of protective legislation in general and upon the minimum wage in particular. During Rose Schneiderman's presidency in the 1920s, the WTUL devoted itself almost exclusively to legislative activity.

The difficulties these women faced were not uncommon. Most

members experienced some conflict between feminism and unionism. Policies also reflected this clash during the first decade of its history. From 1903 to 1914, the WTUL minimized the special problems of women in the work force and concentrated on integrating them into the labor movement as workers; at a later period, its members worked hard to implement demands that were relevant only to women workers: suffrage and protective legislation. For members, explanations for the oppression of working women were always couched in either/or terms: either a working woman was exploited as a worker or she suffered as a woman. What the WTUL needed was an policy which came to terms with both facets of the situation confronting women workers. Such a policy was never realized, and the WTUL remained split. Caught between two alternatives, members were frequently unable to define their purpose or their role.

In short, the WTUL had only limited success in achieving its goal of an egalitarian cross-class alliance. Although it went further than any other women's organization in establishing sustained relations with working women and in grappling with the problems of a feminist alliance, its internal affairs were rarely harmonious. In part, the WTUL's difficulties can be attributed to conflict between allies and workers. Neither group satisfactorily resolved the dual commitment to the labor movement and the women's movement and that failure also contributed to the difficulties of establishing a cross-class alliance.

NOTES

1. Mary Dreier, "Expansion Through Agitation and Education," *Life and Labor* 11 (June 1921): 163.
2. The New York Women's Trade Union League was an autonomous organization, but it was closely related to a larger body, the National Women's Trade Union League of America. The same individuals founded both organizations in late 1903.
3. *Weekly Bulletin of the Clothing Trades*, March 24, 1905, p. 2.
4. Rheta Childe Dorr, *What Eight Million Women Want* (Boston, 1910), p. 5. For a good discussion of the changes in American feminist ideology from the mid-nineteenth century to the early twentieth century, see Aileen Kraditor, *The Ideas of the Woman Suffrage Movement* (New York, 1965), ch. 3.
5. See, for example, Gertrude Barnum, "The Modern Society Woman," *Ladies Garment Worker* 2 (June 1911): 8. "All women before the laws of the country . . .

are of equal rank or lack of rank, being classed without exception with children, idiots, and criminals. With a common sense of injustice, feminine descendents of Patrick Henry, Tom Paine, and Thomas Jefferson ignore social differences and march shoulder to shoulder in campaigns to secure their 'inalienable rights' — to secure the fullest possible social equality with man.''

6. Leonora O'Reilly to the Executive Board, Women's Trade Union League of New York, January 14, 1914. Women's Trade Union League of New York Papers, New York State Labor Library, New York, New York (hereafter cited as WTULNY Papers).

7. Some historians who have dealt briefly with the WTUL have interpreted the discord within the organization and the shift from labor organizing to legislative activity as the result of class conflict betwen allies (and/or social reformers) and working women. William Chafe argues, for example, ''Reformers viewed the WTUL's primary function as educational, and believed that the interests of the workers could best be served by investigating industrial conditions, securing legislative action, and building public support for the principle of trade unionism. Female unionists, on the other hand, insisted that organizing women and strengthening existing unions represented the League's principal purpose. One group preceived the WTUL as primarily an instrument of social uplift, the other as an agency for labor organization.'' Chafe, *The American Woman, Her Changing Social, Economic, and Political Roles, 1920-1970* (New York, 1972), p. 71.

8. The New York WTUL was never a large organization. Although it counted several hundred women among its dues-paying members in the years after 1907, few played active roles in the day-to-day work. In the years from 1903 to 1914, about twenty women formed a core group of members. These women made policy, served as officers, organizers, and speakers, and set priorities. Although the composition of this core group changed from year to year, most of them devoted most of their time to the organization for at least several years. Using the extant lists of executive board members, officers, and committee members, it is possible to reach some conclusions about the changing class composition of the core membership group. This discussion on membership is based on a more complete treatment in Nancy Schrom Dye, ''The Women's Trade Union League of New York, 1903-1920'' (Ph.D. dissertation, University of Wisconsin, Madison, Wisconsin, 1974).

9. Women's Trade Union League of New York, *Annual Reports*, 1909-1910 to 1913-1914. For a more detailed discussion of membership, see Dye, ''The Women's Trade Union League of New York, 1903-1920.''

10. Letter to Leonora O'Reilly, 1908 (O'Reilly's statement is in the form of a note written to herself on the back of the letter), Leonora O'Reilly Papers, Schlesinger Library, Cambridge, Massachusetts (hereafter cited as Leonora O'Reilly Papers).

11. William English Walling to Leonora O'Reilly, December 1903 (O'Reilly's handwritten note on the back of the letter), Leonora O'Reilly Papers.

12. This statement is based on the compilation of biographical information on the WTUL's core membership group. For more complete information, see Dye, ''The Women's Trade Union League of New York, 1903-1920.''

13. Mary Beard to Leonora O'Reilly, July 21, 1912, Leonora O'Reilly Papers.

14. Report of the Organizer, Women's Trade Union League of New York, October 1915, WTULNY Papers.

15. Laura Elliot to Leonora O'Reilly, March 1911, Leonora O'Reilly Papers.

16. Pauline Newman to Rose Schneiderman, July 16, 1912, Rose Schneiderman Papers. Tamiment Library, New York University, New York, N.Y. (hereafter cited as Rose Schneiderman Papers).

17. Minutes, Executive Board, Women's Trade Union League of New York, January 25, 1906, WTULNY Papers.

18. See, for example, Violet Pike, *New World Lessons for Old World People* (New York, 1912); Gertrude Barnum, "A Story with a Moral," *Weekly Bulletin of the Clothing Trades*, November 20, 1908, p. 6; Gertrude Barnum, "At the Shirtwaist Factory, A Story," *Ladies Garment Workers* 1 (June 1910): 4.

19. Pauline Newman recorded her impressions of the election in three letters to Rose Schneiderman. Pauline Newman to Rose Schneiderman, (1914,) Rose Schneiderman Papers.

20. Ibid.

21. Laura Elliot to Leonora O'Reilly, March 1911, Leonora O'Reilly Papers.

22. Women's Trade Union League of New York, *Annual Reports*, 1910-1911, 1911-1912. In both years, Pike is listed as a union representative for the Bookkeepers, Stenographers, and Accountants Union.

23. U.S. Congress, Senate, *Report on Condition of Woman and Child Wage-Earners in the United States*, "Wage-Earning Women in Stores and Factories," S. Doc. 645, 61st. Cong., 2d sess., 1910, vol. 5, pp. 18, 25, 144. Senate investigators pointed out that New York City had the smallest proportion of self-supporting women of all the major cities investigated.

24. Gertrude Barnum, "Women Workers," *Weekly Bulletin of the Clothing Trades,* July 13, 1906, p. 8.

25. Mary Dreier to Leonora O'Reilly, June 19, 1908, Leonora O'Reilly Papers.

26. Other historical studies have touched upon this phenomenon. See, for example, Christopher Lasch and William Taylor, "Two Kindred Spirits," *New England Quarterly* 36 (Winter 1963): 23-41.

27. This interpretation differs from brief accounts of the WTUL in other works. See, for example, Kraditor, *Ideas of the Woman Suffrage Movement*, ch. 6, and Chafe, *American Woman*, ch. 3.

28. New York State, Factory Investigating Commission, *Fourth Report of the New York State Factory Investigating Commission, 1915* vol. 1, p. 774; Helen Marot, *American Labor Unions, By a Member* (New York, 1915), ch.5.

29. Harriot Stanton Blatch to Samuel Gompers, December 30, 1905, American Federation of Labor Papers, Wisconsin State Historical Society, Madison, Wisconsin; Harriot Stanton Blatch, *Challenging Years* (New York: Putnam, 1940).

30. See, for example, Leonora O'Reilly to Executive Board, Women's Trade Union League of New York, January 14, 1914, WTULNY Papers.

31. National Women's Trade Union League, *Proceedings of the Second Biennial Convention*, 1909, p. 26.

32. Leonora O'Reilly to Mary Hay, December 29, 1917, Leonora O'Reilly Papers.

33. Leonora O'Reilly's statement was quoted in a letter from Pauline Newman to Rose Schneiderman, 1914, Rose Schneiderman papers. Newman wrote, "Mrs. Robins wanted Nora [Leonora O'Reilly] to tell her what she thought of the candidats [*sic*] but Nora said that, 'this you will never now, but I can tell you what I think of the League, it ought to die, and the sooner the better.' "

34. Minutes, Special Meeting, Executive Board, Women's Trade Union League of New York, November 19, 1915, WTULNY Papers.

35. See, for example, Pauline Newman to Rose Schneiderman, February 22, 1912, Rose Schneiderman Papers.

36. Pauline Newman to Rose Schneiderman, April 17, 1911, Rose Schneiderman Papers.

INDEX

About the Editors

Milton Cantor, professor of history at the University of Massachusetts, Amherst, has written primarily in the areas of American constitutional law and labor history. Among his earlier publications are *Main Problems in American History, Men, Women and Issues,* and *Black Labor in America.*

Bruce Laurie is an assistant professor of history at the University of Massachusetts, Amherst. His articles have appeared in such journals as *Labor History* and *Journal of Social History.* He is currently preparing a book on working-class culture in Philadelphia.